14/8/20 Rd
LA- 3/2/20
19/4/21

Please return/renew this item by the
last date shown to avoid a charge.
Books may also be renewed by phone
and Internet. May not be renewed if
required by another reader.

www.libraries.barnet.gov.uk

BARNET
LONDON BOROUGH

FREE LUNCH

'*Free Lunch* doesn't claim to be comprehensive, but it is comprehensible, and that's much more important. It's vital that citizens understand the economic forces they experience. *Free Lunch* achieves that aim, eloquently and without "useless complications".' *Guardian*

'Smith ... is an amiable and talented dining companion' *Observer*

'Free of jargon, obfuscation and interminable subordinate clauses, his prose is just the job.' *Times*

DAVID SMITH is Economics Editor at the *Sunday Times* and broadcasts regularly on radio and television. His previous books for Profile include *The Dragon and the Elephant* and *The Age of Instability*. He has won several awards, including the Harold Wincott award for Senior Financial Journalist of the Year, and is a visiting professor at Cardiff and Nottingham universities. Born in the Midlands, he now lives in London.

ALSO BY DAVID SMITH

The Dragon and the Elephant
The Age of Instability

FREE LUNCH

EASILY DIGESTIBLE ECONOMICS

David Smith

P

PROFILE BOOKS

This edition updated in 2012

First published in 2003 by
Profile Books Ltd
3A Exmouth House
Pine Street
Exmouth Market
London ECIR OJH
www.profilebooks.com

10 9 8 7 6 5 4 3 2 1

Typeset in Garamond by MacGuru Ltd
info@macguru.org.uk
Printed and bound in Great Britain by
CPI Group (UK) Ltd, Croydon, CRO 4YY

A CIP catalogue record for this book is available from the British Library.

ISBN 978 1 78125 011 2
eISBN 978 1 84765 946 0

MIX
Paper from
responsible sources
FSC® C020471

For Jane, Elizabeth, Emily, Richard and Thomas

Contents

Appetizer

This is a book about economics. I used to say that as a half-apology, knowing that economics had to work quite hard to compete with other subjects, not to mention most other things in the bookshop. Things are different now, thanks to the global financial crisis that began in the summer of 2007 and was far from over in the run-up to its fifth anniversary as this was being written. The crisis came like a whirlwind, damaging everything in its wake but also shaking up perceptions, including those about economics. Everybody has a view on the crisis, and most people have something to be angry about, about bankers, regulators, politicians and even economists. Apart from the fact that the repercussions of the crisis will live in the memory for decades, its effects are real. Would we have had severe cuts in public spending and tax hikes in the absence of the crisis? Would, to take a simple example, the coalition government in Britain have been emboldened enough to introduce big increases in university tuition fees? Would there have been a coalition government at all, a rarity in Britain, in the absence of the crisis? The crisis drew into sharp focus questions about how modern economies operate. It marked a shift from the easy, credit-driven growth of the 1990s and 2000s into something very different. Banks were safe, staid institutions, were they not? No, and in the autumn of 2008, the western banking system came very close to collapse. This was the time when at a practical level the cash machines almost did not get refilled, the supermarket shelves almost were not restocked, the wages not paid. It was very close to a full state of economic emergency, in Britain and in other countries.

So, without wishing that kind of crisis on anybody, it seems to me that it taught us that everybody should take an interest in economics, and not just at times of great turbulence. The crisis, you will find, makes appearances throughout this book but it does not dominate it. For this is a book about economics. And it is a book about economics quite unlike any other. There are no tricky diagrams of the kind that leave you wondering whether the page has been printed the right way up. There are no complicated mathematical equations. Unless something can be easily explained, it has no place in this book. Above all, at a time when we all need to know some economics, it is intensely practical. This book will not necessarily make you a millionaire – I always say that the only economists you see driving Rolls-Royces are wearing chauffeurs' caps – but it will tell you about the process by which we become, mainly, better off, apart from when those crises hit. It is also, I hope, good fun.

The aim of this book is to fill a gap, just like a good lunch. For years, at the *Sunday Times* and elsewhere, readers had been asking me to recommend an easily digestible book on economics, either for non-economists or for those whose grasp of it is a little rusty. Until now I have found it difficult to do so. There are some excellent textbooks on economics, some of which I shall recommend later, but they are intended for formal courses of study, with teachers offering a guiding hand. This is different. I hope that many students will read and profit from *Free Lunch* but in a way that complements formal study rather than replaces it. There are, too, some excellent works describing recent economic history but these can be difficult, if not impossible, in the absence of the building blocks. An account of, say, Alan Greenspan or Ben Bernanke's time as Chairman of the Federal Reserve Board in Washington needs the context of knowing something about monetary policy and how central banks are supposed to operate it. Similarly, trying to judge whether an assessment of the success of the government's management of the economy is fair or unfair requires a few basic tools.

Why have I called it *Free Lunch*? It is not, whatever you might think, a sneaky attempt to increase sales by passing off a work on economics as an addition to the ever-popular and expanding catalogue of cookbooks, although that would not be a bad idea. Rather, it is because the one snappy phrase from economics most people will have heard of, even if they are unaware it has anything to do with the subject, is: 'There's no such thing as a free lunch.' You never, in other words, get something for nothing. As I am a journalist often required to lunch, not always enjoyably, it has always been close to my heart. It is such a famous phrase but its origins are unclear. While it is often attributed to the American economist Milton Friedman, of whom more later in the book, the *Oxford Dictionary of Quotations* lists its authorship as Anonymous, first coming into circulation in American university economic departments in the 1960s but making it into print, not in a text-book or learned article, but in *The Moon is a Harsh Mistress*, a 1966 novel by the science-fiction writer Robert Heinlein. It is likely, however, that the phrase was in use much earlier than this. The *San Francisco News* used it in a 1949 editorial, itself reputed to be a reprint of one written in 1938, while the legendary New York mayor Fiorello La Guardia said it in 1934, albeit in Latin. As for the origin of the idea, bars in the west of America commonly offered free lunch to patrons buying a certain amount of alcohol, notably during the gold rush. Those who stayed sober soon worked out that they were paying for their lunch with what they were being charged for beer or whisky.

Does 'There's no such thing as a free lunch' work as a piece of economics? Most of us can think of cases where we have apparently got something for nothing. That bus fare you did not pay, or that £10 note you picked up on the street, for example. But think about it. The free fare has a cost, not just in the risk of prosecution but also in that fare-dodgers mean, in the long run, higher fares for all, including you. As for that windfall £10, I would not pretend that there is some higher economic authority guaranteeing that every-body's lucky gains and losses even out exactly over time but it is likely that something approximating to that is close to most peo-ple's experience. Any gambler will tell you how hard it is, over time, to stay ahead of the bookmaker; any stock market investor that it is difficult to beat the index consistently.

Let me give you another example of the 'free lunch' idea at work. If you have just bought this book, thanks, and you have proved that there is, indeed, no such thing as a free lunch. If you have borrowed it from a friend, you are obliged to them, and your payment will probably be to have to lend them something of yours. If it is from a library, you are paying for it in taxes, or will eventually do so. And if you have stolen it then shame on you, but you are paying for it with a guilty conscience and you might get caught. My contract with you is that, in return for obtaining this book, by the time you've read it, you will know as much economics as you will probably ever need and more than the vast majority of the population. Except, of course, in the unlikely event that everybody else reads it too. That would put me in a monopoly position, although not for long, because economics tells us that we would then see a flood of entrants into the market of similar works. Economics could become the new cookery.

At one level the book is an aid to reading newspapers, particularly the financial pages, and understanding (and being able to see through) the economic claims and counter-claims of politicians. Why are we interested in inflation, the level of interest rates, the balance of payments and the budget deficit, and what do they really mean? Why are we interested in some of these things more than others, and at certain times rather than others? No longer when you see economic stories on the financial pages (and increasingly the front pages) should your reaction be to turn over. The only newspaper or magazine economic reports that should be hard to understand are those that are badly written. When you hear a politician saying that this year his or her government is spending a record amount on the health service you will be able to scream at the TV, as I do: 'But that's been the case virtually every year since the National Health Service was created!' – or at least it was. Every voter should know some economics.

There is, however, more to *Free Lunch* than that. When I urge school or college audiences to study economics, it is not just because some such knowledge is essential for modern living. Rather, it is because the way that economists think about and analyse problems in a logical way is useful in so many areas. Watching economists at work is not always a pretty sight and the jokes about their indecisiveness are legion. President Harry Truman yearned for a one-handed economist because every one that he knew said: 'On the one hand this, on the other hand that.' You could, according to the hoary saying, lay every economist in the world end to end and never reach a conclusion. This is unfair, confusing the invaluable ability of economists to be able to see the other side of the argument with an apparent inability to reach decisions. Thinking like an economist means approaching problems in a logical manner, replacing assertion with analysis. This book will not turn you into a professional economist overnight but it will encourage you to think differently about things.

Free Lunch, like all good meals, comes in several courses. It can be digested at a single sitting, taken a course at a time or, if you like, dipped into from time to time by snackers. This second edition is rich enough to risk, towards the end, a nasty bout of indigestion. Even so, I hope very much that you enjoy it.

2

Starters

Many books on economics begin by saying something like: 'Economics is about the allocation of scarce resources between competing demands.' Or, according to a very good and widely used textbook: 'Economics is the study of how society decides what, how and for whom to produce.' These are splendid definitions and undoubtedly correct as far as they go but they suffer from two important drawbacks. The first is that it is not until you have studied quite a lot of economics that you really understand what they mean. The second is that they are, for me, just too limited. Economics dominates and shapes our daily lives, even when we are not aware of it. It is all encompassing. This does not mean that we exist only as economic men and women, or are obsessed by money. It does mean that there is no getting away from economics. We refer, after all, to countries as 'economies'. I like the definition used by the great English economist Alfred Marshall (1842–1924) who said economics was the study of people 'in the ordinary business of life'.

Much of it also comes back to food, which is why I like the title of this book. Anne Sibert, professor of economics at Birkbeck College, London and, at time of writing, a member of the Icelandic central bank's monetary policy committee, once used a restaurant analogy to explain how speculative frenzies – financial bubbles – build up in the stock market. There are two restaurants in a town, the Ritz and the Savoy. Albert does not much mind which one he goes to but chooses the Ritz. Ben, coming next, is leaning slightly towards the Savoy but, seeing that Albert is at the Ritz, decides that it must be better. Catherine is also persuaded by Albert and Ben's choice that the Ritz must be the place, and so is David. By the time we get halfway through the alphabet, to Mary, everybody has chosen the Ritz and nobody the Savoy. But then Neville, who is next, has a very strong preference for the Savoy, partly because the Ritz is by now very crowded. Olivia, seeing Neville's choice, follows him, so does Peter, and so do the rest, right through to Zak. And then something strange happens. Halfway through their meal, all those who chose the Ritz hear that everybody else is going to the Savoy. They leave, in a rush, to go from one to the other, to the Ritz's chagrin. Think of all those who initially chose the Ritz as people who invested in dot.com shares during the late 1990s, or the rush by banks and other institutions into dodgy mortgage-backed securities in the 2000s, and then think of the rush to get out as they realised they had invested in worthless companies or securities, and you have a pretty good analogy for how bubbles build up and are burst.

Anyway, this is holding things up. The waiter is hovering and the meal is about to start. What shall we talk about? According to journalistic folklore, the only thing the middle classes talk about when gathered together at dinner parties is the level of house prices. Bubbles also come into any discussion of house prices too. The global financial crisis that began in the summer of 2007 had its roots in America's housing market and led to a sharp fall in house prices in Britain. So let us take the housing market as our starting point.

Houses versus potatoes

Most conversations about the housing market will include several elements. One person will assert that house prices have risen too much and are about to fall, while somebody else will claim that they have a lot further to rise. There is bound to be an argument over whether it is better to put your money into housing or stocks and shares. Everybody will count their good fortune to be already several rungs up the housing ladder, and not a first-time buyer struggling to scrape together a deposit for a home. These conversations change. Prior to 2007, people might also have commented on how easy it was to get a mortgage, with few questions asked. After that it became much harder, with many more questions asked. Home ownership was one of the great economic developments of the twentieth century. From a tiny minority of owner-occupied homes a hundred years earlier, the share of owner-occupied properties in England – people either owning their home outright or buying it with the help of a mortgage – peaked at 71 per cent in 2003, before slipping back to 67.5 per cent by 2010. Canada, the

United States and Australia have similar proportions at just below 70 per cent. In Spain it is a little higher, almost 80 per cent, while in Germany it is much lower, only just over 40 per cent, with home-buying usually occurring at a later age. One issue that emerged during the global financial crisis was whether some governments, notably the US government, had pushed home ownership too far.

Housing will always be an obsession, particularly in countries where home ownership rates are high. Unfortunately, as markets go, the one for housing is quite complicated. Imagine for a moment that the middle-class obsession was with the price of potatoes, which had risen to a very high level. Both the economist and the non-economist – the former after long years of study, the latter instinctively – would know how to analyse this. If the price of potatoes is very high, many people will decide they are spending too much of their income on them and switch to alternatives, such as rice and pasta, reducing potato demand. High prices discourage people from buying, while low prices encourage them. The effect on potato suppliers is, however, the opposite. High prices are an encouragement to supply more, while low prices act as a disincentive. Of course, it may not be possible to conjure up extra supplies instantly, although these days the supermarket chains operate very long storage times for so-called fresh foods. One reason why the prices of fresh produce traditionally varied so much from season to season was because supply varied between glut and shortage, depending on weather conditions and the extent to which farmers had responded to price signals (for example, planting more in response to this year's high prices).

The point, returning to our dinner table conversation about potatoes, is that if their prices have risen to very high levels compared with competing products, this is unlikely to last. Demand will fall, because other foods look relatively cheap. Supply will increase because it looks as if there is more profit to be made in potatoes. The net result will be lower prices. There's quite a lot of economics in all that but the only things to remember are, firstly, that whereas the higher the price, the lower in general the demand, the opposite is the case for supply. The second is that prices are determined by the interaction of supply and demand. In our example potato prices will fall by enough to make people want to buy more of them but not by enough to discourage suppliers from increasing their output. The price mechanism really is wonderful, ensuring that supply and demand match up, that the market achieves equilibrium, or balance. Markets tend towards equilibrium, towards the balancing of supply and demand, though they may take a while to get there. Remember that and you are well on your way to understanding market economics.

Housing and 'lemons'

It would be a strange and rather sad meal if the guests sat around talking about potatoes, so let us return to house prices. Many people think that the unusual thing about housing, indeed, is the extent to which prices have risen over time. In the 1930s, while much of Britain was suffering in the Great Depression and prices for everything including houses were falling, a great building boom was under way in and around London, creating suburbia. New Ideal Homesteads sold three-bed semis in Sidcup, Kent, for £250, houses that would cost you about one thousand times that at close to £250,000 in the 2010s. Modern Homes sold rather grander properties in Pinner, Middlesex, for between £850 and £1,500. To buy one of these eighty or so years later would cost over £1 million. These changes are dramatic but then plenty of things have increased in price over time. My first pint of beer (consumed at a very young age) cost the equivalent of ten pence. Now it would be thirty to forty times that or more. Inflation, the rise in the general price level, means that we look back with nostalgia at the prices we used to pay. All that has happened to house prices is that they have risen more rapidly than prices generally – they have outpaced inflation – and there is an explanation for that, which I shall come on to.

What is unusual about housing, a peculiarity it shares with only a few other things such as antiques, fine art and vintage wine, is that its price rises even as you own it. Housing, to economists, is not just something you 'consume', it provides warmth, shelter and a place to sleep – it is also an asset. Contrast what happens to house prices with other, apparently very solid, products. Most fall in price, either because they deteriorate with use or become obsolete. Try selling a ten-year-old computer. It is well known that if you buy a new car, it will usually be worth about 20 per cent less than you paid for it the moment you drive it out of the showroom. A famous article in 1970 by the economist George Akerlof, 'The Market for Lemons' – lemons in this case being American for 'dud' – explained why this was. Any buyer being offered a nearly new car by its owner would immediately assume that there must be something wrong with it, that it is a lemon, and thus will not be prepared to pay anything like the full price for it. This applies even if the car is perfect. Only sellers really know whether a car is perfect or not, buyers can never really be certain. Economists call this 'asymmetry of information' (one side has full knowledge, the other does not) but the jargon is not essential. The effect, as Akerlof explained, was to drive down prices across the whole market. Buyers will tend to assume, unfairly perhaps, that all second-hand cars are 'lemons'. And as long as this is the case, sellers have little incentive to sell good quality second-hand cars. Akerlof was jointly awarded the Nobel Prize for economics in 2001 (to be accurate the Bank of Sweden Prize in memory of Alfred Nobel) and, interestingly, the big car manufacturers have made an explicit effort to correct this lemon effect in the market. They now offer extended warranties on new cars (even lifetime warranties, though with strings) and special guarantees on the second-hand vehicles sold by their dealerships.

When we talk about the housing market, we are talking by and large about a second-hand market. New houses are built every year but their number is tiny, perhaps a 1 per cent increase in a good year in supply in relation to the existing housing stock in Britain. The net addition to that stock each year, taking into account properties removed from the market by demolition or conversion into offices, is even smaller. Why, if most houses are second-hand, do they not suffer from the lemon effect? Some, it should be said, do. Periodically, parts of Britain suffer from devastating flooding. In some cases such flooding is a once in a hundred years event, though other areas are affected every few years. One immediate consequence of the increased incidence of flooding, experts say, is that properties in areas prone to it become more difficult to sell, or only sellable at significantly lower prices, because people willing to put up with flood risk would require some compensation for doing so. In the late 1980s, in response to strong demand, Britain's house-builders built thousands of tiny boxes and called them starter homes. In the 2000s, builders went similarly over the top in building urban apartments in many of Britain's regional cities such as Birmingham, Leeds and Manchester. Like flood-prone houses, these subsequently became hard to sell. They became lemons.

In general, though, second-hand houses do not suffer in this way. Even if they need money spent on them, as they usually do, and even if that money exceeds anything revealed by the structural survey, which it usually does, buyers are not deterred, for two reasons. One is that, except in extreme circumstances, the cost of repairs and improvements usually represents only a small fraction of the cost (and therefore to the buyer the value) of the property. The second is that people are willing to spend money on their houses because they see this as maintaining or improving an asset that is going to go up in value. As an aside, a perennial debate in the property pages is whether you ever get back in the eventual selling price of the house, what you have spent on double-glazing, a conservatory or a kitchen. In other words, does your house sell for a sufficient amount more than the unimproved property down the road? To an economist, that may be a sensible question for a property developer to ask himself, but it does not have a lot of relevance to the ordinary home-owner. This is because the gains from any improvements fall into two categories: the 'consumption' of those improvements in the form of more warmth, comfort or space; and the effect on the value of the property. Splitting the two is very difficult indeed, not least because it will vary according to individual preferences.

While we are at it, let us nail another newspaper (and dinner party) favourite. Can you compare the rise in the price of your house and that of investments in the stock market? The answer is no, unless you have a way of valuing the non-financial benefits – warmth, shelter and so on – you have received from housing along the way, which share certificates do not offer. Not only that but, on the other side, most people do not take out a mortgage to buy stocks and shares (although when investing they do forgo the interest they could have obtained from putting their cash in a deposit account). It is a case, and I hesitate to introduce more fresh produce into the discussion, of comparing apples and pears. Even for professional landlords, the calculation is not easy. Most measures of long-run stock market performance assume share dividends are not taken as income but reinvested. The equivalent for a landlord would be that rental income was immediately invested in additional properties, and the comparison would then be between the rise in the value of an entire property portfolio, not any single house, and that of the stock market.

We have got this far without addressing a rather important question. People are prepared to spend money on their houses, not just because they want to live in more comfortable and spacious surroundings, but also because they think they are investing in an appreciating asset. History tells us that they are right to think that but it does not explain why. Let me try.

Why house prices rise
One of the most enduring economic relationships is that between house prices and people's incomes. House prices rise because

incomes do. The house price–earnings ratio – the ratio of average house prices to national average earnings for full-time workers – has averaged just over 4 since 1980. So if average earnings are £25,000–£30,000, house prices might be expected to be roughly four times that. It is easy to see why this relationship should exist. Suppose house prices had not risen and were stuck at their 1930s level. Someone on average earnings could buy several houses in the London suburbs a year, instead of buying one and paying for it over the twenty-five years of a mortgage. We are back to supply and demand. In this case rising demand does not mean that everybody wants to own a string of houses. It does mean that the amount they could afford to pay for their semi has increased hugely and, more importantly, so has the amount others can afford to pay. Competition among buyers, all of whom have been able to pay more over time, pulls house prices higher.

The house price–earnings ratio is not perfect, though some people follow it slavishly. Many more women work, accounting for nearly half of employment, so their income should also be taken into account in estimating household income. In a significant number of households the woman is the main breadwinner. It is also the case, as will be explained below, that over time the proportion of 'equity' in the housing market (that proportion of a property's value not accounted for by the mortgage) increases. So the house price–earnings ratio should be on an upward trend. Even so, incomes are clearly the key factor in determining house prices. Rising incomes pull house prices higher and incomes have risen steadily, and by about 2 per cent a year more than inflation (in other words in 'real' terms) for as long as anybody can remember (though they fell as a result of the crisis in both 2010 and 2011). Only rarely do real incomes fall. When it happened in 2011, the 1.2 per cent fall in real household incomes was the biggest since 1977. Mostly pay and other sources of income outstrip inflation. Certain groups of workers do better than others. I am old enough to remember the first £100-a-week professional footballer. Now the top-paid players get an eye-watering £300,000 a week or more in pay and sponsorship deals. I shall return later to the reasons why earnings usually rise faster than prices. One entertaining way of demonstrating that they do is by reference to the time an average person has to work to earn enough to afford certain products. Thus, in 1900 the average worker had to toil for a couple of hours to earn enough to buy a loaf of bread. Today, it is about five minutes.

In 2010, the Halifax (part of Lloyds Banking Group) looked at house prices over the previous fifty years. The average house price had risen from £2,507 to £162,085. This was faster than inflation, representing an increase of 273 per cent in 'real', or inflation-adjusted, terms. It was also a little faster than the growth in earnings. There is also an institutional element in the relationship between house prices and incomes. Banks and building societies base their mortgage lending decisions on the income, and therefore ability to pay, of the borrower, offering an advance that is a multiple of annual salary. That multiple can be as high as four, five or six times salary – and the lenders were criticised for offering that and sometimes more in the run-up to the financial crisis – although the average is roughly three. Interestingly, the ratio of house prices to incomes is usually significantly higher for older people who have been homeowners longer than for first-time buyers. This is because, while for first-time buyers the mortgage covers a high proportion of the value of the property, longer-term homeowners have usually built up capital, or 'equity', in their house. Someone buying a £100,000 house on an £80,000 mortgage has £20,000 of equity. If the value of the house rises to £200,000, the amount of equity increases to £120,000, and so on.

I said the housing market is different. Why, as in our potato example, do housebuilders not respond to high prices by sharply increasing the supply of new houses? And why does this not bring prices down, as it would for other products? The answer, as already noted, is that new houses account each year for only a tiny proportion of the existing housing stock. Land, to go back to some of those definitions at the start of this chapter, is a scarce resource. And planners ensure that, as far as building is concerned, it remains so. If there were no planning restrictions, and any farmer could sell a few fields for housebuilding, the housing market would be more like the market for potatoes. Big increases in supply would, from time to time, be followed by significant price falls. The planners, by preventing this from happening, help ensure rising house prices. Most of the 2000s were, apparently, strong for the housing market, with prices rising strongly and mortgage demand buoyant. It was a weak decade, however, for housebuilding. In no year did the number of houses completed by private housebuilders exceed 200,000. It is possible to stretch available living space a little, by converting houses into flats, or offices and former factories into fashionable lofts. But the general point still holds. New supply is very small in relation to the size of the market. To economists, supply is 'inelastic' – it responds only slowly to rising prices – whereas if builders were able to flood the market with new properties in response to high prices it would be 'elastic'.

Two prices for housing

We have got this far without touching on something rather important as far as housing is concerned. When people talk about their own house, they usually know how much they paid for it. They usually have a rough (or very precise) idea of how much it is worth. But, as every homeowner knows, as important as price paid and current value is the monthly mortgage outlay and that, in turn, depends on the level of interest rates. An easy way of demonstrating this is as follows. Suppose I buy a house for £200,000, on a full repayment mortgage worth 100 per cent of the value of the property (not that easy to obtain any more), and pay for it over twenty-five years at an average interest rate of 10 per cent. The total cost to me in monthly payments over the period is £550,839. If, on the other hand, the average interest rate were 5 per cent, repayments over twenty-five years would be £354,762. The difference is nearly as much as the original price of the house. Before anybody jumps up and down, £200,000 now is clearly worth a lot more than £200,000 spread over twenty-five years. Newspaper competitions sometimes offer choices of prize money in the form of either a large amount upfront or a somewhat smaller amount paid weekly for life. There are few takers for the latter. The economic principle behind this is a bit like the old proverb: 'A bird in the hand is worth two in the bush.'

Suppose you had the choice between £200,000 now or £400,000

in twenty-five years, which would you take? Before you opened this book your instinct may have been to go for the larger sum. Armed with some economics, however, the kind of calculation you would make would focus on the rate of interest you could earn on that money over the period. At a 4 per cent interest rate (which used to be thought of as quite low), £200,000 invested now would rise to £400,000 in fifteen years. At a rate of just over 2.5 per cent – and until the crisis, UK interest rates had not been that low since just after the Second World War – it would double over twenty-five years. Put another way, if you were asked what £400,000 in twenty-five years was worth to you now, the answer might be, depending on what you expect interest rates to do, a much smaller sum, and probably rather less than £200,000. This is known in economics as the present value of a sum received in the future. The number you have used to come up with it is called the discount factor – how much you would be prepared to trade money upfront for a stream of income in the future. It is most commonly used in decisions about investment. In this case it tells us that to match the offer of £200,000 now, and assuming a 4 per cent interest rate, something rather more than £400,000 would have to be offered in twenty-five years. On the other hand – an expression I promise to use only sparingly – if you expected interest rates to stay for a quarter of a century at the 'emergency' level of 0.5 per cent the Bank of England reduced them to in March 2009, you might accept an offer of rather less than £400,000.

I have digressed and time is moving on. The central point is that while the initial price of a house will be the main factor in the amount of a mortgage, the level of interest rates determines how much that mortgage costs. This is where analysis of the housing market gets quite interesting. Many amateur observers of the market, and quite a few professionals, have a blind spot when it comes to this. A fierce debate raged in Britain for years in the run-up to 2007 and the crisis about whether the boom in house prices then underway was about to come to a sticky end, as its predecessor did in the early 1990s. A little nervousness was in order. Peaking in 1989, house prices fell by between 20 and 30 per cent over the next four years, and by much more in some areas. Those who had bought near the top, and quite a few more, found themselves in 'negative equity' where the value of their property was less, by a considerable amount in some cases, than the mortgage they had taken out to buy it. This, the opposite of the equity enjoyed by most homeowners in their houses, affected more than a million households. A fall in house prices of this kind had not happened in Britain since the general deflation (a period of falling prices for everything) of the 1930s.

As in 1989, said the worriers, the ratio of house prices to incomes had stretched higher. Surely this presaged an imminent collapse? The trouble with this was that it ignored the crucial factor of interest rates. In 1989, interest rates rose to 15 per cent. In the 2000s they fell as low as 3.5 per cent, even ahead of the crisis. The implication, in terms of monthly mortgage outlays, was huge – people could afford to borrow more while paying a smaller proportion of their income in payments. They could afford to 'gear' themselves up. Maybe they geared themselves up too much but at least part of the recovery in house prices from their low point after the crash of the early 1990s could be seen as a gradual adjustment from the high interest rates of the 1970s and 1980s to the much lower rates that prevailed from the 1990s. These lower rates provided an argument for a permanent upward adjustment in the normal ratio between house prices and incomes.

They also provided a challenge for the Bank of England. When Gordon Brown gave the Bank operational independence in 1997 –which meant control over the instruments of monetary policy to meet an inflation target set by the government – some regarded it as a significant political risk. Would not the Bank, obsessed with achieving the inflation target, make life miserable for homeowners? Did Bank independence presage a period of uncomfortably high mortgage rates? In fact, the opposite happened. The level of interest rates needed to achieve the inflation target was low enough to produce a house-price boom, with house-price inflation touching more than 25 per cent in 2002 and 2003 and remaining generally high in the post-independence period. The Bank was criticised for ignoring house-price inflation, a criticism that increased when it was required to target a measure of inflation, the consumer prices index, which did not include a house-price component. The episode led to puzzlement at the Bank and the Treasury but had an easy answer. Without the volatility of interest rates of the past, and with their level apparently set permanently much lower, home-buyers were prepared to take the risk of mortgaging themselves heavily. Stability in consumer price inflation and interest rates led to instability in house prices. The general point, however, still holds. Sharply rising interest rates will tend to be associated with a weakening of housing demand, and vice versa when rates are falling. The real world, however, can be a complex place.

Housing in the crisis

The final chapter of this book will have much more to say on the global financial crisis that began in the summer of 2007, led to huge economic turbulence and cast a pall over the economy for years. It is impossible, however, to leave a discussion of housing without some mention of it. In the United States, where the infamous sub-prime mortgages provided the trigger for the crisis, housing was central. Sub-prime mortgages are low-quality loans, or at least loans to low-quality borrowers. America's housing market is different to that in Britain in that, in general, prices rise in line with inflation rather than earnings. There are two main reasons for this. One is that supply of new properties is much less constrained in America, so builders can respond quickly to demand. Another is that, since the 1970s, the growth in median wages, in real terms, has been much more subdued, and thus much closer to general inflation, than in Britain. So, when US house prices rose very strongly in real terms in the late 1990s and the first half of the 2000s, it should have set alarm bells ringing. Even so, the post-war history of the United States showed that national house price falls were both rare and modest. That provided no reassurance at all, however. From their peak in 2006 to the middle of 2011, US house prices fell by roughly 35 per cent, echoing the Great Depression. The big rise in prices that preceded the crash was undone. People would think more carefully about the American housing market in future.

In Britain the experience was rather different. The rise in prices that preceded the crisis was more pronounced than in America. In real terms, prices rose by 162 per cent between late 1995 and the autumn of 2007, according to the Nationwide Building Society. Britain's housing market looked particularly vulnerable because of the reliance of mortgage lenders on 'wholesale' sources of funding. Retail funding, consisting of savings' deposits by individual customers, was the traditional way building societies and banks funded mortgages. Wholesale funding means borrowing directly from the financial markets, or bundling mortgages together into what are known as asset-backed securities to sell to investors and raise funds. In the first half of 2007, on the eve of the crisis, between 60 and 70 per cent of new mortgages came from these wholesale sources. This was, however, also the source of funding that froze when the financial crisis erupted. At a stroke, two-thirds of the supply of new mortgages in Britain was cut off.

It was not surprising, in these circumstances, that house prices fell – and sharply. Cutting off the supply of credit to the housing market is a bit like cutting off its circulation. Combine that with the fact that prices had risen much faster than incomes and were overvalued, and a fall was guaranteed. Between October 2007 and February 2009 prices fell by a little over 20 per cent and were widely predicted to carry on falling. Then something surprising happened. House prices stabilised and began rising. By April 2010 they were more than 10 per cent up on a year earlier and, while they subsequently levelled off, they had behaved in an unexpected way. The episode is worth recalling as a reminder that economies do not always follow the script. It is also a useful exercise in explanation. Why did house prices not continue falling? One reason was the actions of the Bank of England, which cut Bank Rate to a record low of just 0.5 per cent – cutting one of the prices of buying housing – and embarked on a £200 billion programme of electronically creating money, or 'quantitative easing', of which more in later chapters. Another factor, however, brings us back to basic economics. Demand matters, so the loss of two-thirds of new mortgages was a significant problem for the housing market. Supply matters as well, however. The supply of new housing by builders, which had not kept up with demand in the run-up to the crisis, halved. There was also, however, a more important supply phenomenon. In the previous housing recession of the early 1990s there had been waves of forced selling, as homeowners, hit by high interest rates and unemployment, had no choice but to put their properties on the market. This happened to a much lesser extent in the 2008–9 recession because interest rates were cut sharply, unemployment rose by much less (though the recession was deeper) and lenders decided it was better to keep people in their houses rather than repossess the homes of borrowers who could not keep up with their mortgage payments. This resulted in what I describe as a low-activity equilibrium. Equilibrium is when demand and supply are in balance. In this case, both demand and supply were weak, leaving house prices nervously balanced between the two. Unusual things happen. Economists do well if they can explain them.

Intelligent observations

Sorry to have gone on so much about housing. It just shows that when you get into a conversation about these things it can be hard to stop. What it also shows is that a little bit of economics can take you a long way. No longer do you have to wonder uneasily whether the pub bore might be right when he tells you that house prices are going to fall for the next thirty years. Just ask him whether he thinks incomes are going to fall over that period, and why that should be. No longer, too, do you have to smile politely when somebody suggests that, irrespective of the level of interest rates, house prices are too high. You know better. And when you see one of those newspaper articles asking whether houses or shares are the better investment, either read it with a superior smile on your face or just turn the page. This is what economics is about, replacing assertion with argument, anecdote with analysis. Sometimes, when very unusual things happen, it is also about searching hard for cogent explanations. And as we shall see, it can be applied to very many things 'in the ordinary business of life'.

Interest rates and incomes are vital to the housing market but we have not talked about what determines them. That will come soon. In economics, as most people know, the study of individual markets is known as 'microeconomics', while both interest rates and the growth of incomes are 'macroeconomic' variables – concerned with the overall economy. Actually housing is a bit unusual in that respect too. While economists would regard the market for potatoes or, say, the housing market in Milton Keynes, as the preserve of microeconomics, the housing market in aggregate is so important that it makes it into the macroeconomic arena. All will become clearer when we look at how economic policy works. Time, however, is moving on. On to the main course.

3

Main Course (1)

Rude of me, I know, but I have not yet introduced you to the other guests at the table. Meet Mr and Mrs Rational – economic man and economic woman. They are not a bad couple, even if everything they do can be a bit predictable. I shall come on to them in a moment but let me just set out the aim of this main course. It is easy to get the idea that economics is about the billions of dollars flowing around the world's financial markets, or whether the Chancellor increases public spending or taxes by a billion pounds or two, but human behaviour is at the heart of it. The aim, then, is to start with the behaviour of economic men and women like them and try to build up from that to a picture of how the economy as a whole works. If that sounds a bit daunting, it will not be. Let us just start at the bottom and work our way up. Time to tuck in.

Behaving economically

Many people have trouble with the idea that human behaviour is predictable. Surely, most will say, it is inherently unpredictable. Economic man or woman may be acceptable in the textbooks but do they really exist in real life? If you are like me there are plenty of times when you will have made a stupid purchase (one of the 'lemons' of the last chapter) or some other bad and apparently unfathomable economic decision. On a more mundane level, how can economics explain why I choose to buy a new shirt on a whim, or walk to work rather than catch the bus? An aerial view of Oxford Street would surely show us scurrying around haphazardly, like a colony of ants.

Apart from the fact that there is nothing haphazard about the way a colony of ants behaves, the essence of economics is that human behaviour follows predictable patterns. When the price of something falls, for example, we will tend to buy more. There is nothing difficult or surprising about that. Even so, it appears that many see it as pseudo-scientific mumbo jumbo. Denis Healey, Britain's Chancellor of the Exchequer from 1974 to 1979, perhaps one of the most torrid periods for the economy in modern times, found plenty to criticise in the economic advice he was given. He declared his intention of doing for economic forecasters 'what the Boston Strangler did for door-to-door salesmen – to make them distrusted for ever'. As for economics in general, he was far from convinced of its usefulness. He wrote in his autobiography, *The Time of My Life*: 'I decided that while economic theory can give you valuable insights into what is happening, it can rarely offer clear prescriptions for government action, since economic behaviour can change from year to year and is different in one country from another.'

Healey was not being as damning as he thought. His central point that behaviour can change from one year to the next and differs between countries, is not one that any economist would have difficulty with. In the period he was in charge inflation rose to a peak of more than 26 per cent, the stock market plunged by two-thirds in value, the world economy had to try to cope with a quadrupling of the price of oil and Britain, apparently on the brink of bankruptcy (although countries default on their debts rather than going bankrupt) had to seek help from the International Monetary Fund – as Greece, Ireland and Portugal had to do more than three decades later in the eurozone crisis. What was changing was not so much fundamental economic behaviour as the forces acting on that behaviour, which were outside previous experience. There is another point, and it is one we shall return to, which is that rational behaviour can mean behaving differently at different times in response to similar circumstances. If you have bought a dud timeshare holiday once, you probably would not do so again, even if faced with the same inducements. If the price of oil quadrupled again, you would want to take your money out of the stock market. This kind of learning process is part of rational economic behaviour.

Predictably unpredictable
What about that unpredictability point? Behavioural economics, a relatively new branch of the subject, is all about exceptions to the rational rule. So, for example, it can explain that people are heavily

influenced by others' behaviour. Even if we know something is not a sensible decision, we might do it if other people are, perhaps for fear of being left out. We may also do things because we have always done it this way, and old habits die hard. Our motivation may be non-economic; we may do things that are economically irrational because we think it is good for wider society. Some rational decisions are hard to work out and often people lack the skills to do so. That, perhaps, is why so many buy dud savings products and invest in dodgy shares. The wider point is that most of us believe there is a large element of whim about what we do. I shall return to behavioural economics later.

How can anybody explain or predict why, on a given day I decided, perhaps with this meal in mind, that my wardrobe would not be complete without a purple-and-green striped shirt? What if everybody decided to buy one of those shirts on a particular day and then nobody decided to buy any shirts for a week? The answer is that, as long as there are enough of us, the unpredictable behaviour by some will cancel out. Even on an individual basis, we are not as unpredictable as you might think. An economist may not be able to predict the exact day you buy that shirt, and he may not be able to explain your appalling taste in colours (although he could go a long way towards doing so). But he knows, given your income, that you will buy a certain number of shirts over a period. This is why firms spend so much acquiring information on people's spending patterns and bombarding us with marketing literature that taps into those patterns. If everybody behaved haphazardly there would be no point in doing so.

Carrots and sticks

In his excellent book *The Armchair Economist*, Steven Landsburg writes: 'Most of economics can be summarised in four words: "People respond to incentives." The rest is commentary.' We have been here a little bit before, in the discussion in the last chapter on potatoes, and why they are different from houses. When potatoes fall in price we are likely to buy more of them and vice versa. Just to add to the confusion, incentives are popularly known as carrots and disincentives as sticks. Why do most of us keep working when there are much more pleasant things to do? Because the carrot of a gradually rising income bobs gently in front of our nose, while the stick of an alternative life of destitution brings up the rear.

The most obvious example of incentives is the one already described. When the price of something falls we will tend to buy more of it. There are exceptions to this rule but not many. In the 1990s, when a price war broke out between newspapers in Britain, many economists thought that newspaper proprietors were effectively throwing money away because people simply did not buy papers on price. Because the cost of a paper represented such a low proportion of income, a little like the usual textbook example of a box of matches, demand was expected to be unresponsive to changes in price, or 'inelastic'. In fact, it turned out to be quite elastic, demand for *The Times* increasing in response to price cuts, with the overall broadsheet market expanding when other newspapers followed suit. It was not, however, a strategy that newspapers stuck with, eventually deciding that it was worth sacrificing some circulation in favour of the revenue from a higher cover price.

Economists are always looking for exceptions to the rule. In the nineteenth century Robert Giffen noticed that for certain basic commodities, such as bread and potatoes, demand appeared to go up when prices rose. In very special circumstances, it worked. Imagine a family on very low incomes with a diet of potatoes and meat. When the price of potatoes goes up – but is still well below that for meat – their response is to cut out some of the meat and replace it with a larger amount of potatoes. Higher prices mean more, not less, demand. There may have been a real-life example of this during the Irish potato famine.

Giffen's observation earned him a place in the economics equivalent of the Hall of Fame, with certain goods being known as Giffen goods. Economists have, however, found it hard to identify sustained examples of them. It is a curiosity rather than a rule.

So-called inferior goods can also break the normal rule. Tripe (cow's stomach) used to be part of the regular meat diet of many people, particularly those on modest incomes, in the Midlands and the North. As people's incomes rose and the relative price of other meats fell, they were able to move on to chops, joints and even steaks. It did not matter that the price of tripe was falling, because demand also fell. These things, it should be said, can come full circle. Later, when French cuisine came to Britain in a big way, tripe became a delicacy much in demand at the best restaurants. Again, though, we should not get hung up about this. While it may have been true that over time the demand for tripe fell in spite of lower prices, on any given day during that process a butcher cutting his price could expect to sell more. You have to distinguish the short- and long-run effects.

Fish and chips

Paul Krugman, the American economist who is always worth reading, has a good example of the effects of changing tastes and incomes. His short paper, 'Supply, Demand and English Food', tries to answer the question of why restaurant food in Britain, which 'used to be deservedly famous for its awfulness – greasy fish and chips, gelatinous pork pies and dishwater coffee', had suddenly got better. His conclusion was that industrialisation and the shift of huge numbers of people from the country to towns and cities, had made people in Britain forget about wholesome food, and accept inferior, processed alternatives – canned vegetables and preserved meats – which were easier to ship and store. Prosperity rose but tastes did not change, mostly because people knew no better. According to Krugman, who is only half joking: 'Because your typical Englishman, circa, say, 1975, had never had a really good meal, he didn't demand one.' Only when people began to travel more widely, and began to experience other countries' cuisines, did they demand better quality. 'So what does all this have to do with economics?' asked Krugman.

Well, the whole point of a market system is supposed to be that it serves consumers, providing us with what we want and thereby maximising our collective welfare. But the history of English food suggests that even on so basic a matter as eating, a free market economy can get trapped for an extended period in a bad equilibrium in which good things are not demanded because they have never been supplied, and are not supplied because not enough people demand them.

Fun, and surely this must be right. It is interesting to speculate whether these bad equilibriums have become rarer because, via the Internet as well as increased international travel, people are better informed about what is available elsewhere. The point of much marketing and advertising is to convince us that new products will lift us to a higher level of satisfaction, a good equilibrium.

Pricing to sell

Having wandered off down a little byway, it is worth returning for a moment to the central point. Why do we buy more of something when its price falls? With the exception of Bill Gates and a fairly limited number of other very rich people, most of us are limited in what we can spend by our income; we are subject to a budget constraint. Within that constraint, we allocate our spending on the basis of necessity and desire – some on food, drink, travel, books, entertainment, and so on. I buy a certain number of CDs every year. I could buy more if I chose to eat a little less but I am happy with the way things are. I have made my choices. To economists, I am 'indifferent' between the number of CDs I buy and the number of meals I eat. Odd word, I know, but all it means is that, for a given level of income and pattern of prices, this combination of spending is right for me.

Now what would happen if the price of CDs were to halve? At the very least you might think that I would buy twice as many, because I could do so while devoting the same proportion of income to their purchase. I could, though, buy exactly the same number and use the money so released to buy nicer meals, travel more, or go to the cinema more often. I could even save more. If

I did that, the cut in prices would have had no effect and our rule would have been broken. So what would one expect? Within my own pattern of spending, CDs have suddenly become cheap relative to everything else. The cost of other things, expressed in terms of CDs, has gone up. So my future desired pattern of spending will be for a higher proportion of CDs relative to other things. Economists call this the 'substitution' effect – shifting spending patterns in favour of things that have fallen in price or, in the opposite situation of a rise in prices, away from products that have gone up. We demonstrate the substitution effect every time we buy more of an item emblazoned with special offer signs at the supermarket.

There is also, however, another effect. The halving of the price of CDs has made me better off. Why? Before the price cut, my income allowed me to buy food, housing, clothing, travel and so on, plus about twenty CDs a year. Now, that same income allows me all those things plus forty CDs. The fall in price is equivalent to an increase in my income. In that respect, it is like any other increase in income. So, just as I would not spend all of a pay rise buying more CDs, neither will I do so in this case. This is known, unsurprisingly, as the 'income effect'. What it means, for me at least, is that the most likely result of a halving of the price of CDs will be quite a big increase in purchases of them (but not a doubling) and smaller increases in my consumption of everything else. In the opposite situation of a rise in the price of CDs, assuming no change in my income, all of the above would be reversed.

A good real-world example of this goes back to the previous chapter. When interest rates fall, one of the prices (and the costs) of housing – the one that affects household budgets – has come down. The substitution effect of this is that you think of buying a bigger house, and some people do so. The income effect is that you have become better off, a fall in interest rates being equivalent to a rise in the borrower's income. And, because you are better off, you spend more on items other than housing. That is one of the ways that monetary policy traditionally works, as we shall see later.

Getting satisfaction

Before moving on, time to tackle a little puzzle. What determines what we spend our money on? Why some things rather than others? Many people would answer 'need' to this question. Britain's Office for National Statistics, which produces the annual Family Spending Report, found that in 2009 the average household spent £455 a week. A significant proportion of this was on what most would think of as necessities: with £58.40 going on transport; £57.30 on housing, fuel and power; and £52.20 on food and non-alcoholic drink. The average household spent smaller amounts on clothing and footwear, package holidays, furniture and other durable goods, and alcoholic drink. It also spent £57.90 a week on recreation and culture. The interesting thing about this was that 2009 was a depressed year for consumer spending. In the midst of the deepest recession in Britain in the post-war period, spending by households fell. Even so, spending on non-necessities, particularly if you regard recreation and culture as not essential to survival, remained high, and was almost the biggest single component of household spending. This is why we should always treat claims about current economic conditions that draw historical parallels with a pinch of salt. If things are bad now it is from a higher base; there is no real comparison with the 1920s and 1930s or the austerity period that followed the Second World War. Earlier generations would not have had the luxury of devoting an eighth of their weekly spending to recreation and leisure. Feeding and housing the family would have taken up most, if not all, of their income. Prosperity has brought with it an increase in consumer choice. We can go to the opera (although a ticket at the Royal Opera House costs more than the average family's weekly leisure spend), or get fat on the sofa watching televised football.

Taking all the above as read, we still need to answer the question: why do we spend in the way we do? It may seem trivial but it was something that obsessed many of the great economists of the past, particularly in the nineteenth and early twentieth centuries. They were concerned with the satisfaction or 'utility' people obtained from consuming things. Some even believed it could be precisely measured. In general, the more of something we consume, the less satisfaction or utility we will get out of each extra one. One bar of chocolate a day is fine for me but a second I could take or leave. After a third I would feel queasy and after a fourth I would be quite ill. The amount of utility we get from each extra one, each 'marginal' one, falls. This is known as diminishing marginal utility – the more you have the less you want another one. It can even go negative. After six cups of coffee in a morning, I would pay somebody to drink the seventh I was offered. Diminishing marginal utility does not apply to everything. Collectors may get more satisfaction out of the final acquisition that completes a set than the first that began it. One harmless bit of fun economics opens up is thinking of exceptions to the rule. Are addicts, for example, subject to diminishing marginal utility?

Utility does allow us to answer some of the great mysteries of our time. Why, when there are so many wholesome alternatives around, do people buy barely nutritious convenience food? Why don't students blow their entire loan in frenzied partying in the first week of term? Why do old men who drive cars in the middle of the road always wear trilby hats? Actually I cannot help with the third one (and if anybody can, let me know) but I can with the other two. It all has to do with utility. What we all try to do, subconsciously – although I have met a few strange economists who do it consciously – is try to maximise our utility. In other words, we try to get the most out of what we spend. I would not be doing this if I spent my entire income on Mars bars, because diminishing marginal utility would kick in quite quickly. It may be that I could do it by alternating fillet steak with Pot Noodles. I suspect, however, that many aficionados of Pot Noodles maximise their utility by alternating them with copious quantities of beer in the student bar. As for why those same students do not blow their student loans in the first week, it is because it would not maximise their utility to have one glorious but soon forgotten binge and live on nothing for the rest of the year.

Incentives work everywhere

The idea that 'incentives work' underpins much of economics. It is also a basic tenet of economics that can be extended to other areas of life. Gary Becker, an American economist, won the Nobel Prize for economics in 1992 'for having extended the domain of microeconomic analysis to a wide range of human behaviour and interaction, including non-market behaviour'. Some of the ways incentives work are fairly obvious, if nevertheless controversial. How do you reduce the murder rate? Some would say by making the death sentence mandatory for all convicted murderers. I shall leave to you the question of whether this would, in turn, give juries an incentive not to convict. Crime and punishment are areas where the incentive model can be widely used. What is the best way of stopping people speeding in their cars? Is it to try to persuade them of the dangers of driving too fast or is it to install speed cameras on every stretch of road and slap heavy fines on transgressors? Government policy in Britain, having tried the former for many years, took to emphasizing the latter, before politicians began to worry that they could be accused of waging war on the motorist. Road safety, in fact, is an area where incentives could be used more widely. Safe and conviction-free drivers already benefit from lower insurance premiums than their more dangerous counterparts. Why should not the government extend this incentive principle by varying rates of road tax depending on the safety record of the driver? Road safety is also an area, however, where incentives may operate in a perverse way. Do seat belts make people drive more carefully or, knowing that they are better protected in the event of a crash, more dangerously? Would the best way of ensuring safe driving be to require every vehicle to be fitted with a large spike in the centre of the steering wheel, as has been suggested, because nobody would then take any risks?

There are more entertaining examples of incentives. Why, in most western societies, is polygamy banned? On the surface it looks like a case of men, against their own self-interest, legislating in favour of women, ensuring they are not forced to share a husband. This assumes, however, that polygamy is a state desired by most men, which is debatable. It also ignores the fact that, in any society where there is a roughly equal number of men and women, polygamy will mean that, for every man with five or six wives there will be four or five sad and lonely ones without any wives at all. There is also the strong possibility that wives in a polygamous marriage will be less loyal, ready to respond to the blandishments of a richer man down the road. Incentives work, and men can do without that kind of competition. Men have an incentive to outlaw polygamy. You can extend this to plenty of other areas. Were more liberal attitudes towards the position of women in the workforce driven by fairness, or by the desire of many men to be able to spend their afternoons on the sofa, watching the racing on television?

Steven Landsburg, in one of his regular pieces for *Slate*, the online magazine, offered another interesting angle on the role of incentives in society. Why, he asked, is there so much obesity around, particularly in America? The usual explanations revolve around the malign influences of TV, cars and fast food (including the defining moment when the standard unit of consumption for teenagers became, not the four-ounce hamburger, but the Big Mac at twice the size). These are all good reasons. Lack of exercise in childhood, with fewer children walking to school, often results in obese teenagers. But why do people stay obese? Why don't they lose weight when they realise how dangerous it can be to carry too much fat around? According to Landsburg, it is because they have lost the incentive to lose weight. And incentives, as we know, are the key to economic behaviour. He writes:

> *Here's one plausible story: The nineties saw the advent of drugs like Pravachol and Lipitor that can dramatically cut your cholesterol and increase your life expectancy. With medical advances like that, who needs to be thin? Of course obesity is still bad for you – but it's not as bad for you as it used to be. The price of obesity (measured in health risks) is down, so rational consumers will choose more of it. With the success of the human genome project, even greater advances are just over the horizon, making obesity an even greater bargain. Today's expanding waistlines might reflect nothing more than a rational expectation of future progress against heart disease.*

Landsburg also offered, perhaps tongue in cheek, an explanation of why low-fat foods contribute to obesity.

> *Suppose a scoop of ice cream a night would add 10 pounds to your weight, and you've decided that's not worth it, so you don't eat ice cream. Now along comes a low-fat ice cream that allows you to eat two scoops a night and add 10 pounds to your weight. That's a better deal, and a perfectly rational being might well opt for it. So when low-fat foods come along, some people sensibly decide to become fatter.*

Economists, you see, have an explanation for almost everything. Why do tall people tend to be more successful in life? The usual explanation is that employers favour them, particularly in leadership positions. There is, however, little evidence of that. And if there was evidence of such discrimination, short people could legitimately cry foul. The key, according to researchers at Pennsylvania State University, is that what matters is not height in adulthood but height during adolescence. Tall adolescents are usually picked for school sports teams, are chosen as prefects and, for boys at least, often fare better with the opposite sex. It is during adolescence that, thanks to their height, the tall acquire both confidence and leadership qualities. This may also explain, incidentally, why some short people have risen to the top. Either they are reacting against the discrimination they perceived when they were younger or they were tall for their age during adolescence and then stopped growing. Does it work as a general rule? Ask around.

Work or leisure?

Finally in this section, let me come to a question of incentives that causes much debate among economists. When somebody wins a large sum on the football pools, the Lottery or *Who Wants to Be a Millionaire?*, the question usually asked is: will your winnings mean that you will give up work? There is another question, to which I shall return later in the book, which is: will this money make you happy? In response to the work question, the answer is either the heart-warming but probably unrealistic: 'I won't let it change my life', or the more usual: 'You bet your life I'm giving up work.'

Very few of us win large sums of money, although the prospect of doing so gives us an incentive to play the lottery or do the pools, however long the odds. But many of us are faced with smaller versions of this kind of decision. Suppose, at a time of negligible inflation, you receive a 25 per cent pay rise. The choice is between being better off financially or, instead, working four days a week instead of five and enjoying the same standard of living as before. A manager could, in other words, reward his best staff by paying them more, only to find that he then sees less of them.

This is known as the 'work–leisure trade-off' and it is quite interesting and important. By leisure, by the way, we do not mean just going to the cinema or lounging around the pool. It also includes those hours you spend sleeping, washing up or vacuuming the stairs, in other words all non-work hours. If you spent all the time working, not only would you be very tired, there would be no time to spend the money you had earned. That is one end of the spectrum in terms of the work–leisure trade-off. If you did not work at all but spent all your time on the beach, you would have no money to eat. That is the other end of the spectrum. For most people there will be a trade-off between work and leisure somewhere in the middle. To go back to the earlier discussion of why people spend in the way they do, people will be 'indifferent' between a certain amount of time spent in work, say forty hours a week, and a certain amount of leisure, the rest of the week. When wages rise people are indeed better off, and could work fewer hours. On the other hand, leisure has become relatively more expensive – think how much you could be earning while you are relaxing – creating an incentive to work longer hours. The balance between these two effects, the income and substitution effects, will determine whether higher wages result in longer or shorter hours.

On the face of it, the long-run evidence suggests that higher wages do result in fewer hours worked. I described in the last chapter how incomes have risen in real terms – they have outstripped inflation – but alongside this we have also seen a decline in hours worked. In the past 150 years or so, a typical manual worker's week has dropped from well over sixty hours to forty or fewer, with a corresponding reduction in the standard white-collar week. Prosperity brought with it a demand for greater leisure – the income effect dominated the substitution effect. To remind you how this works, the rise in income has, in effect, made it possible to buy more leisure time, and this is what most people have chosen to do. This is despite the fact that leisure time has become more expensive in terms of what the worker could have earned by, say, working Saturday mornings.

Interestingly, many would testify that this process came to an end towards the end of the twentieth century, with many managerial and white-collar staff being required to work far longer than their statutory hours of employment, and to take work home. More people took second jobs, notably in America and Britain. Yet another change took place, if only temporarily, during and after the UK recession of 2008–9. Unemployment rose by much less than feared, because employees were willing to work fewer hours (and take less pay). A smaller amount of available work was spread over a larger number of people. The fall in employment was only just over a third of the drop in gross domestic product. It remains to be seen if this represented a lasting change. There are also big variations in working hours, even among industrial countries. Americans work nearly 1,800 hours a year on average, compared with roughly 1,400 in Germany and about 1,650 in Britain. The differences are accounted for by variations in both weekly hours and holiday entitlements.

Work and tax

All this is rather important, particularly when it comes to economic policy. In the 1980s, when Margaret Thatcher was in office in Britain and Ronald Reagan was in the White House, there was great stress on the role of incentives and on how they could be sharpened by means of income tax cuts. The argument was that if you allowed people to keep more of their earnings – in effect boosting their wages – they would work harder. If you hit them with punitive rates of tax, on the other hand, they would work less hard. Embarrassingly for the British government, a piece of research commissioned by the Treasury, carried out by Professor Chuck Brown of Stirling University, found that the opposite was true. When taxes were cut, it either made no difference to people or they worked fewer hours. But when taxes went up, they were obliged to work harder to maintain their level of (post-tax) income. A furious debate ensued, after which there was no clear winner. Most people, it turned out, were in no real position to alter their hours of work, these being fixed by the firm they worked for. The more difficult question, whether lower taxes meant they worked harder during their allotted time – in other words that they raised their productivity – is still not conclusively settled. There was, however, other evidence. Britain's top rate of income tax was reduced to 40 per cent in 1988 and appeared to have a positive effect by encouraging more international companies to locate in Britain, particularly in financial services. It also reduced the incentive among individuals to engage in expensive tax planning. This and a stronger rise in earnings among the higher-paid than for the population as a whole resulted in a rise in the proportion of income tax revenues coming from higher-rate taxpayers. In 1978–9, when the top rate of income tax was 83 per cent, 11 per cent of income tax revenues came from the top 1 per cent of earners. By 2009–10, with a top rate of 40 per cent, the proportion had more than doubled to 24 per cent. This was, though, the final year of the 40 per cent top rate. It was raised to 50 per cent from April 2010 by the Labour government, as one of the measures to reduce the budget deficit. Business warned that the move would have serious disincentive effects, while the incoming coalition government in May 2010 promised to examine whether the higher rate of tax generated a net increase in tax revenues, in the event cutting it to 45 per cent from April 2013.

I shall return to tax later. One area where tax changes do appear to have had a clear effect on people's appetite for work is in the case of women. In Britain married couples used to be taxed jointly. A woman getting a part-time job would be taxed at her husband's highest marginal tax rate, which in the 1970s in Britain could be as high as 83 per cent and for most of the 1980s was, for higher-rate taxpayers, 60 per cent. In such circumstances many couples decided it was not worth the wife working. Independent taxation, the separate taxation of husbands and wives, introduced in the late 1980s by Nigel Lawson, one of Thatcher's three Chancellors, changed all this. Women had their own tax-free allowance and paid tax at a rate that reflected their earnings, not those of their husband. This made a big contribution to one of the features of

Britain's job market in the latter part of the twentieth century – a huge increase in the number of women working.

We have come a long way and we are not even through the main course yet. I know the feeling, however, when you are halfway through a prestige dinner with the speeches still to come, and you are wondering uncomfortably whether you can make it until the end. I also hate excessively long chapters. It is time for a quick break, and then to welcome a very special guest.

4

Adam – but no apple

In many ways our first celebrity guest is a brave choice. While few economists would quarrel with the choice of Adam Smith as the father of modern economics, many might hesitate before inviting him along as a speaker. This eighteenth-century Scot (1723–90) was almost a parody of the absent-minded professor. Anecdotes that have been passed down through the years tell of him putting bread and butter into a teapot, pouring hot water on it, and then wondering why the tea tasted so foul. Or of him being so engaged in a philosophical discourse while walking along that he stumbled into a tanning pit. Born in Kirkcaldy on the Firth of Forth a few months after the death of his father, the town's customs controller (in the days when the post was grander than now), Smith never married, although he refers approvingly in print to the beauty of 'potato-fed Irish prostitutes' in London. He was no oil painting, as he himself admitted. While in later life women courted his mind, they had to overcome his big teeth and bulging eyes. One female French novel-ist declared him to be 'ugly as the devil'. His private passions have to be a source of speculation because he ordered all his papers to be destroyed on his death.

Smith, like many great thinkers, was not, it seems, a great speaker. Burdened with a harsh voice and an occasional stutter, he was also an unforgiving lecturer. Having spent a miserable few years in Oxford as a student, he chose his native Scotland to pursue his academic career. His lectures in Glasgow used to start at 7.30 in the morning, begin hesitatingly, and then last for hours, with Smith addressing the ceiling rather than the students. He was sometimes seen carrying on such debates with himself, out loud, on street corners. Absent-minded he may have been but he was also hugely influential. Two centuries after his death, his ideas returned to prominence across the world but, in particular, with the election of Ronald Reagan in America and Margaret Thatcher in Britain. Thatcher was said to carry a copy of Smith's *The Wealth of Nations* in her legendary and capacious handbag. The five-volume work runs to nearly 1,200 paperback pages. The Adam Smith Institute in London (from whom you can buy a range of Adam Smith memorabilia) came to the fore as an advocate of pri-vatisation and pro-market policies. The collapse of communism and the triumph of capitalism at the end of the 1980s could be seen as a victory for Smith over Karl Marx. The financial crisis that almost brought down the global banking system in 2008 cast the free market, or at least one version of it, in a rather less favourable light.

Timing is everything

As far as most economists were concerned, Smith had never gone away. It may seem like a conceit to think that economics began in 1776 with the publication of his great work which, to give it its full title, was *An Inquiry into the Nature and Causes of the Wealth of Nations* (which in his lifetime was outsold by his other main work, *The Theory of Moral Sentiments*). There was economics before Smith, now known as pre-Adamite economics. Ancient civilisations had their economic thinkers, as did the Renaissance. Like all great thinkers Smith has been accused of lifting some of his best ideas from his predecessors and near contemporaries. Certainly he was fortunate in some respects. He was offered and accepted a lucrative sinecure from Charles Townshend, a fan of *The Theory of Moral Sentiments* and one-time Chancellor of the Exchequer, who invited him to become tutor to his teenage stepson, the Duke of Buccleuch. On taking up this role, in which he began the twelve-year period of the writing of *The Wealth of Nations*, Smith was able to travel widely with his pupil, and in particular tap into economic thinking elsewhere in Europe. French economists such as François Quesnay were influential. He also spent time with Voltaire.

The important thing about *The Wealth of Nations*, however, hugely ambitious as it was in scope and size, is that it presented the first synthesis of economics in its entirety. It explained why nations should trade with each other and benefit from doing so (opposing the view of the earlier mercantilists who had favoured trade restrictions in the belief that protectionism preserved economic advantage for some countries). It provided an explanation and a justification for the minimum interference by government in free markets within countries. It told governments how they should go about the process of raising taxes. It explained how the Industrial Revolution then in progress would raise prosperity, most notably as we shall see with his famous example of the pin factory.

That, perhaps, helps explain Smith's influence more than anything. He came at a turning point in economic history. Published in the year of American independence, and the beginning of a new world order, *The Wealth of Nations* also coincided with the start of a process in which industrialisation was to provide unprecedented growth in wealth. This, a step-change compared with the economic stagnation of the agricultural age, was also to raise questions about how that wealth should be distributed among the population. Smith, a product of the Enlightenment, provided a template for economic thinking through and beyond the Industrial Revolution that so changed previous notions about the way societies worked.

But what, out of the multi-volume *Wealth of Nations*, should we take as important? Is it Smith's rules, or canons, of taxation, centred on ability to pay? Is it his theory of value? Is it his belief that governments should concentrate on certain basic functions, because most public services are 'unproductive', and that public works such as roads or bridges should be paid for by tolls or fees, not out of general taxation? Important though these are to students of the history of economic thought and in some cases to policymakers today, and while it is the done thing at this point to recommend that people read the full work themselves (few do), there are probably three things we should carry with us from Smith.

The division of labour

Smith was writing at a time when there were very few factories in Britain. Those that did exist were mainly powered by water. The Industrial Revolution had barely begun. Yet he promised to demonstrate how economic changes could occur that would bring 'universal opulence which extends itself to the lowest ranks of the people'. First among these was the division of labour. The pin factory, mentioned above, demonstrates very simply how this operates. Suppose, Smith said, a pin factory employed ten people, each engaged in the entire process of making a pin. The factory would certainly produce pins, perhaps a few hundred a day, but it would not do so very effectively. Now look at the way it actually worked in his day:

> *One man draws out the wire, another straightens it, a third
> cuts it, a fourth points it, a fifth grinds it at the top for receiving
> a head; to make the head requires two or three distinct
> operations; to put it on is a peculiar business, to whiten the pins
> is another; it is even a trade by itself to put them into the paper.*

And so on. Specialisation made each man much more effective. Even in what was essentially a manual process, without the machinery that was to shape industrialisation, huge productivity gains could be achieved. The division of labour, in other words, raised the level of output per worker. Smith's factory produced not a few hundred but tens of thousands of pins each day. It is interesting to think that it took until 1912, when Henry Ford applied his mass production methods to the building of the Model T at his

Highland Park assembly plant in America, methods that meant the time it took to build a car was cut to just ninety-three minutes, for the full flowering of this particular division of labour to occur.

There was more to Smith's division of labour, however, than a management consultant's approach to factory organisation. If we think about the pin factory, the key to raising the productivity of the workers and therefore their prosperity (and that of the owners) was specialisation. But there was no reason, as Smith explained, to think of the possibilities of specialisation as being limited to those within a single workplace.

What determines why people do certain jobs and others do others? In general, because people find something they are suited to, and are good at. What is best for me to do, to try to fix a problem with the plumbing in my house in my inexpert and laborious way? Or to write an article (or probably, given the prices London plumbers charge, two or three articles) to earn the money to pay for the services of a professional? The answer, to me at least, is fairly clear, as I hope it would be to the plumber if somebody asked him to pen an economics piece. The point is that it is much more efficient if each of us concentrates on what we are good at and trades those services. We buy pork chops from the butcher rather than attempt to kill the pig for ourselves.

Extending this division of labour a little further up the scale, it becomes clearly beneficial if there is specialisation by firms. A modern car is made up of many hundreds of components made by different firms. Such specialisation enables the cost of the car to be much lower than if a single firm attempted to manufacture every part. In the 1980s there was a revolution in British industry when manufacturing firms contracted out to independent suppliers many tasks, from cleaning and maintenance to distribution. They were following Adam Smith.

The process does not have to end within countries. The argument in favour of foreign trade, indeed of free trade, is essentially a division of labour argument. With the right investment in hothouses and specialist equipment, Britain could in theory provide for all her wine needs and never import a drop from abroad. It makes more sense, however, to buy it from countries with the climate and expertise to do it better and more cheaply. The basis of trade is that countries specialise in the things they are best at. The gains from trade result from this specialisation. This is why actions to restrict trade usually impoverish us all. What happens if a country is no good at anything? I'll come back to that later.

The invisible hand

The part of *The Wealth of Nations* that every schoolboy knows – or if not they should – gives us Smith's most famous idea. He wrote: 'It is not from the benevolence of the butcher, the brewer, or the baker, that we expect our dinner, but from their regard to their own interest. We address ourselves not to their humanity but their self love.' To understand it fully, it is necessary to tie it to another, related section which, in slightly edited form, reads:

'Every individual who employs capital and labours neither intends to promote the public interest nor knows how much he is promoting it … he is led by an invisible hand which was no part of his intention. By pursuing his own interest he frequently promotes that of society.'

What was this invisible hand? Because of its later importance, you might think there are references to it dotted throughout the pages of *The Wealth of Nations*. In fact, the above is the only one. Some writers have speculated that it could have had religious connotations; others that Smith unconsciously lifted it from Shakespeare's *Macbeth*, where there is a reference to the 'bloody and invisible hand'.

There is no need to get too fancy about this, however. What Smith was sketching out was the market mechanism, the laws of supply and demand we have already touched on, although it was left to later economists to fill in the details. This was no paean of praise to businessmen. Whenever they met, he wrote, 'the conversation ends in a conspiracy against the public, or in some contrivance to raise prices'. The point was that the market did not let them get away with it, or at least not for long. Customers would abandon profiteers in favour of competitors offering lower prices. Attempts by groups of firms to fix prices by agreement – forming a cartel – would fail as long as it was possible for new firms to enter the market and undercut them. The invisible hand is the market, and through its operation the best possible, or optimum, outcome is achieved.

Of course, in any economy, there will be lots of different markets, not only for all the various products and services but also, for example, for labour. One of the great debates sparked off by Smith was, in fact, over labour. What was to stop workers being permanently exploited in this new Industrial Revolution, of being paid no more than necessary for the very basics of existence? Smith pointed out not only that competition for workers among employers would make this unlikely but also that the process of industrialisation, and of the development of mass market products, would require that workers – as the new consumers – be paid above the subsistence level, and increasingly so. He was right. The market did not put an end to worker exploitation but the Industrial Revolution marked the start of the rise of modern mass prosperity. As we shall see, Karl Marx had rather different views on this.

Liberty

It is hard to overstate the importance of Smith's contribution to economics. As its founding father he provided a template for the subject. He also provided an underlying philosophy that endures to this day. That philosophy was that economic freedom and liberty provides the best of all possible worlds, through the operation of the invisible hand. Attempts to interfere with that freedom, by introducing restrictions, or allowing monopolies to operate, will make us all poorer than we need be. Governments, even if they mean well, will usually end up making things worse. This did not mean that there should be no government at all – Smith favoured strong and clear laws, properly policed – but it did mean limiting its role. He would have had no truck with government being directly involved in the production process by owning firms.

When, advocated by the likes of Margaret Thatcher, Smith came back into vogue, it was easy to see why. The market, it seemed, had taken a back seat. The UK had, in the thirty or so years since the Second World War, become a heavily controlled economy and one in which the state played an increasingly dominant role. Monopoly power had been allowed to develop while, on the other side, unions operated a range of restrictive practices. The policies followed by the Thatcher government, which involved the removal of controls, denationalisation (or as it came to be known, privatisation), and the ending of restrictive practices by both unions and employers, added up to a classic recipe for restoring markets, for giving the invisible hand a chance to operate. Adam Smith would have been proud of her.

Did the process go too far? One of the more interesting features of the financial crisis was the spectacle of bankers with impeccable free market credentials crying out for official action to prevent the system from collapsing. The light-touch regulatory framework under which the City had been allowed to operate was one that assumed that, in acting in their own interests, bankers would not act in such a way that so endangered the wider economy. What happened to the invisible hand? Both sides have a response to this. Critics of the free market say there was a direct line from Thatcher and Reagan to the financial crisis. Free market supporters blame inept regulation for the failure and argue that banks and other financial institutions would have been more risk-averse if left to regulate themselves. One thing we can be clear about – Smith would have had little time for the argument that some banks were too big to fail.

5

Main Course (2)

Welcome back. Before we broke we had made a lot of progress in trying to explain how, as individuals, we behave as economic animals, even when we are not aware of it. All very interesting you might say (at least I hope you do) but how does this fit into the big picture? When people talk about 'the economy', what do they mean? This is a good time to start thinking big, to go from the micro to the macro. Here goes.

So what is an economy?
This is one of those questions, a bit like 'What is life, Daddy?', you hope your children will not ask you. The best way of answering it, given that this is probably not the time for another food analogy, is by thinking of a football match. At one level, a football match is a game between two teams of eleven men lasting ninety minutes, the object of which is to kick a ball into your opponents' goal more

times than they do into yours. Everybody knows, however, there is more to it than that. A football match is about the contributions of individual players, and of the referee and crowd, of the goals, the goalmouth incidents, the fouls, the mistakes, and so on. Put like that, a football match consists of many thousands of actions that go together to make a whole. How do you explain that to somebody who was not there? They can read a match report in the newspaper. If they are real enthusiasts, though, they will examine the statistics – goals scored, shots on goal, red and yellow cards, the percentage of time each team had possession of the ball, and so on. The statistics can never be a perfect substitute for being there but it is the next best thing. So it is with the economy. At its most basic, the British economy is what a nation of just over 62 million people spends, earns and produces. At its most complicated it is millions upon millions of decisions taken by individuals, either for themselves or on behalf of companies. Magnificent though this would be, to observe it would also be impossible. As with football, therefore, it is necessary to boil all these actions down to manageable statistics. For economists, as we shall see later, it is also necessary to develop models of the economy. These simplified or stylised versions of the real thing are similar in concept to architects' models of buildings. An architect's model does not try to capture every detail of the actual building – very few have running water or working miniature coffee machines – but it gives a good idea of what the full-sized building will look like. Economic models try for something similar, though they often fail spectacularly. In the run-up to the financial crisis central banks, finance ministries and other forecasters made extensive use of what were known as 'dynamic stochastic general equilibrium' (DSGE) models. Such models failed to get wind of the crisis coming, mainly because their financial sectors were poorly developed. Some of their more loyal defenders would argue that predicting crises was never their purpose.

Disappointingly, however, when economists say they are building a model of the economy, this does not mean they are getting out the hardboard, sticky-backed plastic and papier-mâché. Models of the economy are usually linked sets of mathematical equations that churn away in the recesses of computers. One of the exceptions, still in existence at the Science Museum in London, was built at the London School of Economics.

In the late 1940s, A. W. 'Bill' Phillips was a New Zealander in his early thirties who had emerged from a Japanese prisoner of war camp (the late Laurens van der Post, once Prince Charles's mentor, was a fellow prisoner). Phillips had suffered near starvation, as was obvious to fellow students, when he came to study at the LSE. He also had difficulty understanding what he was being taught and in particular the flow of money around the economy. So, using Perspex tubes, levers, pulleys and windscreen-wiper motors scavenged from a wartime plane, he built a model of it. It was and is a device of extraordinary complexity. Not only was it a fully working hydraulic model showing money (water) flowing around the system but it also provided a primitive printout, as a pen attached to the machine plotted the results. When Phillips demonstrated the machine to a sceptical LSE audience in 1949, by pouring in red liquid at the top to demonstrate the effects of adding cash to the economy, it was to general acclaim. The model, conceived in an age when computers were still the stuff of science fiction to most people, could simulate the effects of, say, cutting taxes or boosting government spending. *Punch*, the humorous magazine, said a Phillips machine should be installed in every town hall in Britain. 'The machine is taller than the man in the street and wider and heavier and much, much cleverer,' it said. 'Using coloured water (a convenience denied the man in the street) it reacts obediently to every morsel of economic information communicated to it, and records, with its mechanical pens on its calibrated charts, the subtle impact of a slump in the second-hand ship market, the slightest hint of a boom in soap, emery wheels or white fish.' Phillips did not make machines for every town hall but did make fourteen of them. The Ford Motor Company bought one, and so did Harvard. Phillips went on to become an influential economist, known also for the so-called Phillips curve – the inverse relationship between wage inflation and unemployment. Computers, initially bigger and more unwieldy than his machine, took over the job of running models of the economy, which was a pity. Anyway, let me return to the question of trying to pin the economy down a little more closely.

Adding it all up

Until about 100 years ago, economists knew, or thought they knew, what the economy was but they had no means of measuring it. When William Gladstone was Chancellor of the Exchequer in the nineteenth century he had no difficulty in finding things to talk about. Most modern Chancellors manage to get through their annual Budget speeches in about an hour. Gladstone made one of his last more than four hours, and this was without the benefit of the kind of macroeconomic statistics that are regarded as essential today. Britain's Central Statistical Office, now called the Office for National Statistics, was not set up until 1941, because it was recognised that there was an urgent need for accurate and timely statistics on production, particularly of munitions, and of the supply–demand situation for scarce food. During the war Britain effectively became a command economy with 70 per cent of it government-controlled. The statistical tradition continued and was extended in peacetime. Today, within a few weeks, we know to one decimal place how much the economy grew in the most recent quarter. The figures, like most economic statistics, are subject to revision but they are still testimony to how far the art of measurement has advanced.

Most people, understandably, do not worry overmuch about whether the economy grew by 0.2 or 0.8 per cent in the latest quarter, leaving such matters to those whose job it is to pore over the statistics. It does matter, of course. The economy's long-run growth rate has been about 0.6 per cent a quarter, or about 2.5 per cent a year, though there is a debate about whether it can grow at that rate in the aftermath of the financial crisis and against the backdrop of an ageing population. Assuming the 'trend' growth rate remains 2.5 per cent, if it stayed at this rate, year-in year-out, you would expect unemployment to remain steady. Why? Every year the population of working age goes up a little, either because of natural increases or immigration. More importantly, each year we become more productive, increasing our output by 2 per cent or so, compared with the previous year. A lot of people do not believe this and think they have stayed about as productive as they have always been. Think, though, of the way technology has replaced so many basic clerking functions in offices. I shall say more on productivity later. If the economy did not grow at all, or did so only slowly, then rising productivity would mean fewer workers were needed, hence rising unemployment. If it grows roughly in line with productivity, unemployment remains stable. Higher growth rates should mean falling unemployment, and vice versa. If the economy shrinks even for a quarter (negative growth is the clumsy term most economists use for this) the worry would be recession. If it grew by 1.5 per cent in that quarter, the worry would be 'overheating'. All this will become clearer later.

The most useful thing about macroeconomic data and in particular the national accounts, is not the precise information they give us about any single quarter or year. It is, rather, that they give us an invaluable framework for thinking about how the economy is constructed. If it were possible to observe the economy from above, it would consist of many millions of transactions by people spending, producing and earning. That is exactly what gross domestic product (GDP), the main measure of the size of the economy and of changes in that size – economic growth – seeks to measure. GDP is the sum of everything produced in the economy, hence gross domestic *product*. To avoid double counting, however, it is necessary to subtract at each stage the value of the inputs that have gone into producing a product. The chef in our expensive restaurant assembles and cooks the meal. He could not do it, however, without the vegetables supplied from the market that morning, the meat from the butcher or the gas and electricity supplied by the power company. His output, for the purposes of measuring GDP, is the value added to these various inputs. The same applies from the very largest company, making billions each year, to the smallest sole trader. The principle is exactly the same as value added tax, VAT. Some people, indeed, prefer to talk, not of GDP, but of 'gross value added'.

Hang on though, where do earning and spending fit in? Do they fit in? The answer is that they do. GDP is often known as national income. The two are not precisely the same but broadly similar. GDP, as well as being the sum of everything produced in the economy, or at least the value added at each stage of production, is also the sum of incomes earned. It is easy to see why this should be. The income of our chef, assuming he is also the owner of the restaurant, is the amount we have paid him for the meal less the income earned by his suppliers and, say, the rent for the premises (the landlord's income). The value of the income earned by the various players equals the value of production.

You may ask at this point how this relates to your own circumstances. Suppose you are a salaried employee for a profitable firm. Your income, plainly, goes to make up GDP. But what about the profit the company makes? What about the tax you pay? Profit is easy enough. That is either reinvested, in which case it generates income for the suppliers of capital equipment. Or it is distributed to shareholders in the form of dividends, which means income for them. Tax is a little trickier. On the face of it, it simply represents the income of government. In practice, the way to think about tax is in terms of the income it generates as the government converts tax into public spending, thus providing income for doctors, nurses, teachers and civil servants, as well as payments to state pensioners and people on welfare benefits. These last are known as 'transfer payments' because they simply transfer money between taxpayers and beneficiaries.

It really does all add up. GDP is not only the value of everything produced (the value added) in the economy but also the sum of incomes received. It is also, and I have left what I regard as the most useful until last, the sum of spending.

The most useful equation in economics

So how does spending fit in? Again, the important thing to avoid in measuring the economy is double counting. What we are therefore concerned with is 'final' demand. When you or I buy a car, we have probably read the brochure beforehand detailing all the features and accessories it comes equipped with. What we are concerned with, however, is the entire product. Few people would buy a car and then remove the radio to sell it, or the spare wheel (many no longer have one). Similarly, the purchase of all these components by the manufacturer does not feature in GDP. Such purchases are known as 'intermediate demand'. The car could not be made without them but they are subsumed in final demand.

Does that mean that spending by consumers is all that matters? After all, if we are talking about final demand, it would seem natural that most of that comes from you and me when we shop. Consumer spending, or household consumption as it is now known by official statisticians in Britain, does indeed account for the lion's share of GDP, but not all of it. In the year 2010, for example, UK consumer spending totalled £919 billion (that's £919,000 million).

That in itself is quite an interesting figure, being the equivalent of nearly £15,000 for every man, woman and child in the country. GDP, however, was higher than this, at £1,455 billion. So consumer spending accounted for most of it, 63 per cent, exactly the same proportion as ten years earlier. I have used Britain as an example but this is typical of most advanced economies. Consumers drive our economies. After the September 11 2001 terrorist attacks on America the key question for economists was whether consumers would lose their nerve. Later, with the global financial crisis, the question throughout the advanced world was whether credit-starved consumers would ever spend as freely again as in the past. Incidentally, you often hear economists and pundits gravely opining that whether the economy slows or not depends on the consumer. I have done it myself. As you can see, there is nothing terribly profound about this. As a matter of simple arithmetic it mainly does depend on the consumer. The rate of growth of consumer spending depends mainly on the rate of growth of income (this is known as the 'consumption function') and the ability of households to borrow to finance their spending. Consumer spending can throw up some curiosities. In 2011 there was a rush to buy tickets for the 2012 Olympics and this was big enough to have an impact on GDP. But, while the tickets were bought in 2011, the statisticians decided they would not affect GDP until 2012, when the games took place. Mostly it is rather more straightforward than that. But where, apart from consumers, does the spending that makes up GDP come from?

The next most important category, in Britain at least, is spending by government. Again, this is quite typical. The national accounts showed that for the year 2010 the government 'consumed' £336 billion. This is a big number but it is also a little puzzling. As a proportion of GDP it is 23 per cent (compared with 19 per cent a decade earlier) but, as many people will know, both public expenditure and tax in Britain are usually thought of as being roughly 40 per cent of GDP, and public expenditure was pushed close to 50 per cent of GDP under the impact of recession and crisis in the period 2009–11. If spending were really only 23 per cent of GDP, taxes could be much lower. What has happened to the missing 25 per cent or so? The answer is that for GDP purposes it is necessary to exclude transfer payments, such as state pensions and benefits, which account for a lot of government spending but which, in economic terms, are the government handing money to other people to spend. This is not true, by the way, of the salaries of public sector workers such as teachers or nurses. When the government pays these, it is buying the services of these professionals, just as your purchase of the services of a plumber counts as part of consumer spending. To include transfer payments in GDP would be double-counting and would not be within the spirit of this measure of economic activity. They are not received in return for currently producing something, even though in the case of pensions, the right to them has been earned as a result of production (and paying taxes) in the past. This complication is the reason why I always refer to public spending as being 'the equivalent' of 40 or 50 per cent of GDP. Think about it. If consumer spending is 63 per cent of GDP, it is quite hard for public spending to be a further 50 per cent on top, given that the components have to add up to 100 per cent.

The other missing bit of government spending comes in our next GDP category, investment. When a business buys a computer, that is investment. When a household does so, it is consumer spending. Most investment in Britain is done by the private sector, on plant, machinery, vehicles and so on. But government, often now in partnership with the private sector, also carries out investment. New hospitals, roads, government computers, for instance, are investment – or 'gross fixed capital formation', as statisticians usually describe it. Investment in productive capacity, as every businessman knows, is vital for long-run economic growth. For many years it was thought that Japan's economic success was due to high levels of investment, averaging 30 per cent of GDP. Japan's two lost decades since the early 1990s have raised the question of whether, as far as investment is concerned, it is possible to have too much of a good thing, though China is also a very high-investment economy, particularly when it comes to infrastructure. Investment in Britain in 2010 totalled £214 billion, or nearly 15 per cent of GDP, a relatively low proportion.

Adding up the proportions of spending by consumers, spending by government and investment gives us, for 2010, 63 plus 23 plus 15 per cent, or 101 per cent in total. Give or take 1 per cent for rounding, it appears we have got to GDP. Well, we would have but only if we lived in a 'closed' economy with no overseas trade. Remember that what we are measuring, albeit via different categories of spending, is gross domestic *product*, in other words the value of spending on goods and services produced in Britain. That Nintendo games console, Audi or BMW car, iPad or iPod included in consumer spending – quite a lot of them actually – should not be part of Britain's GDP (although the proportion of the selling price that reflects distribution costs within Britain and the retailer's profit should be). At the same time, there are plenty of products and services produced in Britain but consumed in other countries. GDP therefore also has to reflect exports and imports. Exports are goods and services made here but consumed elsewhere. Imports are made elsewhere but consumed here.

In 2010, exports totalled £429 billion, equivalent to 29 per cent of GDP. We add this £429 billion to the totals for consumer spending, government outlays and investment. Imports, on the other hand, were £478 billion, 33 per cent of GDP. We take this away from our GDP total. The fact that both exports and imports were roughly a third of GDP shows that Britain is an open economy, as it has been for centuries. Both America and Japan, the world's first and third economies at time of writing (Britain was in sixth place), have much smaller export–import shares. China, the world's second largest economy as of 2010, had exports that year equivalent to 29 per cent of GDP, similar to Britain. The fact that imports exceeded exports shows that Britain was running a significant trade deficit, of roughly 4 per cent of GDP.

This book is intended to be an equation-free zone, but I cannot let this section go without just writing down what has been spelt out above. Strictly speaking it is not an equation at all, but an 'identity', and it is: $GDP = C + G + I + X - M$. C is consumer spending, G government spending, I investment, X exports and M imports. Sometimes you will see instead of GDP, the letter Y (for reasons that have never been entirely clear to me), for national income, but the meaning is the same.

Why is this so useful? First, it provides a simple way to understand explanations of the various types of spending that drive the economy. Second, anybody trying to forecast what will happen to the economy will first need to predict what is likely to happen to these expenditure components of GDP. All the main models of the economy are based around this simple identity. It also provides, with the accompanying statistical information, a rough idea of the orders of magnitude involved. A 1 per cent rise in consumer spending, for example, increases GDP by about 0.6 per cent, but it would take an increase in investment of over 4 per cent, or a rise in exports of more than 2 per cent, to produce the same effect.

Does it really add up?
Sharp-eyed readers who have been working out GDP for themselves will have noticed that they come up with an answer nearly £40 billion short of the £1,455 billion we are looking for. There are two reasons for this. One is that the statisticians in Britain separate out from other consumer spending the small amount of spending by non-profit institutions – charities and not-for-profit companies – on behalf of households. The other is that some of what is produced in any given year is not sold but goes into stocks, or inventories. Inventories can be important in determining quarter-on-quarter or year-on-year movements in GDP. At the onset of recession, for example, there is often an unplanned build-up in stocks of unsold goods. But the big picture for GDP is provided by our five other components: C, G, I, X and M.

There is one other little complication. Much of what we spend our money on is subject to tax. Taxes such as VAT and excise duties are known as 'indirect' taxation whereas taxes on income, most obviously income tax and also National Insurance, are known as 'direct' taxation. Included in the total for consumer spending, for example, will therefore be a significant indirect tax element. Many goods, roughly half, are subject to VAT at 20 per cent. In theory the government could temporarily boost GDP simply by increasing VAT, although the subsequent effect should be to make us spend less. Because of this tax complication, economists usually distinguish between GDP at 'market prices' – the prices that are actually paid – and another measure, GDP at 'factor cost', which is those same prices excluding the tax element. The difference between the two measures is simply the amount of indirect taxation; in other words, GDP at market prices less indirect taxes equals GDP at factor cost. Again, there is no need to worry about this distinction. The two measures will not show much variation when it comes to measuring economic growth except when there are big changes in indirect taxation such as in 1979, when Margaret Thatcher's Conservative government increased VAT to 15 per cent, from the old rates of 8 and 12.5 per cent, or in 1991, when the Conservatives raised VAT again, from 15 to 17.5 per cent, or in 2011, when the Conservative–Liberal Democrat coalition increased it to 20 per cent. The market price–factor cost difference is worth keeping by you, however, if only for one-upmanship purposes, invaluable in economics.

Does housework have any value?
All the above, I hope, will have seemed entirely logical. There is, however, a long-running debate in economics about whether GDP,

and closely related measures, are comprehensive enough. In November 2010, Britain's National Statistician launched a forum on Measuring National Well-being, precisely because of the fear that GDP does not go far enough. The aim was to develop new measures 'intended to cover the quality of life of people in the UK, the environment and sustainability, as well as the economic performance of the country'. It remains to be seen how far this exercise goes and the extent to which other measures will come to be seen in future as alternatives to GDP. Already the World Bank produces a range of human development indicators for member countries, intended to monitor changes that are not necessarily captured by GDP or other conventional economic measures. As it says:

'It is important to look at human development indicators side by side with income or consumption measures. Information on trends in human development indicators can supplement the information obtained from consumption-based surveys for a better understanding of poverty performance. In particular, such information can provide additional texture to the poverty results by showing how changes in income or consumption are reflected in such tangible outcomes as, say, child mortality or school enrolment.'

There is a more basic problem with GDP, which is that plenty of activity goes unmeasured in the economy. This is not just the kind of activity that people deliberately keep away from the taxman, the so-called black economy – thought to be worth between 5 and 15 per cent of GDP in most countries – but also much more mundane things. If two of us go to the local park and exhaust ourselves playing tennis for a couple of hours then, apart from the small amount we have paid to hire the court and perhaps buy a tube of new balls, the effect on GDP is negligible. If, on the other hand, two professionals slog it out for a considerable amount of prize money on the Centre Court at Wimbledon, there is quite a sizeable GDP effect. Many would say this is as it should be. Plenty of people are prepared to pay good money to watch the professionals but you could not give away tickets to witness my efforts.

Much more difficult questions arise in respect of housework. Mr Jones, a gentleman of some means, employs a housekeeper, Miss Williams. She is courteous and efficient and he pays her a good wage. She is also very pretty. Soon the inevitable happens and love blossoms over the feather duster. They marry and, while she carries on much as before with the housework, he stops paying her a wage. After all, in marriage what is his is hers. The effect, however, is to reduce GDP. Before the marriage part of his spending was on her housekeeping services. And, while she was paid out of his income, her earnings counted separately for GDP purposes. These effects, which are identical, reduce the expenditure and income measures of GDP respectively, while the value of her output is also apparently lost to the national economy.

Can this be right? Plenty of people think not. For almost as long as there have been national accounts, there have been people arguing for the inclusion of non-paid housework, as well as the many other unpaid but useful activities without which the economy would grind to a halt. Work on a so-called 'genuine progress index' in the province of Nova Scotia, Canada, found that people put in 941 million hours a year on domestic chores and primary childcare,

1,230 hours per adult. This was 25 per cent more than the 707 million hours a year of paid work in Nova Scotia. When the researchers valued this unpaid work at the prevailing pay rates for domestic work and childcare they found it added up to just over half of measured GDP. Including this unpaid work, in other words, would push up the level of GDP by half as much again.

As they put it:

Work performed in households is more essential to basic survival and quality of life than much of the work done in offices, factories and stores, and is a fundamental precondition for a healthy market sector. If children are not reared with attention and care, and if household members are not provided with nutritious sustenance, workplace productivity will decline and social costs will rise. Physical maintenance of the housing stock, including cleaning and repairs, is also essential economic activity. Yet this huge unpaid contribution registers nowhere in our standard economic accounts. When we pay for childcare and house cleaning, and when we eat out, this adds to GDP and counts as economic growth and 'progress'. When we cook our own meals, clean our own house and look after our own children it has no value in our measures of progress.

It is a persuasive argument, and it has its echoes in the currently fashionable debate about the 'work–life balance', that the way we have come to work and live overstates the economic and social value of time spent at the office (it usually is the office) or factory. Unfortunately, there would be very real problems in trying to include unpaid activity in the national accounts. GDP, as we have seen, is made up of a huge number of recorded transactions. What happens when there is no recorded transaction? Do we assume that a husband will pay his wife the going market rate for doing the housework (or, if he is a house-husband, vice versa)? If so, why should the couple not just employ somebody to do the job? If the value the husband or wife puts on the housework is less than the market rate, how much less is it? We really do not know and it would be very difficult to find out. Official statisticians have enough trouble trying to monitor recorded transactions. GDP may be an incomplete measure of the amount of activity in the economy but for the moment it is the best we have. Despite these problems, the UK's Office for National Statistics tried in 2002 to estimate the value of unpaid work in the home, including food preparation, washing, ironing, transporting children around, and so on. Its estimate was £700 billion. While stressing that its estimate should be treated with caution, it noted that the value of this so-called household production at the time was equivalent to 77 per cent of adjusted GDP, even bigger than in Canada.

Shoppers and savers
As far as individuals are concerned, they have so far been seen in action at both microeconomic and macroeconomic levels, as workers helping in the production process, as earners and of course as spenders, quite big spenders at that. What has not yet been touched on is the role of individuals as savers. We know that this is important. Look at the personal finance pages of any newspaper, or the size of that part of the financial services industry which is supported

largely by personal saving. Over the long-term (1950–2010) households in Britain saved an average of just over 6 per cent of disposable income (take-home pay), although this proportion, known as the saving ratio, varies hugely from year to year. The saving ratio can be negative, when households borrow more on aggregate than they save, or run down their existing savings. Saving, encouraged by successive British governments via tax relief on, for example, personal equity plans (PEPs), tax-exempt special savings accounts (TESSAs) and individual savings accounts (ISAs), is generally regarded as a good thing. Most governments provide some form of incentive to save. If there has been a shift in recent years it has been away from the self-interested encouragement by governments of saving in products such as Premium Bonds and National Savings Certificates, which are a way of packaging and thus funding government debt. Most obviously in wartime but also at other times, people have been persuaded to help the government to fund its debt by buying bonds, war loans, or other products. When the financial crisis pushed up government debt and deficits sharply, from 2009–10 onwards, the government needed some such additional funding from individuals though the vast majority was through the issue of government bonds (gilts) to financial institutions. Mostly these days, governments are keen to encourage saving not only for its own sake but also to provide the resources for productive investment. In a closed economy with no government, the only source of funds for investment, in fact, would be from the amount people put aside for saving. Things are rather more complicated in an open economy with no capital controls (which means that funds can and do flow in and out of the country) but the general point still stands.

Countries with very low saving ratios are generally either not investing enough or they are excessively dependent on funds flowing in from overseas. At the tail end of the long US economic boom of the 1990s, when the saving ratio dropped to zero alongside still-strong investment, many economists expressed concern that this was not a sustainable situation. In the event, investment fell sharply when the economy slowed. Britain's saving ratio fell progressively in the run-up to the financial crisis, from more than 10 per cent in 1995 to 2 per cent in 2008. Households were busier acquiring debt than saving. Japan once provided an example to the rest of the industrialised world, with saving as well as investment equivalent to about 30 per cent of GDP in the early years of its post-war revival. After its 'bubble' economy burst in the late 1980s, by which time the saving ratio was in the high teens, there were periods in the 1990s when the Japanese economy could have done with consumers spending more and saving rather less. Japan, it seemed, was a living example of what is known as 'the paradox of thrift', usually identified with John Maynard Keynes, of whom more later. The paradox is that, while a high level of saving is beneficial in the long-term, providing the funds for investment and therefore for strengthening the economy's ability to grow, in the short-term more saving (and therefore less spending) means a lower rate of economic growth, which may itself discourage firms from investing. Japan's saving ratio did come down very substantially, to just 2 per cent by 2008, before picking up slightly. Some economists predict that Japan, once one of the world's highest savers, will end up with a negative saving ratio, its ageing population (it has the oldest median age of any country) drawing down more from past savings than it is putting in.

What makes people save?

Surely it cannot be patriotic duty that makes people save, or a need to ensure there are sufficient funds for productive investment to take place. It is not hard to find reasons for saving – putting money away in case of unforeseen emergencies (the 'precautionary' motive for saving), such as a temporary loss of income, or the 'rainy day' of legend. Or people save for future eventualities, such as school or university fees, or for retirement. Milton Friedman, most famous as the intellectual parent of the monetarism of the 1970s and 1980s, gave us the permanent income hypothesis. This advanced the argument that people have a firm idea of what their permanent or long run income is, and how much they want to spend out of that income to maintain a certain standard of living. If in one year they receive a large bonus, they are too canny to regard that as part of their permanent income, and so will save a significant proportion of it by buying financial assets. If in another year their pay is cut because times are tough, they may also treat that as temporary, maintaining their spending by drawing down savings. Saving varies according to what people actually earn in relation to their permanent income.

If this sounds a bit too good to be true, Franco Modigliani and Albert Ando offered their life-cycle hypothesis of saving behaviour. At its simplest this is just a story about pensions. People build up savings during periods when they are earning most and run them down when their earnings stop, during retirement. We are spenders rather than savers in childhood, accumulate savings during middle age (or give some of it to our own children to spend) and run down savings in old age, probably leaving some spare at the end to pass on to the next generation. The life-cycle hypothesis fits many people's experience quite neatly. It can also accommodate variations. Young couples save to buy a house or flat but when the children arrive, and the wife's earnings may stop for a while, they stop saving, probably for some time. The life-cycle hypothesis, which like all good ideas is very simple, is profound in its implications as Angus Deaton, the economist, set out in his Princeton University Rome lecture in 2005. While much of economics is prone to revision and going out of fashion, it has endured. As he put it:

> It is life-cycle theory that helps us think about a host of important policy questions about which we would otherwise have very little to say. One of the most hotly debated issues today, in both Europe and in the US, is how societies should collectively make provision for the increasing numbers of elderly. How does government provision interact with private provision? Is a state pension a substitute for private retirement saving and, if so, to what extent? How do changes in retirement behavior affect the economy? Do social security systems affect the age at which people retire, and with it, the amount of wealth in the economy? How does a stock market boom affect people's spending and saving? More broadly, anyone who thinks about economic development has to think about the role that saving plays in economic growth. Is thrift the wellspring of growth, or simply its consequence? What about demography? Will the ageing of China bring down its saving rate and bring its growth to a halt? Is that what happened in

*Japan? Is the wealth of the nation simply a vehicle for
retirement provision?*

There is an interesting debate to be had when it comes to housing. Everyday discussion of the economy tends to distinguish
between people's investments in financial assets – stocks, bonds,
long-term savings accounts – and in housing. The former is often
regarded as saving, the latter as consumption. When share prices
soar it is a sign of economic health. When house prices do so, it is
a sign of danger, of irresponsible behaviour. This distinction
between financial and physical assets is, however, hard to sustain.
When people buy a house, they are engaging in the household
equivalent of a company investing in new factory or office premises. Buying a home, it could be argued, is the ultimate long-term
investment, with monthly mortgage payments being the equivalent of a regular savings plan.

Saving behaviour in aggregate both influences and is influenced
by what is happening in the wider economy. High unemployment
appears to encourage more saving, because people fear they are
going to be next in the redundancy queue. Low inflation seems to
be associated with low levels of saving, ideally because individuals
have more confidence that the money they have already put aside
will not be eaten away by rising prices. It may also be that savers
are affected by what is called the 'money illusion'. When inflation
is low, interest rates are also usually low, making the rates offered
on savings accounts look unattractive. It is, of course, an illusion.
An interest rate of 10 per cent at a time of 8 per cent inflation is
lower in real terms (after allowing for inflation) than a 5 per cent

rate when inflation is 2 per cent, but such illusions can be surprisingly powerful. In March 2009, however, savers were entitled to feel aggrieved when the Bank of England reduced interest rates to 0.5 per cent, the lowest in an existence dating back to 1694. Bank Rate had never before been below 2 per cent. Though savers could obtain interest rates somewhat higher than this 0.5 per cent Bank Rate, mainly from banks and building societies desperate to attract funding, few could achieve a rate higher than inflation, before or after tax. For those who had built up a stock of savings during their working lives, to live on in retirement, this was hard.

Many of the basics are now in place. Indeed, we have touched on some fairly sophisticated stuff. We still need to look at what lies behind the behaviour of two other important sets of players, firms and the government, but that will build on what has already been described. First, we have some more guest speakers.

6

Classical recipes

When we left Adam Smith, it was with an optimistic view of the world. As long as economic freedom was maintained, prosperity would follow. Our next three speakers, all of whom came after Smith, present a much more mixed vision. The first, Thomas Robert Malthus (1766–1834), known as Robert Malthus, was certainly responsible for giving economics its gloomy reputation. It is not clear whether the writer Thomas Carlyle had only Malthus in mind when describing economics as the 'dismal science', but it is a label that survives to this day in spite of the fact that most economists are cheery souls. A rather good American economics website and blog is called Dismal Scientist. Also on the bill are two other great economists from the classical era, mainly the nineteenth century, David Ricardo (1772–1823) and John Stuart Mill (1806–73).

Malthusian gloom

Everybody, I suspect, is familiar with the basic ingredients of Malthus's gloomy vision, although most know little about the man who came up with it. Robert Malthus was born into a well-to-do family in Guildford, Surrey, in 1766, one of eight children. He was blessed not only with intelligence but sporting ability. He was also good-looking, making the most of it by wearing his hair in long golden curls tinged with pink, a kind of strawberry blonde of his day. The effect was rather spoilt when he ventured to speak, a cleft palate he had inherited from his father giving him a high-pitched, whining voice. Malthus excelled in his studies of mathematics and natural philosophy at Cambridge, becoming a fellow of Jesus College before taking holy orders. He gave up his Anglican priesthood in 1804, however, in order to marry Harriet Eckersal, ten years his junior, although he used the title Reverend in later life, partly to deflect criticism of his views. A year later he took up the post of professor of modern history and political economy at a college established by the East India Company, making him the world's first economics professor (Adam Smith held chairs in logic and moral philosophy), and probably the world's first professional economist.

By then Malthus had already published the first version of the paper that was to make his name. 'An Essay on the Principle of Population, as It Affects the Future Improvement of Society, with Remarks on the Speculations of Mr Godwin, M. Condorcet and Other Writers' is a mouthful, and usually shortened to just 'Essay on Population'. To set it in context, Condorcet, or the Marquis de Condorcet (1743–94), was an eighteenth-century French philosopher who had taken Adam Smith's optimistic view of the future and run with it. He saw a future of strongly rising industrial and agricultural production, in which population and living standards would increase together. William Godwin (1756–1836) was born into a strict Calvinist family, trained as a minister, but became a writer and thinker with unconventional views, including regarding marriage as slavery (although he married twice, the first time to the writer Mary Wollstonecraft, who shared his views on marriage – Mary Shelley was their daughter). Godwin also shared Condorcet's optimistic vision of the future and if anything was more utopian in his vision. More importantly, Malthus's father Daniel, the wealthy Surrey squire, was very taken with Godwin's vision.

The 50,000-word 'Essay on Population' was therefore written by the younger Malthus to settle a family argument, although his father was so impressed he published it at his own expense. The core of Malthus's pessimistic case is contained in just a few sentences of the Essay. He wrote:

I think I may fairly make two postulata. First, that food is necessary to the existence of man. Secondly, that the passion between the sexes is necessary and will remain nearly in its present state. Assuming, then, my postulata as granted, I say that the power of population is indefinitely greater than the power in the earth to produce subsistence for man. Population, when unchecked, increases in geometrical ratio. Subsistence only increases in an arithmetical ratio. A slight acquaintance with the numbers will show the immensity of the first power in comparison with the second.

The acquaintance with the numbers he was talking about means that food production, he predicted, would increase arithmetically (2, 4, 6, 8, 10, 12, etc.), while population would rise geometrically (2, 4, 8, 16, 32, 64, etc.). If you have ever owned rabbits, you will get the point. Something had to give, and in Malthus's view the choice was between voluntary restraint on population growth, which he was sceptical about, and something much more nasty, population being controlled by war, pestilence, plague and, perhaps most of all, famine. As for ordinary workers, about whom Smith, Condorcet and Godwin had been so optimistic, Malthus saw their prospects as grim. Workers would not see any rise in living standards; instead they would be stuck at subsistence levels or even below them. Indeed, the sheer grimness of their lives, during periods of which 'the discouragements to marriage and the difficulty of rearing a family are so great', would be one way of keeping population down. Dismal indeed.

Was Malthus wrong?
When I first came across Malthus, in the early 1970s, it seemed that while he might have got his timing wrong, his predictions of a world in which population growth would outstrip food supply chimed in with warnings (which are still around today) that this would be the condition, if it were not already, of much of the Third World. This debate will not go away, with the United Nations predicting in 2011 that the world's population will rise from 7 billion to 9.3 billion by 2050, and to 10.1 billion by 2100. Sharply rising world food prices, in 2008 and again in 2010–11, appeared to suggest growth in population was outstripping the world's ability

to feed itself, though there were a number of explanations for this, including floods and poor harvests. Some saw climate change and its impact on food production as the additional ingredient in the gloomy Malthusian vision.

In fact, Malthus got two important things wrong. The first was to underestimate the scope for technological advance in the production of food and to misunderstand the biological nature of food production – why should the population of humans rise geometrically but the population of, say, sheep for meat eating, rise only arithmetically? Malthus also got the causes of population growth wrong. Although he wrote on the brink of a huge increase in world population, from under 1 billion in 1800 to roughly 7 billion now, this was not due to lusty peasants breeding indiscriminately but to medical advances and rising living standards (including the availability of better and more plentiful food), which both reduced infant mortality and increased average life expectancy. The pattern has been for rising living standards to be associated with smaller, not larger, family size.

Thus, while Third World famine may look like a Malthusian nightmare, his predictions were too pessimistic. The problem in developing countries is not that there is a global shortage of food and they, as the poorest, are missing out. It is that the distribution of the available food between countries is so uneven. There will be more on that vexed question towards the end of the book.

Not just population
While Malthus's population predictions may have been wrong, his contributions on the subject were invaluable. As well as being the

world's first professional economist, he was probably also its first demographer. Those were not his only claims to fame. Malthus gave us the 'law of diminishing returns', again derived from his agricultural observations. There are two ways of looking at it. One is that if ten men work a piece of land they will get a certain amount of produce out of it. Increasing the number of workers to twenty will increase the size of the crop but is unlikely to double it because there is only so much the land can produce. The average output per worker falls because after a certain point the *marginal* product of an additional worker – the amount by which he increases output – is smaller than that of the man who came before him. Another way of looking at the same thing is to take the view that most fertile land is already in use at any given time. Raising output would therefore require bringing into play stony, less fertile land, which would produce less. That was why Malthus was gloomy about food production. He may have been wrong on that but the law of diminishing returns was and is an important piece of economics.

Finally, Malthus took on another Frenchman, Jean-Baptiste Say, with another argument that went against the opinion of the time. Say (1767–1832), a follower of Adam Smith, said that not only does the market mechanism ensure that supply and demand meet for individual products but that this was true for the economy as a whole. Say's Law, sometimes described as 'supply creates its own demand', or rather that the act of producing goods – paying the wages of workers and so on – will mean there is ready demand for those products. In the aggregate too, supply will equal demand. General over-production, or glut, was impossible. Malthus disagreed. He saw little danger of glut for essential products such as food. But he thought that glut, or 'over-production', was perfectly possible for other goods. So, by extension, was unemployment. Given that unemployment in Britain may have risen to more than a million after the Napoleonic wars (huge for the population of the time though we do not have precise figures), he appears to have had a point. He also had a remedy, advocating 'the employment of the poor in roads and public works'. In this he was to anticipate John Maynard Keynes, the most famous economist of the twentieth century, by more than a hundred years. Malthus is buried in Bath Abbey, and there is a lengthy epitaph to him in its entrance which describes him as 'one of the best men and truest philosophers of any age or country'. The burial places of the classical economists are often worth a visit. Adam Smith has an impressive memorial stone in Canongate Kirk, Edinburgh, near one end of the city's Royal Mile.

David Ricardo

Ricardo, a contemporary of Malthus, has a biography that reads like that of a character out of Dickens, or perhaps Trollope. One of a large number of children of a wealthy stockbroker, with roughly twenty brothers and sisters (the exact number is not known), he was born in London, a few years after his father, a Dutch Jew, had left Holland for the City. Ricardo junior appears to have had only an informal education but one that was sufficient to prepare him for entering the family firm at the age of fourteen. All went well until, at the age of twenty-one, he fell in love and married a Quaker girl, thus outside his Jewish faith, a course of action that was to see him dismissed from the family firm and disinherited. But Ricardo was clever and resourceful, establishing his own firm of stockbrokers and building a highly successful business. He was also a man of culture, reading widely, and in his twenties discovered Smith's *Wealth of Nations* and began to develop his own approach to economics. By the age of forty-two he had accumulated enough wealth to retire (he ranks as the world's richest economist – adjusting for the prices of the time – in a profession that throws up relatively few millionaires). He had a string of properties, most notably Gatcombe Park in Gloucestershire, the home of Princess Anne, daughter of the Queen. A few years after he retired he bought himself a seat in Parliament – as was common in his day – and was regarded, unsurprisingly, as the leading expert on economics in the House of Commons. He did not, however, have much time to develop his political career, dying at the young age of fifty-one.

Ricardo and trade

The bit of Ricardian economics that everybody should know about, and many do, is the law of comparative advantage. Smith argued that the division of labour explained why specialisation increased economic output and therefore prosperity. Ricardo developed this, in the setting of international trade, into a fully-fledged theory. That countries should specialise in what they are best at seems beyond dispute; it did not need an economist to point this out. But what happens when one country is more efficient than another in everything? Should it produce all those products? And is the other obliged to put up tariff barriers to avoid being swamped with imports from the more efficient country? Ricardo's answer was 'no' on both counts, and he used economic arguments to campaign for free trade in general and the repeal of Britain's nineteenth-century Corn Laws in particular.

The example he used is by now famous. Suppose two countries, England and Portugal, are trading just two products, wine and cloth. Portugal, with the benefit of sunshine, is obviously good at producing wine – it takes twenty-five workers an average of a day's work to produce a barrel. England, in contrast, is inefficient at producing wine, 200 workers being required to produce the same amount, even leaving aside questions of whether it would taste as good. Obviously it is best for Portugal to produce wine. But look too at cloth. In Portugal it also takes twenty-five workers a day to produce a roll of cloth. England is more efficient at producing cloth than wine but not as good as Portugal – fifty workers are needed to produce a roll. So what should happen? Portugal has *absolute* advantage in both products. Is the game up for England? Ricardo explained that, in these circumstances, there would be a net gain in output if Portugal switched production from cloth to wine and England did the opposite. Why? Suppose you start in a situation where, with the same number of workers available in each country, Portugal is producing 1,000 units of wine and 1,000 units of cloth each day. Less efficient England is, by contrast, producing only 500 units of cloth and 125 units of wine. If England switches all its wine workers to cloth production, it will make an extra 500 units of cloth, making 1,000 in all, but no wine. Portugal would in such circumstances, produce more wine (to satisfy the English market), and a little less cloth. Its total production of both products would remain at 2,000 units, while England's production would have risen from 625 to 1,000. 'World' output would have gone up. The central point was that what matters in trade is *comparative* advantage, not absolute advantage. Ricardo's law of comparative advantage explains why it is beneficial for countries to trade in every circumstance.

Many people have trouble with this idea. Why should the Portuguese want to buy cloth that is less efficiently produced than their own product? The answer is that the price of English cloth will be determined by 'world' levels. English cloth workers, because they are half as efficient, will tend to be paid half as much as Portuguese workers. The Portuguese will thus be able to afford to buy a significant proportion of the increase in world output. There is still a gain for England and its workers, though, from moving from appallingly inefficient wine production to cloth. It is a 'win–win' situation. It is still the essential argument for globalisation, for all its faults, being a good thing.

Ricardo and economics
Although the law of comparative advantage stands as Ricardo's most enduring contribution, there was much more to his economics than that. Because of his expertise in finance, he was the first to take the subject beyond the polemic, 'political economy' approach of his day and into areas both more abstract and more scientific. With his complex ideas and ready intelligence, Ricardo was the first to introduce difficult mathematical concepts into the subject – a move that some critics say started the rot. Anybody trying to understand an equation-filled academic paper on economics today should perhaps blame Ricardo.

While the law of comparative advantage offered an upbeat assessment of the gains from trade, much of Ricardo's vision, like that of his friend Malthus, was gloomy. He helped develop the law of diminishing returns, and like Malthus he also had a pessimistic view of the future. Ricardo's 'corn model' was concerned with how wealth was distributed, not how it was created. In an approach that was to provide Marx with the basis of his economic theories, Ricardo saw the battle over the distribution of the economic cake as more important than the size of the cake itself. Income would be divided between wages, profits and landlords' rents. If wages rose, profits would fall, and vice versa. In the long-run, he suggested, landlords would be likely to gain at the expense of workers, whose wages would not rise much above subsistence level, and profits, which would be insufficient to encourage investment in new production. As a result, it was hard to be optimistic about long-term economic prospects.

Finally, Ricardo also gave us an approach that has gained favour in recent times. For years economists have puzzled about why, after Japan's 'bubble economy' burst in the late 1980s, successive efforts by the Japanese government to boost the economy through tax cuts and extra public spending have failed. The answer, developed by modern-day American economists such as Robert Barro, is that such measures have no effect because people know they will have to pay for them later in higher taxes. An increase in the budget deficit is exactly matched by a rise in the surplus of the private sector. Because Ricardo suggested something similar, this is known as Ricardian equivalence. The classical economists, it seems, still have a great deal of relevance.

John Stuart Mill

John Stuart Mill, who has been described as the most important liberal thinker of the nineteenth century, is often not thought of as an economist at all. His greatest book, *On Liberty*, was a work of philosophy. There is a question of how much of an original thinker, and how much of an interpreter and populariser, Mill was on economics. Perhaps it was just a matter of timing. His *Principles of Political Economy*, published in 1848, was the standard text on the subject for nearly half a century.

Mill was always destined for great things. His father James was a well-known political economist and the Mill household regularly played host to Jeremy Bentham (1748–1832) and David Ricardo, friends and mentors. It was an intellectual hothouse that, he reflected later in life, gave him a twenty-five-year head start on his contemporaries. The younger Mill was reading the classics in their original Greek at the age of eight, by which time he was already familiar with Latin. He began to study economics at thirteen and, in his late teens, edited Bentham's writings into a five-volume collection, *On Evidence*, for which effort he suffered a nervous breakdown. Bentham, whose embalmed body is usually on display in the main entrance hall at University College, London, the result of a bizarre stipulation in his will, was famous for 'utilitarianism'. This sounds more forbidding than it need be. At its most basic, utility is merely usefulness. Used in the sense Bentham intended it, however, it is, more than that, a way of expressing pleasure, happiness and satisfaction, or merely meeting needs. Different economists, it should be said, have interpreted the meaning of utility in different ways but the principle of Bentham's utilitarianism was 'the greatest happiness for the greatest number'. It is easy to see how that principle still applies. When a new public project such as Terminal Five at Heathrow is planned, it is customary to conduct a cost–benefit analysis – if the benefits exceed the costs the 'greatest happiness' is achieved and the project goes ahead. If not it is abandoned. After the Chancellor unveils his Budget proposals each spring, there is always analysis of the 'winners and losers'. Any Chancellor aiming for a long political life will always ensure the former exceed the latter. Later economists were to develop the Bentham–Mill framework into an entire field of the subject – welfare economics. Economists refer to a 'Pareto' optimal situation, after the French-born economist Vilfredo Pareto (1848–1923). This is a situation in which nobody can be made better off without making others worse off. Utility plainly applies to the individual, as well as the population as a whole. Like the law of diminishing returns, the law of diminishing marginal utility tells us that the more we consume of something – chocolate and coffee were the examples used earlier in the book – the less we get from each extra one.

Mill built on this utilitarian tradition in his work (he soon got over his nervous breakdown and joined his father working for the East India Company, which seemed to offer plenty of opportunity for freelance thinking and writing). Apart from a slightly odd view about economic growth – he thought the Industrial Revolution was just a temporary interlude after which the economy would return to a 'stationary state' – his great contribution was in demonstrating that while economic laws applied in certain areas, they did not in others. 'The laws and conditions of the production of wealth partake of the character of physical truths,' he wrote. 'There is nothing optional or arbitrary in them. It is not so with the distribution of wealth. That is a matter of human institution solely.'

How much was produced in an economy, in other words, was determined by economic laws. But there were no laws that set down how the wealth so created should be distributed among the population. This was new. Mill, taking Ricardo's line that, unchecked, most wealth was likely to find its way to landlords, was unhappy even with the idea of private property. Most of all he thought that society could arrange the distribution of wealth in a way that would bring the greatest happiness to the greatest number. In this he was a 'utopian' socialist. Socialists seeking fairer shares for all took his analysis up more generally.

7

Cordon bleu business

As we have looked at how consumers go about deciding what and how much to buy, and how the various components of gross domestic product fit together, it has so far been taken for granted that firms will always be willing to supply goods and services. That is not a bad description of the way things are. In real life there is always somebody willing to meet the needs of customers, to fill a 'gap in the market'. Adam Smith's 'the butcher, the brewer and the baker' are driven to provide us with meat, beer and bread by the prospect of making money and if they did not, somebody else would. If we were not sitting in this particular restaurant there would surely be another, owned by different people, but probably every bit as good. In many instances, firms will themselves create the market through new products, advertising and promotion. That is the way the capitalist system keeps ticking over. That observation does not, however, help us much in terms of explaining what makes businesses function, how they go about deciding how much to invest, how much to produce, and at what price. Perhaps we should start by asking a very basic question. Why do we have firms at all?

Companies and individuals

We consume as individuals, or families, so why don't we produce in the same way? Actually, many of us do. There are about four million self-employed people in Britain, effectively one-man or one-woman businesses, including everything from plumbers and electricians through to IT contractors, journalists and top entertainers. The process by which businesses grow can easily be seen if we start with a one-man business. John the builder begins on his own, putting up garden walls. Soon somebody, impressed with his work, asks him to build a house extension. He is happy to do so but needs to take on a couple of staff. The job is successful and more orders result. Soon he has three house extensions on the go at the same time. Not only does he take on more workers but he effectively becomes the manager, supervising all three projects but doing much less of the building work himself. A contract to build a house follows, then another. Then, with the help of the bank and one or two friends with money to invest, he buys a plot of land to turn into a housing development. Now he does not just employ builders but also accountants and marketing people. A few years down the road and John has become a public limited company, a plc, quoted on the Stock Exchange and with housing developments across the country, his bricklaying days long gone.

Most firms can trace their history in something like that way.

Many other one-man businesses, of course, remain happily in that state, or opt instead for what they see as the security of employment. There are many more self-employed people than firms employing others, and there are roughly ten times as many employees in Britain as there are self-employed people. The majority of people work for somebody else, whether it is a firm or a public sector organisation. To find the reason for this, we need look no further than Adam Smith. He explained, with the example of the pin factory, how specialisation, the division of labour, increased efficiency and thus dramatically lowered costs. A sole trader could still produce pins but would be unable to compete on price with the factory. That is why many self-employed people and very small businesses emphasise the special or bespoke nature of their service – you pay more but you get something better, or at least more individual. In many cases production is simply outside the scope of an individual. Much as I would love to write, edit, design and print a national newspaper, it is not a task that can be undertaken by one person. The fact that there are certain minimum personnel requirements in many areas of production, and in quite a lot of service industries, does not necessarily mean that people have to be organised into what we usually think of as a firm, with an owner-manager, or with managers and outside shareholders. Journalists and printers could, for example, organise themselves as a collective. There are partnerships and member-owned mutual organisations, such as the traditional British building society, although they are a dying breed. The John Lewis Partnership, a very successful retailer, is owned by its employees (who are the partners). John Lewis exists to make a profit, as do all firms, though the business landscape also includes non-profit organisations and social enterprises. But let us think of conventional firms, and the way they go about making profits.

Counting costs

The costs of running a business are easy enough to determine, consisting of wages, raw materials and components, power, distribution (getting the goods to customers) and rent. There is also the cost of investment, expressed in terms of 'depreciation'. If a business buys a computer costing £1,000 and it is reckoned to have a five-year life, its annual cost averages out at £200. It depreciates in value by £200 every year until, by the end of five years it is worth nothing. It is usual to split the costs faced by a firm into 'fixed' and 'variable'. Fixed costs will include those of buildings and of equipment already bought. Variable costs include wages, which vary according to the number of people employed and the hours they work (although in many companies the basic salaries of permanent staff are effectively a fixed cost). Other variable costs include those for materials and components, energy use and distribution. Variable costs rise in direct proportion to the amount produced, unlike fixed costs. The bigger the output of the firm, the smaller the amount of fixed costs for each unit produced. So part of the costs involved in making a car are those of the premises in which they are made. The more that can be produced, the more such costs fall per car as the rent for the factory is divided among a larger output. Fixed costs per unit of output only start rising if production gets to a level where the original factory is not big enough and a new one has to be acquired.

Spreading fixed costs over a larger amount of output is one of the most important sources of *economies of scale*, the tendency for the cost per unit to fall as output rises. Big firms can do things more cheaply than small firms. Assembly-line cars are cheaper, even if they do not have the same cachet, as hand-made ones because the more specialised a task – for example fitting the hub-caps on a car – the more efficient an individual worker becomes at doing it. There are other sources of economies of scale – a full lorry does not cost much more to run than a half-full one, but the full one's costs are spread across twice the amount of goods. Management costs, and those of advertising, are similarly spread over a larger amount of output. This process does not, however, continue indefinitely, or else the ideal situation in every industry would be one giant firm, a monopoly.

Diseconomies of scale, in other words rising unit costs, also apply after a certain point. One would be the cost of acquiring another factory, described above, although if the new factory quickly became employed to full capacity that would soon pass. Another would be the tendency, above a certain size of company, for lean and efficient management to be replaced by layers of bureaucracy. A growing firm will also have to look further afield for its customers. Transport costs may rise and markets become more distant from the source of production. Wage costs may rise because the pool of workers with the right skills is used up and because big firms are more likely to be unionised than small ones. And so on. A bestselling book of the 1970s, which is still in print, was E. F. Schumacher's *Small is Beautiful*, subtitled 'a study of economics as if people mattered'. It encapsulated the view that bigger was not always better, or necessarily more efficient.

Making profits

Why do firms aim to make profits? While there is a body of literature that says managers are motivated by a range of things – the
size of the firm, or their part of it, the size of their office, the size
of their company car, even the attractiveness of their secretary
(which can apply equally to male and female managers) – profit is
at the root of it. Without profit, why should anybody set up in
business, when a more lucrative and less stressful life would be
available working for somebody else? And why would any investor
put cash into a business that makes no money, when it could generate a safe return in the bank? It is not, perhaps, as clear-cut as
that. Many people set up in business because the option of paid
employment is closed off to them. Think, for example, of former
bankers, clutching redundancy cheques, who fulfil their lifetime
ambition to open a restaurant or wine bar. The failure rate of such
ventures, not surprisingly, is quite high. Even bankers, before they
got their banks into trouble in the financial crisis, were driven by
the profit motive, albeit an exaggerated version of it, rather than
an anarchical desire to collapse the system. As for investors and
profits, the willingness in the 1990s of people to put money into
dot.com firms that were not making money, and had little hope
of doing so, appeared to give the lie to the view that investors are
interested only in profitable companies. Then again, investors
would doubtless have said they were investing, not on the basis of
current profits but instead because of future potential. They probably also believed that, because they spotted that potential sooner
than everybody else, there would be every opportunity to make
substantial capital gains on their shares.

Leaving such quibbles aside, the textbook aim of firms is to maximise profits. It is also, pretty much, the real-world aim. This seems
simple enough. 'Annual income twenty pounds, annual expenditure nineteen nineteen six, result happiness,' said Dickens's Mr
Micawber. 'Annual income twenty pounds, annual expenditure
twenty pounds nought and six, result misery.' But, while Dickens
pointed out that being in the black is better than being in the red,
there is a little more to it than that. Fortunately, economists can
help. They can explain to firms how to maximise their profits, and
it is surprisingly simple. To do so, we need just two tools.

The first is concerned with expenditure, or costs, the second with
income, or revenue. The idea that costs vary with the amount produced has already been touched upon. Fixed costs tend to fall per
unit of output as production increases. Variable costs are likely to
rise in proportion to output but may then start to increase faster. For
example, it may be necessary to pay workers overtime rates, higher
than basic pay, to increase output above a certain level. The key
point is that at every level of output it will be possible to calculate the
marginal cost – the cost of producing one extra unit. A typical pattern would be that marginal cost will tend to fall up to a certain level,
so that it costs less and less to produce each extra unit, but then
begins to rise. Marginal cost, then, is our first essential tool.

The other is marginal revenue, its direct counterpart on the
income side of the firm's accounts. Just as it is possible to calculate
marginal cost, so the same can be done for revenue. Marginal revenue is simply the extra revenue, at any point, from an additional
sale. Think, say, of new season winter clothing. A few fashion vic-
tims will buy it as soon as it hits the stores, in August or early

September. Many others will wait until the mid-season sale in October or November, when prices are first cut. Plenty more will hold on until the January sales, when they are cut further. Finally, some who care nothing of fashion will buy in the spring at a factory outlet sale at rock bottom prices. Each time the marginal revenue, the income from each extra sale, declines.

So how do you know how much to make to maximise profit? The answer is not only easy but it is also, unlike some economics, sound common sense. You stop increasing production when you are on the point of losing money on any extra sales. You do not, in other words, sell anything at a loss. As long as the extra revenue from an additional sale exceeds the cost to you of generating that sale, carry on raising output. Once the extra revenue merely equals your additional cost – marginal revenue equals marginal cost – it is time to call a halt. Actually, this is easier than it sounds for many businesses. The original Mini, in production from 1959 to 2000, and one of the most famous and innovative cars of all time, was said to have made a loss on every vehicle sold. This may have been an urban myth, originating with an exercise carried out by Ford in the early 1960s, which concluded that the cost of building the car was £30 more than the selling price. The car, made under the ownership variously of British Motor Corporation, British Leyland and Rover, was said by its manufacturers to have always turned a profit when the costs were properly allocated. BMW, the final owner of Rover and the original Mini, kept the name for a new and more obviously financially successful vehicle.

Thinking about the example of the clothing firm, this is a case in which the price varies, and the firm controls how much it varies over time. For most companies this is not the case. The market – the collective decisions of competitors and consumers – determines the price. Marginal revenue (price) remains the same, however much the individual firm produces. Thus, all that is necessary is to ensure that output does not rise beyond the point where marginal cost is equal to that price. Any further increases in output will mean the firm is subsidizing customers by selling at a loss. You can make this point with diagrams but I do not want to make this look at all like a textbook. For those who are curious, most textbooks will provide a picture.

Let me just clarify one thing that puzzles a lot of people. By increasing production to the point where marginal revenue merely equals marginal cost, firms are still making profits. This is because before they get to that point they will have made lots of sales where marginal revenue exceeds marginal cost, probably by a substantial amount. By producing to the point where there is no additional profit, they are ensuring they have squeezed every bit of profit out of the market they are in.

Do businesses actually behave like this?
I have met very many business people over the years, some excellent and others not so good. The better ones, incidentally, are usually pretty hot on economics. The mediocre ones usually converse in management-speak, talking of 'growing the business', 're-engineering', 'low hanging fruit', 'networking' and the rest. But, good or bad, I cannot recall a single businessman telling me that his aim in life was to make sure his marginal revenue equalled his marginal cost. There are a few reasons for this. One is

that economics has to try to simplify a complicated real world. Businesses will operate a number of strategies, for example deliberately selling at a loss over a number of months or years in order to build market share and drive out competitors. Such strategies are easier, of course, if the business can draw on financial support from another part of the operation. Or, to take another example, supermarket chains often sell certain goods, so-called 'known-value' items such as bread and milk, below marginal cost, in the knowledge that they can recoup the lost profits elsewhere, in products where consumers are less aware of prices. Another reason is that not all businesses maximise profits, even when they think they are doing so. The fact is however that matching marginal cost and marginal revenue is one of the building blocks of business, even if it is implicit in the decisions businesses make rather than explicitly stated. The clothing retailer in the example above knows fairly precisely the prices he or she needs to be able to achieve at various times during the selling season in order to maximise profit. The retailer also knows that there are things that do occur in real life that complicate the task. A mild autumn, for example, when few people buy winter clothes, would make it very hard to maximise profit. These complications aside, in the end businesses that ignore the economic rules will not survive long.

Theory and practice come together in areas such as economies of scale, which provided the rationale for mass production, for Henry Ford's assembly lines, and therefore for industrial development in the twentieth century. Perhaps the best area where theory and practice come together, however, is in the field of competition. It is a rather interesting area.

Playing the monopoly game

We learned from Adam Smith that firms can take advantage of customers, particularly by colluding on prices. Smith argued that the market would be enough to take care of such behaviour. Governments, however, have found that markets need a little help to prevent anti-competitive behaviour. In Britain the Competition Commission (the old Monopolies and Mergers Commission) is, as it describes itself, 'an independent public body which conducts in-depth inquiries into mergers, markets and the regulation of the major regulated industries, ensuring healthy competition between companies in the UK for the benefit of companies, customers and the economy'. It operates in tandem with the Office of Fair Trading (OFT), the country's competition watchdog, which has the power not only to initiate investigations but also to fine companies it suspects of stitching-up the market – running cartels – up to 10 per cent of their turnover, and prosecute, with the threat of imprisonment, directors who obstruct its investigations. Some of this was influenced by America, where a tough anti-trust regime has been in place for decades. There has also been a strengthening of the EU-wide competition regime. Competition policy is one of the most important functions of the European Commission in Brussels. The job of Competition Commissioner is one of its most senior roles and there is a separate Director-General for Competition. Across the world, competition authorities have been given greater powers, as well as the ability to impose financial sanctions that hit offending businesses directly.

There are two reasons why governments are keen to crack down on monopolies. The first is that they believe they act to the detriment of consumers, charging them higher prices than if there were lots of companies competing for custom. The second is that lack of competition is seen to be damaging in another way. Competition is vital for economic efficiency. Monopolies, because they have the market to themselves, can become bloated and inefficient. This, in turn, affects the country's ability to compete with others, the nation's 'competitiveness'. As an aside, you will have noticed by now that there is a tendency in economics for similar words to have quite different meanings. In this case, competition refers to the extent to which different firms are able to compete for business in a particular market. A contestable market, to introduce another term, is one in which it is easy for firms to enter (or leave). Competitiveness means the ability of one country's economy (or the individuals and firms than make up that economy) to compete with others.

Why is lack of competition, monopoly, bad for consumers? After all, if economies of scale are involved to any degree, will it not be the case that bigger is cheaper? Ford, which would doubtless love to have a complete monopoly of the car market, could claim that adding to its already very long production runs would bring down the cost of each car produced. It would also save on the vast amounts of advertising it employs to try to convince customers its products are better than those of General Motors, Toyota or Fiat. A benign monopolist would surely give us the best of all worlds.

The problem, apart from the fact that the idea of a benign monopolist is probably a contradiction in terms, is that it would not be the best of all worlds, by a long way. For one thing it would deprive consumers of choice, and choice is in itself a significant benefit. More importantly, monopoly is likely to mean higher prices. Why is this? The best way of thinking about it is to compare two extremes. One is 'perfect' competition, a situation in which very many firms compete in an industry, each producing identical products, and none big enough to influence the price with its behaviour. Each firm produces to the point where its marginal cost equals marginal revenue, so this is also the situation for the industry as a whole. Each firm has to accept the price set by the market and that price, by the magic of competition, not only maximises the profit of each individual firm but it is also lower than would be charged by any monopolist.

This is because the monopolist, in contrast, can influence prices. Let us suppose that Ford, which we assume for these purposes is the sole supplier to the UK car market, could sell 1 million cars a year at £20,000 each but 2 million at a price of £10,000. It cannot, by the way, sell the first million at £20,000 and the second at £10,000 because the first million customers would not wear it. The more the company supplies, the lower the price gets. The monopolist's demand curve (the lower the price the more customers will want to buy) is the same as that for the industry as a whole. He, in other words, is the industry. So what does the monopolist do? What he does is simply follow the standard rule, by also producing to the point where his marginal cost and revenue are equal. The monopolist, however, is unusual: the extra revenue he gets from selling, say, an additional car, has to take into account the fact that producing more in a given period will lower prices across the board. This is easy to demonstrate. Say Ford worked out that it could sell 1,000 cars a week at a price of £20,000, but to sell 1,001 the price has to drop to £19,999. The marginal revenue from the 1,001st is, in effect, £19,999 less £1,000, £18,999. Why? Because the £1 price cut on the 1,001st also has to apply to the first 1,000 off the production line but not yet sold.

Two things result from this. The first is that a monopolist will produce less than would be the case in a perfectly competitive market with lots of firms fighting for their share. The second is that prices will be higher. For the perfectly competitive firm, marginal revenue is equal to the price in the market. For the monopolist, price – in this case £19,999 – is higher than marginal revenue (£18,999). There will be a limit to the extent a monopolist is prepared to reduce prices. This is why monopolies are bad for consumers.

Real-world competition

Textbook ideas of competition and the real world are rather different. There are very few cases of firms being so powerful and dominant that they can maintain a permanent monopoly position, in which barriers to entry are so formidable that potential competitors are permanently deterred from trying to take them on. There are plenty of examples of temporary monopolies, such as when a company has developed an entirely new product, particularly when it is protected by patent. Typically though, such monopolies do not last, even with patents. The makers of the Rubik cube, an immensely popular puzzle, enjoyed a brief and hugely profitable monopoly in the 1980s before competitors and black-market copies moved in. So did Laszlo Biró, who in 1938 invented and marketed the first ballpoint pen. We may still often call such pens 'Biros', just as for many years we called vacuum cleaners 'Hoovers' (perhaps we call them 'Dysons' now), but the market in them is no monopoly, in fact it is highly competitive. Some monopolies do, however, survive. So do plenty of examples of oligopolies – industries where there are just a small number of competitors, perhaps four or five.

In Britain it is common to talk of the Big Four high street banks, currently HSBC, Barclays, Lloyds Banking Group and Royal Bank of Scotland (the last two were part-nationalised in the financial crisis). In food retailing, too, it is common to talk of the Big Four: Tesco, Sainsbury, ASDA and Morrisons. In 2011 the Big Four banks had nearly three-quarters of all personal current accounts and almost 80 per cent of small-business lending. The four biggest supermarkets had 76 per cent of the grocery market. Both sectors have been the subject of regular investigations by the competition authorities to try to detect whether they are engaged in collusive, or cartel-like, behaviour. A cartel is when a group of firms, big enough to dominate the market, plot together so that they collectively act as a monopoly, setting higher prices and achieving monopoly profits. The OFT, on its website, invites people to inform on those they suspect are engaging in cartel activity, giving them immunity from prosecution for doing so. Anti-competitive behaviour does not necessarily involve cartel activity. The OFT successfully pushed through a change in the early 2000s which significantly reduced the prices of many over-the-counter medicines. In that case, while high prices were benefiting the pharmaceutical companies, they existed because, thirty years earlier, small chemists had persuaded the government that resale price maintenance (the fixing of prices by the manufacturers) should be allowed to prevent them being driven out of business by the bigger pharmacy chains. The OFT's view was that this was a restrictive practice that acted against the interests of consumers. In the case of banking, the Independent Commission on Banking, which reported in 2011 along with the EU authorities, together with them recommended action to increase competition. It included the forced disposal of hundreds of bank branches, notably those of the Lloyds Banking Group, which during the financial crisis had acquired Halifax Bank of Scotland (HBOS), a leading rival.

When it comes to cartels, the real-world example most people think of is the Organisation of Petroleum Exporting Countries, OPEC, which has in the past successfully restricted output in order to raise world oil prices, most dramatically in 1973–4 and 1979–80. There is, however, a question about whether OPEC, which controls about 40 per cent of world oil supplies (but a rather bigger proportion of oil reserves), has a sufficiently dominant position to act as a true cartel. In recent years it has relied on the co-operation of non-OPEC oil producers to achieve its aims. Experts predict, perhaps worryingly, that OPEC's dominance of world oil supplies will increase significantly during the twenty-first century. OPEC itself claims to have just under 80 per cent of the world's proven crude oil reserves.

Monopolies and privatisation
One of the problems economists have with monopolies is that there is often a trade-off between the efficiency that can arise from having one large supplier, most notably economies of scale, and the risk, indeed the likelihood, that monopolies will exploit their

position. What happens, for example, if the optimum size of an industry, in terms of efficiency, is just one big firm? What happens if there is a 'natural' monopoly? In Britain the traditional response to this problem was to accept the argument that there were certain natural monopolies or, at least, sectors where competition was wasteful and inefficient. What purpose could be served, it was argued, from having two companies competing to send gas along adjacent pipelines to supply homes, factories or offices? Or two or more sets of electricity cables? The solution, therefore, was to allow monopolies in these areas but, in order to ensure they did not make excessive profits, bring them under public ownership. Many of Britain's nationalised industries, most brought into public ownership by the 1945–51 Labour government, were monopolies. But, being controlled, they did not make profits at the expense of the consumer. Many, in fact, did not make profits at all.

The existence of public sector monopolies, in gas, electricity, water, coal, rail, telecommunications and other areas, created a problem for the Conservative government when it wanted to privatise them in the 1980s. On the one hand, their monopoly status made them highly attractive to investors with an eye on the potential profits these industries could make once transferred to the private sector. On the other, there was a risk of creating Frankenstein's monsters – great bloated but hugely profitable firms, dominating the supply of essential services. The approach to this problem evolved over time. British Telecom, in which the government in 1984 first sold shares, was transferred to the private sector as a monopoly. It was given its own regulator, Oftel (later absorbed into Ofcom), vital to oversee the conduct of such a huge monopoly, but the regulatory regime for the first few years was a loose one. Investors made a lot of money. Gradually, through the privatisations of gas, electricity and water, a more sophisticated approach evolved, allowing enough in terms of potential profit to achieve a successful sell-off but introducing stiffer competition at an earlier stage. By the time the government privatised British Rail in 1996, it believed the process had evolved enough to allow competition from day one. Thus, the nationalised British Rail was broken up into three broad segments, one company with responsibility for the track, signalling, stations and land, Railtrack; a whole series of train-operating companies running different services; and rolling-stock leasing companies, which took on BR's locomotives, carriages and trucks and leased them to the operating companies. The result was not only the instant break-up of a monopoly but, many would say, a fragmentation that led to many of the subsequent problems of the railways. After a series of accidents, culminating in the Hatfield crash in October 2000 which was blamed on poor maintenance, Railtrack was put into administration by the Labour government a year later. Network Rail, a so-called 'not for dividend' company limited by guarantee – in other words operating in the private sector but not with the aim of producing returns for shareholders – replaced it. Monopoly can be bad, but you have to take care when dismantling it.

Is the Internet perfect competition?

When the dot.com revolution happened in the second half of the 1990s, industry analysts predicted an explosion in online retailing, or B2C (business-to-consumer) sales, as well as a big increase in

B2B (business-to-business) and B2G (business-to-government) activity – there are probably many more of these acronyms but that is enough. Economists, meanwhile, asked a rather different question. Was the Internet a real-world example of the perfectly competitive market of the textbooks? Its claims to be so were rather good. For one thing, the barriers to entry in the vast majority of online markets appeared to be very low. Anybody could set themselves up as an e-tailer of, say, books, compact discs or downloads, as long as they could buy such products wholesale from the publishers or manufacturers and take on a few people to pack them up and send them off to customers (or in the case of downloads, do so electronically). Compared with the cost of establishing a nationwide network of shops to take on WHSmith, HMV or, increasingly, the big supermarkets, even an all-singing-and-dancing website required only a small outlay. If one requirement of perfect competition is that there are many competitors, the Internet also provided another. One source of monopoly pricing, for any product, is the lack of information available to customers. I can sell you a DVD for £15 as long as you are unaware that, a few miles away, somebody is selling it for £12. To make you aware, my competitor would have to advertise, which would increase their costs. Even then, you might decide it is not worth the journey.

The Internet can provide something like perfect information. It has, in fact, spawned the growth of websites whose specific task is to check prices. These sites are not always comprehensive but they do provide something close to price transparency. It is possible, in a few seconds, to see who is offering the best deal on a product. Add in the fact that geography is far less important – even for people who confine their online shopping to UK sites there is usually no difference in shipping costs whether the supplier is a few miles or a few hundred miles away – and the Internet does indeed start to look like the perfect competition of the textbooks.

So why is it not turning out that way? Online retailing's impact has been significant, though perhaps not as dramatic as some of its proponents expected. In mid-2011, for example, 9.9 per cent of UK retail sales were Internet sales. There has, however, been a wider effect. Bricks and mortar retailers, apart from running their own e-tailing sites, have had to take account of the prices available online when setting their prices in the shops. The Internet has thus been a force for low inflation, and has helped bring about falling prices for many goods (though this may have been a one-off or 'level' effect). It has not yet, however, resulted in perfect competition. Only a minority of online shoppers use price-checking sites (usually free to the customer) before deciding on a purchase. The information is there, if not necessarily comprehensive, but most customers are not making use of it. Those that do not, and even some who do, are still heavily influenced by reputation. They will buy from online retailers they have heard of and whom they trust not to make off with their credit card details. Simply setting up a website is unlikely to be enough to build a strong market position. A good reputation is also required. How do e-tailers go about building reputation? By spending a lot on advertising. Existing retailers start with an advantage in that their names are already known. Those seeking to sell online have to get their name across in another way. Think of the amount of advertising by Amazon, or in Britain a company like lastminute.com, or the extensive marketing by LoveFilm, and you get the point. Amazon's strategy was to erect a barrier to entry by convincing the public, through heavy advertising, that it was *the* books e-tailer. To a large extent it appears to have worked. In place of the barrier to entry of the cost of establishing a network of stores, a new one emerged – the need for advertising budgets stretching into tens of millions. Perhaps this will change again, and the growing sophistication of online shoppers will give us something like a perfect market. But it is not there yet. Amazon's strategy worked and it has remained a pure online retailer. The overwhelming majority of Britain's top fifty online retailers are, however, firms with a high street and shopping mall presence, including Argos, Tesco, Next, Marks and Spencer and John Lewis.

What about companies that do not sell a product but a 'weightless' service? What about online businesses whose product is, say, music tracks or movies that can be downloaded over the Internet? This is an interesting area. Most of the above principles apply. Such services may be weightless but they are not costless. An online music provider, for example, has to invest in web capacity – the greater the demand the bigger the capacity – and in marketing and administration. The economies of scale can be considerable but there are still marginal costs and revenues. It does, however, mean that such markets can be truly global. Thinking of mail delivery times and reliability you might not want to buy CDs or DVDs from a site based in Bombay, Shanghai or Sacramento. That does not apply, subject to network capacity, if the product is simply downloaded.

Business games

The approach that firms took in the online market is an example of a business strategy. Economists in the twentieth century took an increasing interest in such strategies as real-world examples of 'game theory'. The idea of game theory is simple. Whether you gain maximum advantage in a particular situation depends, not just on what you do but on what others do. Amazon's decision to spend so much promoting its name was influenced, in part, by its expectations of what others, including the existing book retailers, would do. Do I open a new supermarket in a particular part of town? Perhaps, but to determine how profitable it is likely to be I would also want to know whether others are planning to do so. Many students are introduced to game theory in the form of the prisoner's dilemma, in which two suspects are questioned about an offence. The obvious strategy for each of them is to plead innocent but rat on the other one. If both do so, though, the authorities are likely to deem them both guilty and give them an extra sentence for dishonesty. Depending on what the other does, the optimum strategy for each individual could be to plead either guilty or innocent but to know which is best he has to form a judgment on what the other will do. In a market of two firms, the best collusive strategy would be for them both to restrict output so as to keep prices high. But if one firm restricts its output while the other pumps out as much as it can, the first firm would be a loser. Guessing, or finding out, what your competitor is up to is all part of the game.

Game theory has attracted some eccentric economists. Paul Strathern called his book *Dr Strangelove's Game* after John Von Neumann, the Hungarian-born game theorist with an extraordinary sex drive who, in the 1950s and by this time confined to a wheelchair, advised the American government on its Cold War strategy in relation to the Soviet Union, based on a game theory approach. In this case, while the best outcome for America might have been to blow up Moscow with no retaliation, 'mutually assured destruction' was the chosen alternative. Von Neumann, together with his colleague Oskar Morgenstern, effectively invented game theory and gave us the 'zero-sum game' – one player's gain was another's loss. John Nash, the brilliant American game theorist, who developed the idea of the 'Nash equilibrium' – the optimum solution for all players in any game – became a shambling drop-out in the 1970s and 1980s after suffering bouts of schizophrenia but recovered sufficiently to be awarded the Nobel Prize for economics in 1994. Nash took game theory on by demonstrating the possibility of 'win–win' outcomes, in which all players could gain. He was the subject of an award-winning film in 2001, *A Beautiful Mind*, in which Russell Crowe played him and narrowly missed out on an Oscar for doing so. Two other game theorists, Thomas Schelling and Robert Aumann, won the Nobel in 2005. Schelling, like Von Neumann, did much of his work on the Cold War balance of military power, though latterly took a close interest in global warming. The issue, he argued, was to persuade people in rich countries to pay for the mitigation of a problem which would have its biggest impact on those in poor nations.

Governments have tried to use game theory in devising ways of allocating licences, for example for oil exploration, to businesses. One of the most interesting examples of the practical use of game theory in a business context came in Britain in 2000 when the government held an auction for third-generation (3G) mobile telephone licences. In designing the auction, the government called on the services of a team of economists specialising in game theory, led by Professor Ken Binmore of the University of London and Professor Paul Klemperer of Oxford. The design they came up with was no ivory tower creation. For nearly two years, using research students as 'players', the team tried different approaches to determine how, under various conditions, the bidders were likely to respond. For the telecom firms bidding for licences, the best outcome would have been that each paid a small amount for the licences on offer but that depended on awareness of how the others would bid. In the event, this battle of the game theorists (the bidding companies also employed their own) turned into a comprehensive victory for the government side. Helped by timing, the stock market's mobile telephone frenzy being at its height, the auction raised the extraordinary sum of £22.47 billion, enough at the time to build 400 new hospitals and many times the sum expected at the start of the process. Within a few weeks, as the telecom bubble burst, the companies were asking for their money back. The fact was that the bidders got their game theory very badly wrong. Even the biggest firms would have done better to hold back when the bidding got out of hand. As Binmore later put it:

Nobody is forced to bid in an auction, and anybody who bids more for a licence than he thinks it is worth is just plain stupid. Claims that the complexity of the auction led the bidders astray do not stand up to serious scrutiny. In our auction, the optimal strategy was absurdly simple: just make the minimum bid for whichever licence would maximise your profit if you won it at that price.

Game theory auctions have been used extensively by the Federal Communications Commission in America to allocate spectrum (their first use was before Britain's 3G sale), while those taking part in eBay and other online auctions are also said to benefit from knowledge of game theory: yet another example of the real-world relevance of economics.

Why firms invest

Bidding in a licence auction is one way in which firms invest, albeit an unusual one. It raises more general questions. Why do firms invest, and what determines the amount they invest? For decades, one of the supposed weaknesses of Britain's economy was under-investment – spending a smaller proportion of GDP on investment than rival economies. The Conservative–Liberal Democrat coalition government produced a *Plan for Growth* in 2011. It noted that 'business investment in the UK has been persistently low by international standards; between 2000 and 2010 it was less than it had been in the previous decade as a proportion of GDP, and was the second lowest across OECD countries. From an already low base, business investment fell sharply during the recession.' This matters to the performance of the economy. On one official calculation, the capital per worker (the amount of equipment available, for example) was some 30 per cent higher in America, 40 per cent higher in France and 50 per cent higher in Germany, than in Britain. Why is this important? Because, as the Treasury puts it:

A high quantity and quality of investment has two key influences. The first is that it increases the level of inputs into the economy – increasing the productivity and hence the earnings of workers in a very direct way. But it is also a vital channel for the introduction of new technology and processes. New investment does not just replace existing machinery, but moves forward production processes by embodying technical change.

Investment by businesses is not, of course, the only source of capital expenditure. Economists would argue that as serious as the legacy of business underinvestment in Britain was underinvestment by government in the infrastructure – roads, railways, hospitals and schools. From 2000 (when net capital spending by government was its lowest as a share of GDP since soon after the Second World War) to 2010, infrastructure spending rose sharply, some of it under the Private Finance Initiative (PFI), under which projects were built, run and financed by the private sector and paid for over time by taxpayers. Leaving that aside, it is clear that a vital ingredient in the long-term success of any economy is an adequate level of investment. It is also essential for the long-term health of any company. But what determines how much firms are prepared to invest? On the face of it, the reasons for company investment are as many and complex as those that determine why we choose, on a particular day, to buy something in the shops. Managers might decide to invest to replace a noisy or worn-out piece of machinery or vehicle. They might, similarly, decide to replace all the firm's personal computers because they are becoming obsolete.

It could be that the firm has decided on a new product range and needs to invest in new equipment to produce it. Or, perhaps, the company has been doing well, is flush with cash, and decides to spend some of it.

In fact, while all these are subsidiary reasons why firms may decide to invest, there is one easy and underlying explanation. Investment will occur when it is expected to generate a sufficient rate of return. A new piece of equipment, in other words, not only has to pay for itself in what it adds to revenue and profit, but it has to generate a return over and above this. How high does that return have to be? That depends on the alternatives. Suppose the level of interest rates is 10 per cent and the cost of a new industrial plant is £10 million. If the firm already has cash of £10 million, it could invest it in the new plant, or it could simply leave the money in the bank, where it will generate a 10 per cent return, equivalent to £1 million in the first year and more, if no money is withdrawn and the value of the deposit grows, in subsequent years. To make the investment worth making, its rate of return has to exceed 10 per cent, probably by a comfortable margin. So the income of the firm as a result of the new investment will have to rise by more than £1 million in the first year, and so on. Economists call this alternative use the 'opportunity cost' of the investment – the return that would have been available if the cash invested had been put to its next best use. The same principle applies if the firm has to borrow the money from the bank. Again that borrowing will not be worthwhile if the investment does not generate a return significantly higher than the cost of the funds. One of the arguments for reducing Bank Rate to a record low of 0.5 per cent in March 2009, apart from the fact that desperate times required desperate measures, was to persuade firms that there were better things to do with their cash than leave it on deposit in the bank.

High interest rates, and in particular high 'real' rates of interest (the interest rate after allowing for inflation – a 15 per cent interest rate with 10 per cent inflation is a 5 per cent real interest rate), tend to discourage investment. Low and stable interest rates are likely to be more conducive to investment. Of course, when it comes to assessing the return on an investment, accountants may struggle to be as precise as economists would like. In the absence of a controlled experiment, could a firm possibly tell exactly what the rate of return is on an investment in twenty new £1,000 computers, and how it would differ if twenty-four had been bought? Probably not, but the same general point applies as with marginal cost and revenue, discussed above. Firms that ignore such rules will, in the end, get into trouble. Managers who invest willy-nilly, without regard for the rate of return, should not expect a very long career in business.

Should firms have a conscience?

One of the interesting developments in recent years has been the recognition by companies that there is much more to corporate life than money. Corporate social responsibility, the idea that it is 'not just profit', is not new in itself. Andrew Carnegie (1835–1919), the Scottish-born American industrialist, is famous for endowing a high proportion of the public libraries in Britain, as well as the Carnegie Institute of Technology, the Carnegie Institution and the Carnegie Hall in America. The Cadbury family in Birmingham was a notable early example of the enlightened company, both in the treatment of its workers – taking them from the slums of the city to work and live among the green fields (back then at least) of Bourneville. They were not the only ones. When religion and business mixed – the Cadburys were Quakers – greater attention to the social obligations of commerce was often the result. By the time of its takeover by the American food giant Kraft in 2010, Cadbury had moved a long way from its roots, and was an international company with a large foreign shareholder base. Even so, the takeover brought widespread protests, based on fears that a paternal British company was being acquired by a hard-nosed American firm. Kraft played the hard-nosed part well. One of its first acts was to close a Cadbury factory at Somerdale near Bristol that it had promised to keep open.

Firms would say they have always taken their wider obligations seriously. Happy and healthy employees are likely to be more productive. Customers will be more likely to buy from firms that are regarded as good corporate citizens – not polluting the environment or exploiting Third World suppliers, for example. Money spent on community projects or charitable work has the useful side effect, perhaps even the main effect, of generating a warm fuzzy image for the business. In recent years, however, such matters have climbed higher up the corporate agenda. Businessmen have become more fearful of the actions of pressure groups, whether they be anti-globalisation protestors capable of disrupting business gatherings or annual general meetings, or environmental pressure groups. When Greenpeace successfully lobbied Shell against the dumping of the Brent Spar oil platform in deep ocean waters, doing so by creating a consumer boycott of the company's products, it was a watershed. The fact that Greenpeace was subsequently shown to have got its facts wrong over the environmental effects of Shell's original plan seemed to matter less than the power it had demonstrated to exert influence over company actions. In 2010, another oil company, BP, found itself in a crisis that for a time threatened the survival of the firm, this time over a genuine environmental catastrophe – a huge oil spill in the Gulf of Mexico. Its reputation in America may take years to recover.

One popular way of looking at this is through the 'stakeholder' model. In this, the owners of the company, the shareholders, are important but they have to take their place alongside others. Thus, there are internal stakeholders in the business – the shareholders plus the managers and workers, but there are also 'external' stakeholders. These include customers and suppliers, but they also include competitors. How so? One company, if it produced shoddy products, would not only risk going out of business but could also drag down the reputation of the whole industry, so it has a responsibility to its rivals. Other stakeholders include the government, the communities in which firms operate, and so on.

At heart this seems uncontroversial. Sensible managers would always want to take into account a range of interests, both inside and outside the company. The 'good company' may even attract a better class of investor, concerned about the ethical context in which he makes his money. According to the government's Business Link website:

*Your business doesn't exist in isolation nor is it simply a way of
making money. Your employees depend on your business.
Customers, suppliers and the local community are all affected
by your business and what you do. Your products, and the way
you make them, also have an impact on the environment.
Corporate social responsibility (CSR) is about understanding
your business's impact on the wider world and considering how
you can use this impact in a positive way. CSR can also be
good for your bottom line ...*

    *Building a reputation as a responsible business sets you
apart. Companies often favour suppliers who demonstrate
responsible policies, as this can have a positive impact on how
they are perceived by customers. Some customers don't just
prefer to deal with responsible companies, but insist on it. The
Co-operative Group, for instance, places a strong emphasis on
its corporate social responsibility and publishes detailed 'warts
and all' reports on its performance on a wide range of
criteria – from animal welfare to salt levels in its
pizzas: 'Reducing resource use, waste and emissions doesn't just
help the environment – it saves you money too. It's not difficult
to cut utility bills and waste disposal costs and you can bring
immediate cash benefits.*

Issues and tensions may arise, both within the different divisions
within firms and in the attitudes of shareholders, if CSR is seen to
dominate company strategies and decisions. CSR, in other words,
is important but should never be the tail that wags the corporate
dog. Managers are good at making profits, or they should be, but

they are not so good at charity work. It is all a question of balance.

The balance of this book requires that we now move on. We have learned some of the fundamental economic explanations about how this restaurant, and other businesses, work, and their role in the economy. There has not been time to explore issues of corporate governance and the interaction between boards of directors and company management. Bank boards were widely criticised for not keeping management in check in the run-up to the global financial crisis. I shall return to this later.

When I first studied economics I used to regard the theory of the firm as perhaps the least realistic part of the subject, a very long way from the cut and thrust of everyday business life. Gradually, however, I have come to see how relevant much of it is. To take an example: if you were contemplating investing in a firm, you would probably want to know something about the strength of its market position, and whether it is able to deter potential competitors, so barriers to entry are important. You would probably also want to know whether its management is focused on controlling costs and maximizing revenue, all of which come straight out of the textbook. Economics is not business studies. But economics and business are intertwined.

Now let us turn to another hugely influential person who had a rather different perspective on the role of business.

8

Mulled Marx

Our next speaker is often not thought of as an economist at all but as a political philosopher, a revolutionary and hero of many a revolution, and the subject of tens of thousands of pilgrimages to his tomb in London's Highgate cemetery. This is a strange omission, when for a time perhaps half the world was run on the principles of Marxist economics. If the late twentieth century was a victory for the economics of Adam Smith (and others), this was only after Marx had run him quite close. The global financial crisis that almost brought the capitalist system to its knees in 2008, and continued to have serious repercussions, gave him a new lease of life. 'Karl Marx got it right, at some point capitalism can destroy itself,' said the economist Nouriel Roubini in the summer of 2011. The crisis did not, however, result in as great a revival as his followers might have hoped.

Any smart restaurant might think twice about admitting Karl

Marx. His spectacular beard, grey-flecked and bushy, saw him depicted in cartoons as Prometheus. To modern eyes his appearance would have been more that of a vagrant or gentleman of the road. His pet name within the family was 'Moor', because of his wild appearance. In fact, the Marxist 'look' may have been based on a statue of Zeus, given to him as a present, which he kept in his study. There was, however, little that was godlike about Marx, who suffered like few other mortals from carbuncles, boils (in places you would not want to know about), liver problems, insomnia, bilious attacks, migraines and respiratory complaints. A Prussian spy given the task of reporting back on Marx from Soho in London noted, with disgust, that 'he very seldom washes himself, combs his hair or changes his clothes' and that he enjoyed getting drunk often. Despite this, Marx fathered six children by his wife Jenny von Westphalen, the daughter of a wealthy Prussian aristocrat; and another by the family maid, Helene 'Lenchen' Demuth. Friedrich Engels, his collaborator and benefactor, took the blame for the latter accident, claiming he was the father. Both Jenny and Lenchen are buried alongside Marx in Highgate. When Marx wrote about poverty he did so from first-hand experience. He was poor for most of his life and three of his children died in infancy. His poverty appears, however, to have been partly self-inflicted. He refused to take a job, even during the long periods he suffered from writer's block, preferring to rely on friends and benefactors, including the long-suffering Engels.

Marx was born in 1818 in Trier, Prussia (now Germany), to parents who, to avoid legal discrimination, had just converted from Judaism to Lutheranism. He studied at the University of Bonn, having already acquired a duelling scar, and came under the influence of Hegelian philosophy. Already, however, Marx was developing his own distinctive approach, which he put into practice as a journalist and then editor of the *Rheinische Zeitung*, a liberal newspaper that was too liberal for the authorities. Marx then set off with his new wife for Paris and Brussels, where he was to co-write the *Communist Manifesto* with Engels, published in 1848. There is a plaque commemorating their stay on the house in Brussels where Marx and Engels toiled, as well as a Karl Marx Museum at his house in Trier. In 1849 the revolutionary thinker came to London, where he embarked on his great work, *Das Kapital*. The first volume of *Das Kapital*, or *Capital*, was published in German in 1867 and sold slowly, although an American edition, published in 1890, quickly sold its 5,000 print run, allegedly because the publisher marketed it as a book that explained how to accumulate capital. The final two volumes of *Capital*, edited by Engels, were not published until after Marx, penniless and heartbroken following the death of his wife, himself died in 1883. Despite this, *Capital* ranks as one of the three most important economics books written, along with Smith's *Wealth of Nations* and Keynes's *General Theory*.

A different kind of dismal scientist

We have seen how some of the classical economists who followed Smith took a far less optimistic view of the way capitalist economies would develop. Malthus saw population growth outstripping food supply, with disastrous consequences. Mill favoured utopian socialism to counter what modern economists would define as market failures in the distribution of income. Ricardo, while providing his famous explanation of why free trade was beneficial, also thought that landlords would be the main beneficiaries of economic growth. Workers would be trapped on subsistence wages. Marx, while borrowing the economic tools of the classical economists, including Smith, had little time for their conclusions. Malthus's grim predictions about population, he said, rested on the assumption that the capitalist system of production would continue. Under a different system there need not be a problem. The only abstract laws of population, he said, existed for 'plants and animals', not humans. Mill's utopian socialism, in the making when Marx was working on *Capital* in the reading room of the British Museum was, to Marx, both wishy-washy and wishful thinking. Marx owed his greatest economic debt to Ricardo. Both believed in the fundamental importance of distribution. If the emphasis in Smith was on the size of the economic cake, and the prospect of it growing considerably over time, Ricardo and Marx were more concerned with how it was divided. Both saw that division as leading to huge tensions. The difference was that Marx took those tensions to what he saw as their logical conclusion.

This logic, Marx's adaptation of the Hegelian 'dialectic', set him apart from other economists. His criticism of them was that they proposed laws of economics as universal and permanent as the laws of physics and chemistry, without realizing that they were describing a temporary phase in economic development. Capitalism, in Marx's view, was a mere staging post on the economic journey from feudalism to communism, its final destination. Did he have a point? While Smith has survived remarkably well through changing economic circumstances that even he could not have dreamt of, and comparative advantage is still as relevant as in Ricardo's day, it is the case, perhaps unsurprisingly, that quite a lot of the economics of the nineteenth century and before has not travelled well. Unfortunately for Marx, that is also true of most of his analysis. Before explaining why, let me sketch out some of that analysis.

The value of labour

Marx, like many of the other economists of his day, took as his starting point the question of value. In his view the number of worker-hours needed to produce a product determined its value. If that sounds slightly odd to a modern economic observer, in an era when we know that the cost of manufacture is only a fraction of what we pay for something in the shops, it still has its echoes today. Take your car to a garage for a repair and the quote you are given will usually consist mainly of the number of hours of labour needed to do the job. Or, on a slightly grander scale, a lawyer's bill will usually be calculated on the basis of an hourly charge multiplied by the time it took for the work. Of course, nobody believes that the amount you pay to the garage goes straight into the pocket of the mechanic, or that the articled clerk who does the donkey work on your legal case gets anything like the huge amount of money you hand over to the firm. And this, essentially, was Marx's point. In any price there is value, determined by a strict interpretation of the cost of the labour required, and there is 'surplus' value, the amount that the owner, financier or landlord of the business obtains as a result of the sweat of the workers.

In the previous chapter I described why businesses operate on the basis of the profit motive. Without profit, potential capitalists might as well leave their money in the bank and spend their time fox hunting or on the golf course. The lure of making more money than was available in the absence of risk provided capitalists with their spur. It provided the basis for investment, without which economic development could not occur. It also gave owners of land (the landlords) incentives to allow their green fields to be turned into factory sites. Profit and rent provided the spur for development. Logical though that looks to us today, economists at the time found it hard to challenge Marx, mainly because his analysis was within a value framework that was their own. To argue that the owners of machinery deserved a return was wrong, said Marx, because the value of that machinery – defined by him as the amount of labour needed to build it – was already taken into account. As for rewards to the owners of land, this hardly came into it. In Marx's view, all property was theft.

While we can quibble with Marx's scheme, it does give us a neat way of thinking about the way he and others saw the tensions inherent in capitalism. The aim of capitalists – and in this Marx lumped owners, financiers and landlords together – was to increase surplus value. If this meant employing women and children to carry out dirty and dangerous industrial jobs, so be it. If it meant employing men to work long hours in poor conditions, that was a sound strategy. The comment of a Manchester businessman to Engels, when Marx's friend was pointing out the filth and squalor in which the working classes lived – 'And yet there is a great deal of money made here. Good morning Sir!' – seemed to sum up the attitude. Marx, though, was keen not to attach the blame to individual capitalists. They were creatures of their time, and of the system in which they operated, and their time was running out. Marx's labour theory of value provided the conflict inherent in capitalism, the battle for fair shares and the inevitability of exploitation. Marx also provided a route map to capitalism's collapse.

Capitalist crisis

On the face of it, Marx's analysis, even if it provided an accurate description of worker exploitation, all too evident at the time in the slums of Victorian England and the abuse and ill treatment of child workers, did not necessarily explain why this process should come to an end. The capitalism described by Marx may have been a kind of industrial feudalism but why, as long as bosses could keep workers under the cosh, should it be doomed to failure? The answer, as he saw it, was that there was a dynamic process at work. Capitalists were not content to rest on their laurels, living off their profits, or 'surplus' value. Instead, they were driven by a need and by the pressures of competition from others to move things forward, by investing this surplus in yet more machinery. Marx was quite poetic about this. He wrote: 'Accumulate, accumulate! That is Moses and the prophets. Therefore save, save, i.e. reconvert the greatest possible portion of surplus value or surplus product into capital! Accumulation for accumulation's sake, production for production's sake.'

This drive to accumulate capital, or as we would describe it, invest, had three important consequences. The first was that some workers would be displaced by machinery. In modern terminology, production changed from being labour-intensive to being capital-intensive, throwing workers in those pre-welfare state days on to the streets. This, the creation of a 'reserve army' of the unemployed was quite important in terms of worker exploitation. As long as there were people out there willing to take a job just to eat, wages could be kept very low. The second consequence was that accumulation would result in a 'survival of the fittest', as weaker firms fell by the wayside and dominance by a few large ones became the norm. Evolution, it seemed, applied as much to capitalist economies as to the natural world. (Marx sent Charles Darwin a copy of the first volume of *Capital*, although he did not receive a response.) The third and most interesting consequence, however, was that the accumulation process itself created problems for the very capitalists instituting it. Marx identified what today would be described as over-investment. Driven by the desire to accumulate and to maximise their profit, capitalists invested more than was necessary. This would drive down prices because other capitalists, with their extra investment and production, would have to compete. The process would be brutal, with small firms being driven out of business by bigger ones. It would also, in Marx's view, be part of a never-ending cycle. Capitalists, it seemed, would not learn from their mistakes. Capitalism was doomed to a declining rate of profit, which would add to the pressure on capitalists to exploit workers. It would also impose instability on the economy, as waves of accumulation – investment – were followed by retrenchment and reductions in jobs and wages.

In the Marxist scheme there were two contradictions inherent to capitalism. The first was that downtrodden workers, earning only subsistence wages, would not provide the market, the demand, for the ever-increasing amount of goods produced by the factories of the capitalists. Marx constructed an elaborate explanation of how the system could remain in balance by producing larger and larger quantities of luxury goods – which the capitalists would sell to each other – but his clear implication was that this was unsustainable. Any economist would agree with him. Mass production requires mass consumption. The more fundamental contradiction lay with the workers themselves. Brought together in factories, often having moved to industrial towns and cities from the country, would they be prepared to accept their exploited plight indefinitely? Marx clearly thought not. He wrote:

> *Along with the constantly diminishing number of magnates of capital, who usurp and monopolise all advantages of this process of transformation, grows the mass of misery, oppression, slavery, degradation, exploitation; but with this too grows the revolt of the working class, a class always increasing in numbers, and disciplined, united, organised by the very mechanism of the process of capitalist production itself.*

The capitalists' own factories would become hotbeds of discontent, revolt and, ultimately, socialist revolution.

Workers of the world …

Marx's tomb carries the slogan 'Workers of all lands unite'. That, or the more usual 'workers of the world unite', provided his rallying call. Out of Marx's *Capital* came, not only a view of the capitalist system as inherently unstable and crisis-ridden, but also fundamentally unfair. His labour theory of value demonstrated that capitalists were parasites on the body economic, getting fat on the surplus value created by their workers. The answer was for workers to control 'the means of production, distribution and exchange', simultaneously eliminating this surplus value (as well as the capitalists to whom it accrued) and enriching the lives of ordinary workers. Socialist parties, as well as communists, took this up. Until Tony Blair successfully abolished it soon after becoming the leader of the Labour Party in 1994, Clause Four of the party's constitution said:

> *To secure for the workers by hand or by brain the full fruits of their industry and the most equitable distribution thereof that may be possible upon the basis of the common ownership of the means of production, distribution and exchange, and the best obtainable system of popular administration and control of each industry or service.*

Exactly how far that committed Labour to Marxist state ownership was long a matter of debate. Co-operatives, for example, would appear to meet Clause Four's requirements. It was, however, used to justify the wave of nationalisation by the 1945–51 Attlee government, which, as described in the previous chapter, took a whole range of industries, including coal, steel and the railways, into state ownership.

In fact, while *Capital* in its three volumes provided the theoretical justification for workers to seize the economic levers and use them, Marx and Engels had already reached this conclusion in the *Communist Manifesto* they co-wrote in 1848. While to modern eyes some of the manifesto's proposals seem revolutionary – a single monopoly state bank, monopoly state ownership of transport and communication and the abolition of property rights – others are quite mild. It proposed a graduated or progressive income tax and the extension of state ownership of factories and other means of production, but not complete control.

How wrong was Marx?

While Marx has been one of the most influential thinkers of the modern era, history has not been kind to his economics, or his lasting impact. The rise of the middle classes in western capitalist societies defied his prediction of workers kept permanently in conditions of near-poverty. Capitalism has been kinder to the masses than communism. There were crises of capitalism, most notably in the Great Depression of the 1930s, and there was of course the Russian revolution of 1917. But Marx's central prediction, of capitalist crises brought on by falling profits, did not stand the test of time. The domino-like fall of communism in Eastern Europe at the end of 1980s, most dramatically with the collapse of the Berlin Wall, and its present minority status, pursued by only a few oddball countries, appear to signal that little more than a century after his death, Marx's star has waned, possibly never to come back. The record of economies run along Marxist lines, ostensibly for the benefit of the workers, was abysmal. Before the unification of West and East Germany in 1990, there was a widespread impression that the economy in the east, the old German Democratic Republic, was quite strong. Only when it was opened up to full view were its weaknesses revealed. Nor has Marx's economics really lasted. Keynes set the tone in the 1930s by describing *Capital* as 'scientifically erroneous' and 'without interest or application in the modern world'. Marxist thought, he said, was based on a misunderstanding of Ricardo's theory of value. That was a little harsh, owing much to the benefit of hindsight. The classical economists were seriously challenged by Marx's critique and, in its time, his work provided an intellectual underpinning to the revolutionaries threatening the capitalism of the industrial age. The capitalists of the period, and their intellectual supporters, would have given short shrift to the suggestion that Marx did not represent a threat.

That is partly why his predictions were wrong. Even if you were to accept an analysis that suggested workers would tend to remain permanently downtrodden, this did not leave revolution as the only solution. Worker power could be and was exerted through other ways, not least through democratic socialist parties. A Marxist analysis would say that capitalism adapted, steering a course that accepted, under pressure, a more equitable distribution of income. Adam Smith would have said that this was always the way it was going to be.

Defenders of Marx, responding to the fact that workers had indeed made economic progress, enjoying rising living standards rather than stagnating on the breadline, used to point to the exploitation by industrial countries of their colonies. Western workers had only prospered, in other words, because of the downtrodden poor elsewhere. There is a flavour of that in the present debate over globalisation. When the richest 200 people in the world have the combined income of the poorest 41 per cent of the global population, or nearly half of the people of the world live on less than $2 a day, the existence of inequality is not in doubt. What is harder, however, is to argue that this emerges from Marx's scheme of things. Inequality arises as much from the inability of so many people to participate in the capitalist process, for reasons I shall come on to later. The links between global inequality and Marx's economics are at best tenuous, at worst do not exist at all.

Marx and the crisis

These problems with Marxist economics aside, it might have been expected that an existential crisis for capitalism, with the near meltdown of the global banking system in 2008, would have been the spur for a Marxist revival. That may happen but at time of writing, three years on, it had not. One of the most energetic interpreters of Marx is David Harvey, a Distinguished Professor at the City University of New York, who in recent years has acquired a beard which would not disgrace Marx himself. Harvey, on his website http://davidharvey.org offers thirteen video lectures which provide a detailed guide to *Capital*. He is also the author of *The Enigma of Capital: And the Crises of Capitalism*, published by Profile, publishers of this book. The book is worth reading. One of its essential points is that capitalism has always been good at reinventing itself, even after the most extreme crises. The biggest danger for capitalism would be to pretend that nothing had changed and to attempt to go back to exactly how things were before 2008. It is, however, unlikely to collapse under the weight of its own contradictions. The book concludes: 'Capitalism will never fall on its own. It will have to be pushed. The accumulation of capital will never cease. It will have to be stopped. The capitalist class will never willingly surrender its power. It will have to be dispossessed.'

9

Paying the bill

Now that Marx has left us, it is time to start thinking about something that can ruin any meal – paying the bill. We are not quite at the end of our meal yet, and some might say this is a contrived title for a chapter about what governments do. But it seems fair enough to me. The government's most important role in the economy is, after all, raising taxation, for which we all have to pick up the bill, and redistributing it in the form of public expenditure. The late Sir Leo Pliatsky, a senior civil servant at the Treasury and Department of Trade and Industry in the 1950s, 1960s and 1970s, called his memoirs *Getting and Spending*, after Wordsworth's 'getting and spending we lay waste our powers'. So let us have a look at the government's core role in the economy, at fiscal policy. Fiscal means 'pertaining to tax' but fiscal policy is both government spending and taxation.

Why governments spend

These days the fact that governments spend many billions each year is taken for granted. As long as there have been governments there has been government spending. It is worth thinking briefly about why this is. The first justification comes with so-called 'public goods'. Public goods are, forgive the jargon, 'non-rival' and 'non-excludable'. Non-rival just means that if I consume something, it does not stop you from doing so. Non-excludable means that if I wanted to stop you from consuming something I had paid for, I could not do so. Many public goods are thus services or institutions that benefit the community as a whole but which the public would be unlikely to pay for on a voluntary basis, unless everybody else was also doing so. Would we pay voluntarily for the police service? Perhaps not if we believed the headlines that say they spend all their time persecuting middle-class motorists rather than catching criminals. Would we fund the legal system, which is necessary but expensive, with all those highly paid lawyers and judges? And, while there is no shortage of patriotism at time of war, citizens might object to the cost of maintaining the armed forces when there is no threat on the horizon. The existence of certain public goods is a type of 'market failure'. If the government did not provide them, they might not exist and a properly functioning legal system, for example, is necessary to the workings of the economy. Proponents of a smaller state would argue that many things that are regarded as public goods would be provided privately if government did not. Some things, however, would not be.

A second type of market failure comes with so-called uninsurable risks. Would a chronically sick person with no income be able to get private health insurance? No, unless the government required insurance companies to provide blanket coverage for everybody within an area. Even then, to spread the risks between the healthy and unhealthy, companies might be required to offer such cover across a very wide area. And if this is the case why should not the government itself offer or at least guarantee such insurance, paid for out of taxation? The same goes for a whole range of risks, including unemployment insurance for the persistently unemployed, sickness pay for regular absentees. Even if the government acts as insurer or purchaser, however, it does not have to be provider as well. The government could buy its entire healthcare on behalf of patients from private sector doctors and hospitals, removing the need for a National Health Service. Governments have sought to do this, but only at the margin. The argument for an NHS funded out of taxation was that only a large organisation (the biggest employer in western Europe) could take advantage of economies of scale, provide healthcare even in sparsely populated areas and train sufficient staff.

While most economists accept that it is the role of government to provide public goods, its role in the areas of uninsurable risks and as a provider of services such as health and education has come to be challenged, although not yet by enough to significantly change the system, at least in Britain. Similarly, governments use taxation and government spending to redistribute income from rich to poor. Free market economists would argue that modern governments have moved well beyond what should be their core competences. There is little prospect, however, of a return to smaller, simpler government. In most advanced economies the global financial crisis resulted in an unintended but greatly expanded role for the state, both in terms of direct intervention to support the banking sector and an increase in public expenditure relative to the size of the economy. Indeed, in Britain it led to commercial banks being brought into public ownership, something that had not happened even in the heyday of nationalisation. It was done, of course, for practical rather than doctrinal reasons.

Spend, and spend some more

Budgetary arrangements differ between countries, notably in the split between central and local, or federal and state, when it comes both to revenue-raising and spending. The basic rules are, however, the same everywhere. Revenues are raised to finance spending. If more revenues are raised than are needed there is a budget surplus. If revenues are insufficient there is a budget deficit and the government – central, local, federal or state – has to borrow to make up the difference. That, in a paragraph, is public finance.

UK government spending, at time of writing, is just over £700 billion a year, in an economy with a gross domestic product (GDP) of a little above £1,500 billion, so public spending is the equivalent of nearly 50 per cent of GDP. The word 'equivalent' is important in this context, as noted earlier. Because not everything in public spending counts towards GDP, notably state pensions and welfare benefits, it would be misleading to say that nearly half of the economy is controlled by the state, though these outlays ultimately have to be paid for out of taxation. It is also the case that the global financial crisis had a profound impact on the relationship between government spending and GDP in Britain and in most other advanced economies. This was both because governments spent to try to mitigate the effects of crisis and recession (or had to do so because rising unemployment pushed up spending on out-of-work benefits), and as a result of the drop in GDP that occurred in recession. The numerator, spending, went up while the denominator, GDP, went down. In Britain's case government spending was equivalent to roughly 40 per cent of GDP before the crisis but, as noted, closer to 50 per cent during and after it.

How do governments allocate spending? It would be wrong to characterise it as pure political horse-trading, though there is a large element of that when it comes to the final decisions. Mostly, however, it is a process similar to that described by Britain's Treasury, in which there is a Treasury-led spending review, a 'process to allocate resources across all government departments, according to the government's priorities. Spending reviews set firm and fixed spending budgets over several years for each department. It is then up to departments to decide how best to manage and distribute this spending within their areas of responsibility.' These spending reviews, carried out every two years though setting spending totals for three years ahead, were established by the Labour government in 1998, to replace the old annual 'blood on the carpet' battles, so called because they threw up deep political disagreements. When the Conservative–Liberal Democrat coalition government was elected in May 2010, however, it quickly held a spending review to fix spending limits for the four years from 2011–12 to 2014–15. It also embarked on some of the most significant reductions in spending in decades, with departments that were not 'ring-fenced' (mainly all of them apart from the National Health Service and the

Department for International Development) subject to average real-terms cuts – in other words, reductions after allowing for inflation – of 19 per cent over four years.

An important distinction is between current and capital expenditure. In the National Health Service, for example, current expenditure would include wages and salaries of doctors, nurses and other staff, and the annual drugs bill; while building a new hospital would plainly count as capital expenditure. The lion's share of government spending is current. In recent years public–private partnerships, such as the private finance initiative (PFI), have been used to try to increase the amount of capital spending but have been criticised for imposing too large a long-run cost on taxpayers.

Before the twentieth century, the story of public spending was essentially one of war and peace. Governments spent, by and large, to maintain armies and such spending rose sharply during times of war, when those armies swelled in numbers. Before the Napoleonic wars, for example, the British government spent about a tenth of GDP, a figure that rose to a third by the time of the Battle of Waterloo. Wars were expensive, and still are, necessitating both higher taxation and, more importantly, extensive and prolonged borrowing. That was not just a pre-twentieth century phenomenon. The burden of financing the Second World War seriously sapped Britain's ability to continue as a major economic power in the post-war period.

Until 1914, public expenditure operated around a peacetime norm of 10 or 11 per cent of GDP. This was the level in the early part of the century, the late Victorian and Edwardian eras. The First World War effectively ushered in a period of state control of the economy and, in its aftermath, public spending did not return to its peacetime norm, instead settling at the equivalent of a little over 20 per cent of GDP. This was not just due to the cost of paying for the war, in terms of the interest on government debt, but also because of the beginnings of a government-provided welfare state. The Liberal government elected in 1906 passed legislation in 1908 introducing state old age pensions, as well as David Lloyd George's 1911 National Insurance Act, which provided elements of both unemployment and health insurance. This ratcheting higher of spending continued during and after the Second World War, a period that saw the Education Act of 1944, the National Health Service Act of 1946 (the NHS came into being in 1948), the National Insurance Act of 1946 and the National Assistance Act of 1948. This was the period when, following Sir William Beveridge's 1942 report, the modern welfare state came into being, with the government taking responsibility for health, education, pensions and a range of benefits, covering unemployment, sickness and other needs. It was also a time when state control of industry was significantly extended. By the early 1950s government spending was equivalent to 30 to 35 per cent of GDP, increasing further to between 45 and 50 per cent by the mid-1970s, as welfare spending rose. The Thatcher government succeeded in reducing it, on average, to about 40 per cent of GDP, which was roughly where it stayed until the global financial crisis. This was despite a long period, beginning in the year 2000, in which the Labour government of Tony Blair and Gordon Brown significantly increased spending, particularly on education and the NHS, which benefited from sustained 7 per cent annual real increases. Government spending rose from the equivalent of 39.9 per cent of GDP in 1996–7 to 41.1 per cent in 2007–8 before increasing substantially. Strong GDP growth in the period leading up to the crisis and an initial 2–3 years of spending restraint after the 1997 general election made Labour look relatively prudent in spite of the very big spending increases. Some argue that the true picture emerged only when the economy fell into recession.

The rise of government spending to about four times its pre-1914 level, relative to the size of the economy, has been accompanied by significant changes in its composition. As recently as 1950, defence was the most important item of government spending, equivalent to 6.6 per cent of GDP, and followed, in order, by social security (5.1 per cent), health (3.6 per cent), education (3.4 per cent) and housing (2.6 per cent). Sixty years later, social security, including state pensions, had the biggest budget (13.3 per cent of GDP), followed by health and personal social services (10.5 per cent), education (6 per cent) and defence (2.7 per cent), on which slightly less was spent than the 2.9 per cent of GDP on government debt interest. The rise of the welfare state is clear, as is the declining importance of defence, the more so since the British government, like others, claimed the 'peace dividend' following the end of the Cold War, though it subsequently became involved in long and bloody conflicts in Iraq and Afghanistan. Housing, important in the period following both world wars – building 'homes fit for heroes' – has become only a tiny part of government spending, following the Thatcher government's successful policy of selling council houses to their tenants, and the transfer of much of the remaining council housing stock to housing associations.

What is the right level of government spending?

Why was it the case that governments used to spend only a tenth of GDP on public services, and much of that on defence, whereas two-fifths is now regarded as the norm? Part of the reason is that in the past there was no universal state provision of education, healthcare and support for the poor. This did not mean there was no such provision. In Britain a network of voluntary organisations, charities, medical aid societies, friendly societies and churches, often acting with local or national government agencies, provided an informal welfare state long before Beveridge. School boards ensured most local children received an education well before the 1944 Education Act. One criticism of the post-war welfare state was that it swept aside many of these highly effective voluntary arrangements. Paying to see a doctor was commonplace, indeed expected. Many operated an informal system of cross-subsidies, making sure their wealthier patients paid but not chasing up the fees of poorer clients. On the first day of the NHS, 5 July 1948, many patients turned up at GP surgeries armed with their six-pences, it not having sunk in that from now on consultations and treatments would be 'free at the point of delivery'. They soon got used to it. Within a few months the cost of the NHS was rising at a rate that alarmed ministers, a pattern that has continued to this day. Aneurin Bevan, the 'father of the NHS' in the post-1945 Labour government, was soon commenting: 'I shudder to think of the ceaseless cascade of medicine which is pouring down British throats at the present time.'

The level of public spending varies over time and it also varies in content. Britain's defence budget, relative to the size of the economy, has steadily shrunk with the dismantling of the Empire. Housing is no longer a priority area for government spending. When the Conservatives were in power from 1979 to 1997, some areas of the welfare state were chipped away and replaced by private insurance, for example indefinitely paying the mortgage payments of the unemployed. A policy was also put in place to reduce the attractiveness of the basic state old age pension, and by implication increasing the incentive to contribute to private arrangements, by linking annual rises in the state pension to prices rather than faster-growing earnings. (Interestingly, the Conservative–Liberal Democrat coalition government announced a restoration in the pension–earnings link in 2010, though alongside other reforms including accelerating planned rises in the state pension age.) Privatisation dramatically reduced the state's role in the UK economy during the 1980s and early 1990s, transferring telecommunications, steel, gas, water and electricity from public to private sectors, whereas the earlier policy of nationalisation had increased it.

The point is that there is no economically determined optimum for the level of government spending. It is a matter of political choice. It is also a matter of national preference. The coalition government elected in 2010 had the aim of reducing spending to the equivalent of 40 per cent of GDP again, which would leave it higher than some countries but lower than others. Most countries, as noted, saw their government spending to GDP ratios rise strongly in the aftermath of the crisis. On OECD figures (slightly different to Britain's own official data), government spending in 2011 was the equivalent of 50.1 per cent of GDP in the UK, similar to Italy (50.5 per cent). It was higher than the United States (41.3

per cent), Spain (42.4 per cent), Japan (42.1 per cent), Germany (45.3 per cent) and Australia (35.6 per cent) but lower than Sweden (51.9 per cent), Finland (54.1 per cent), France (55.3 per cent) and Denmark (58.1 per cent). When the first edition of this book was written, government spending in Germany was significantly higher in relation to GDP than in Britain. The fact that the level of spending is a political choice does not mean, of course, it has no economic effects.

Getting crowded

'There's no such thing as a free lunch' is the motto for this book, and there is no such thing as costless government spending. When Bevan fretted about the embryonic NHS's medicine bill, it was because the market mechanism had been removed. For the first time there was no price constraint – the cost of a visit to the GP or of the medicine itself – on people's healthcare. This is why, when services are funded out of taxation, rationing is common and, indeed, has been a feature of the NHS since its creation. The benefits of government spending are many. Governments can, through taxation, put money to more socially desirable uses. They can spend to keep the economy going during hard times (more of that shortly) or to help out hard-hit regions. However, there are also costs, and one way of thinking about these is in terms of crowding out.

What is crowding out? Right at the very start of this book I picked up on one of the commonly used definitions of economics, the one about it being all about the allocation of scarce resources. That definition is quite useful in the context of government spending, in two respects.

The first is that markets achieve that allocation by means of price. Products that are in short supply will rise in price, restricting the demand for them, and encouraging people to switch to things that are cheaper and more plentiful. 'Free' public services such as healthcare operate in the absence of any price mechanism. Demand, as a result, can be limitless. This is why rationing is so common in public healthcare and other services.

The second way the allocation of resources comes in useful as a concept is in thinking about the way the economy divides up between public and private sectors.

A computer expert employed full-time by the Inland Revenue cannot also be employed by the private sector. The office in which he or she works cannot also be used for commercial purposes. A pound taken in tax and used to fund the NHS cannot also be spent by the individual for half a pint of beer. It has gone. The government, in carrying out public services, stakes a claim on a substantial slice of the economy's resources, whether they are people, property, equipment, or the money to pay for all these things. 'Resource' crowding out occurs when the government's claims on these things act to the detriment of the private sector. When might this arise? Suppose there is a limited number of IT experts and the private sector cannot get hold of trained staff because the government is employing most of them. Or Whitehall departments take all the best office locations in the centre of London. More generally, resource crowding out arises when resources are fully used. If the economy is in a situation of full employment, for example, the private sector will be unable to take on extra staff unless it is able to recruit them from the public sector. If the public sector does not want to let them go, or is recruiting too, the effect will be to push up wages, and therefore both private and public sector costs will increase.

There is another type of crowding out. What happens when governments increase spending at a faster rate than tax revenues are flowing in? In such circumstances governments are required to borrow, to run a budget deficit. All governments borrow, usually from their own citizens in the form of National Savings or from financial institutions and other investors through the issue of government bonds (called gilts in the UK because the certificates originally had gold edging). Borrowing by governments is perfectly normal. The problem arises when governments try to borrow too much. Originally people used to think about financial crowding out in the sense that, if there was a limited supply of funds, the more the government claimed for its own purposes the less would be available for companies to access in order to finance productive investment. In these days of global, free-flowing capital between different countries, it is wrong to think of a narrowly defined pool of money existing only in one country. International investors buy the bonds issued by the governments of other countries. Japanese financial institutions, famously, allowed America to run big budget deficits from the mid-1980s onwards by their willingness to buy US government bonds, so-called treasuries. That role was subsequently taken on by Chinese institutions and official bodies. In 2008 China became the largest foreign holder of US government bonds. Cross-border holdings of government debt do not, however, change the fundamental proposition. The crowding out that occurs can be more subtle but also much more dangerous. Governments that borrow heavily will be regarded with some suspicion by the financial markets, which normally will require a higher rate of interest in return for providing funds. The effect of heavy government borrowing is usually to push up interest rates for all borrowers, which has the effect of crowding out some of them. Curiously, as the global financial crisis unwound the interest rates on UK and US government bonds fell to very low levels in spite of heavy borrowing. One reason for this was that investors saw them as 'safe haven' assets.

This is one reason why, when the euro was established in 1999, it operated under a 'stability and growth' pact, under which member governments were required to restrict their budget deficits to 3 per cent of GDP or below, or face penalties. The fear behind it was that heavy borrowing by one member country could have a damaging effect throughout the euro area. It did not work. The stability and growth pact fell into disrepute when it was ignored by both France and Germany. Both paid for not taking it more seriously. The global financial crisis led to big increases in eurozone budget deficits but particularly those of what came to be known as peripheral economies. The eurozone succumbed to fiscal contagion in May 2010 when Greece had to be rescued by a combination of other eurozone governments and the International Monetary Fund, followed in subsequent months by Ireland and Portugal. The failure of governments to control their borrowing threatened the entire system.

Multiplying government spending
Before moving on to tax, and the 'Budget judgment', one quick point. Our next speaker, John Maynard Keynes, will have a little more to say on this, but it is necessary to qualify very slightly the

effect of government spending. A pound spent by the government cannot be used by you or me to buy books or groceries but some of that pound may indeed end up being spent on such things. How so? Approximately 70 per cent of health service spending goes on wages and salaries. It therefore provides public sector employees with an income, part of which they will use for, yes, books and groceries. There is a 'multiplier' effect. Some of the non-wage component of public spending will be used to pay for supplies or services that, again, will provide somebody with an income. An initial increase in government spending flows around the economy for quite a while. Just like a pebble tossed into a pool, the effects go beyond the initial splash. A pound spent by the government does not, however, produce a pound of spending at the next stage. Some of the income paid out by the health service will be taken by tax, some will be spent on imports, some saved. But the multiplier is a useful idea. Sometimes it is used to justify extra government spending rather than tax cuts, on the ground that cutting taxes for individuals will be subject to quite large leakages because, for example, three-quarters of cars sold in Britain are imported. Government spending, as Americans used to say (some still do), may in such circumstances carry 'more bang for the buck'. Estimates in 2010 by America's Congressional Budget Office had fiscal multipliers ranging from 0.2 for tax cuts for higher income individuals – a $1 billion tax cut would boost GDP by $0.2 billion – to as high as 2.5 for certain kinds of government spending; spending an extra $1 billion could boost GDP by $2.5 billion. In Britain in the same year the Office for Budget Responsibility, the government's independent fiscal watchdog, suggested fiscal multipliers ranging from 0.35

from a change in VAT to 1 for extra spending on the infrastructure. So in its view, expansionary fiscal policy would be unlikely to boost the economy by more than the upfront cost of the policy.

Taxing time – the Budget

Budget day, held in March or April (apart from a brief period in the 1990s when it was held in the autumn), is one of the great occasions in the British political calendar, and the big date in the UK economic calendar. Many other countries have a single day each year when their finance ministers make their annual budget statement. In the United States, where the budget is the product of long and often messy negotiation between the White House and Congress, the process is less clear-cut. The principles are, however, similar the world over.

In the UK the days may have gone when MPs would queue for hours to be sure of securing their place in the House of Commons chamber for the Chancellor's speech, but 12.30 on Budget day, when the speech is usually delivered, is still guaranteed to be one of the few times when it is full to overflowing. The term Budget derives from the French '*bougette*', a wallet or pouch, of the kind Robert Walpole used to carry his papers in when he was Chancellor in the 1730s. Today, Chancellors carry a more familiar red Budget despatch box, holding it aloft for photographers outside 11 Downing Street before making the short journey to the Palace of Westminster. Today too, Chancellors read prepared texts, in the knowledge that a stray word could be misinterpreted in the financial markets. It was not always like this. William Gladstone's legendary four-hour speeches were made from brief notes, one set of which is on display in the Museum of London. Many Chancellors used Gladstone's battered red Budget box, until it was officially retired to the National Archives after George Osborne, the first peacetime coalition Chancellor since the inter-war years, used it for his 2010 Budget.

The Budget is preceded by weeks of speculation, some of it informed, some of it leaked, deliberately or otherwise. Only one Chancellor, Hugh Dalton, has resigned for leaking the Budget. In 1947 he inadvertently let slip some of its contents to a reporter from a London evening paper, who was able to get it into the paper and on the streets before Dalton had told the House of Commons. In 1984 a disgruntled civil servant leaked the entire contents of the Budget to the *Guardian*. A police investigation was launched, but the culprit was never caught. Why the obsession with secrecy? Because some Budget information is market-sensitive and because foreknowledge can allow people to take action. The 1984 leak was important because the Budget contained some important changes to corporate taxation, but also because it included, from midnight on the day of the speech, the removal of tax relief on life insurance policies. The leak produced a two-week rush to take out such insurance, and thus to continue to benefit from the tax break, and cost the government tens of millions of pounds in lost revenue.

Budgets have changed over the years and the amount of documentation accompanying them has expanded hugely over time. Chancellors have always used them to update parliament on the state of the economy and the public finances, and the outlook. This was formalised in the 1975 Industry Act, which required the Treasury to produce two published forecasts of the economy annually. In 2010, the Conservative–Liberal Democrat coalition announced the major reform of handing over the role of economic and fiscal forecasting to its new and independent Office for Budget Responsibility. A large part of the reason for this was to remove the well-founded suspicion that Treasury forecasts, officially the 'Chancellor's forecast' were politically influenced. Otherwise, the Budget will include both tax and public spending changes, even though the latter are supposed to be the province of the spending reviews. The main purpose of the spring Budget, though, as it always has been, is to raise tax.

Taxes and the Budget judgment

In the 2011–12 tax year UK government receipts totalled about £589 billion, a considerable sum. Income tax, introduced 200 years ago by William Pitt the Younger, is easily the most important single tax, bringing in £158 billion. It was followed by National Insurance contributions, at £101 billion. NI contributions, paid by both employers and employees (and the self-employed), are examples of direct taxation. They are levied according to income, as of course is income tax, and have to be paid, unless you have a clever accountant. Indirect taxation, in contrast, can be avoided, usually by the act of not purchasing the goods on which it is levied. If you do not smoke, drink or drive, you will escape the duties and value added tax (VAT) levied on these activities. VAT, which brought in £100 billion in 2011–12, is the third biggest tax. It is harder to avoid but not impossible. Food, books, newspapers and children's clothing and footwear are all zero-rated for VAT purposes. A small person whose only hobby was reading would pay very little VAT. The fourth biggest tax, another direct tax, is corporation tax, the tax levied on the income of companies. It brought in £48 billion. These four taxes together accounted for the lion's share of the government's income, £407 billion, or more than two-thirds of the total. Other significant taxes were excise duties on fuel, alcohol and tobacco, £46 billion; council tax, £26 billion; and business rates, £25 billion.

The 'Budget judgment' is, at its simplest, the net amount the Chancellor intends to raise or lower taxation in the coming year. In practice it can get a little more complicated, because Chancellors often announce deferred tax changes that will only take effect in future years. The principle is, however, the same. I shall come to what determines that judgment but first a small note of clarification. On the face of it, some taxes go up every year. Smokers, drinkers and motorists have got used to the idea that duties, and therefore prices, rise after the Budget. But some taxes also usually go down. Most income taxpayers will find, a month or so after the Budget, a small reduction in the amount of tax they pay. There is an easy explanation for this, and it has nothing to do with the Budget judgment. It is conventional for income tax allowances to be lifted each year in line with inflation, to be 'indexed' (increased in line with the retail or consumer prices index). A parliamentary amendment, the Rooker–Wise amendment, introduced during the high inflation of the 1970s, required Chancellors to do this unless they had good reason not to. Hence the appearance of an income tax cut – in fact just handing back the extra tax you are paying because of inflation – each year. Chancellors, in addition, have a way of getting this money back, mainly by indexing petrol, tobacco and alcohol duties. This is why the prices of these tend to rise after Budgets. It is also why these 'indexation' effects, which are more or less automatic, should be put aside when we are trying to assess whether taxes are being raised or lowered.

On this basis, a typical Budget 'giveaway', an expansionary Budget, might involve between £3 billion and £5 billion of tax cuts, while a tough Budget might raise them by a similar amount. This is small in relation to government receipts – 0.5 to 0.8 per cent – and even smaller in relation to the size of the economy, 0.2 to 0.3 per cent. Some Budgets do go further. In 1988 Nigel Lawson cut the top rate of income tax from 60 to 40 per cent and the basic rate from 27 to 25 per cent. That giveaway was worth, at 2011 prices, £10–11 billion. A few years earlier, in 1981, his Conservative predecessor Sir Geoffrey Howe had raised taxes by a similar amount. Gordon Brown, in his April 2002 Budget, also increased taxes by roughly this amount, mainly through higher National Insurance contributions for both employers and employees, to fund extra National Health Service spending. A more substantial 'giveaway' was announced by Alistair Darling, Chancellor from 2007 until 2010, in response to the global financial crisis. In November 2008 he announced tax cuts and public spending increases worth £25 billion over two fiscal years, 2008–9 and 2009–10. The biggest impact was in 2009–10, with a fiscal stimulus worth more than £16 billion, or over 1 per cent of GDP. The biggest single measure was a temporary reduction in the standard rate of VAT from 17.5 to 15 per cent, to run from December 2008 until January 2010.

From fine-tuning to no tuning and back again
The changes announced by Darling in December 2008 were significant, in that they marked an important change of tack. Until then,

just as the amounts involved in Budget tax changes were generally small in relation to the size of the economy, so too had become the ambitions of politicians. From the early 1950s onwards, under the influence of the followers of Keynes – he will be with us in a minute – 'fine-tuning' was in vogue. The economy was subject to well-observed cyclical fluctuations, lasting about four years. For a year or two things would be slack, then they would pick up, gaining momentum until the point when a boom was under way. These cyclical fluctuations were due to variations in demand, so what better than to try to iron them out by small changes in tax? In a downturn, putting more money into the hands of consumers and businesses by lowering taxes would stimulate spending, thereby lessening the severity of that downswing in activity. Politicians of the day, such as Harold Macmillan, who was both Chancellor and Prime Minister (though not at the same time) used to talk of 'a dab on the accelerator'. In an upturn, when the need was for consumers and businesses to cool their spending ardour, taxes would be raised slightly, 'a touch on the brake'. Why? Because otherwise the economy would carry on growing faster than its long-run rate, unemployment would fall to very low levels and the pressures on capacity would push up inflation. There was even a formal mechanism for fine-tuning, the 'regulator' introduced in the early 1960s, which allowed the Chancellor to vary most indirect taxes – purchase tax (VAT's predecessor) and the excise duties on tobacco, alcohol and petrol – by 10 per cent in either direction between Budgets.

In the years before the global financial crisis, although politicians often talked about tax changes as being timely, fine-tuning through tax had fallen into disuse, killed off by the apparent realisation that it was inefficient. Tax changes, particularly direct ones, can usually be introduced only slowly and then take time to feed through to pay packets. This is partly because Budgets are infrequent, usually only once a year (emergency Budgets smack of panic) and can take time to pass through the parliamentary process. A tax cut introduced during a downturn may actually have its impact in the subsequent boom, when the opposite is required. Fiscal fine-tuning was also killed off by the boom and bust cycles of the 1970s and 1980s. These needed, if it were available, not so much fine-tuning as a new engine. So why did the idea of providing a short-term fiscal stimulus make a comeback in 2008 and 2009 and dominate the macroeconomic debate afterwards? One reason was the severity of the crisis and recession, the worst for the global economy in the post-war era. Another was that monetary policy, the preferred method of short-term control of the economy – experience had shown it was easier and more effective to vary interest rates rather than tax rates – was running out of ammunition. By the end of the winter of 2008–9 most advanced-country central banks had reduced interest rates to zero, or close to it. So a fiscal stimulus, even a temporary one, became the obvious choice.

Fiscal rules
Until the crisis struck, governments tended to operate on the basis of so-called fiscal rules. As already discussed, in the case of the countries that adopted the European single currency, the euro, the Stability and Growth Pact was intended to provide such rules, requiring that countries normally run a balanced budget – with spending and taxation roughly equal – and not allow deficits to exceed 3 per cent

of GDP in other circumstances. The rules, ineffectively policed, were a failure. A similar fate befell the two fiscal rules adopted by Britain's Labour government elected in 1997. The first was the 'golden' rule, that over the economic cycle the government would borrow only to invest – build new hospitals, schools and roads – and not to finance current spending on, for example, the wages and salaries of public sector workers, so that the 'current' budget deficit would be balanced, or better. The second was what it called the sustainable investment rule, which was to hold government debt, the national debt, at a 'stable and prudent' level, in practice below 40 per cent of GDP. Both were maintained, albeit under increasing strain, until the 2007–8 fiscal year but were quickly broken, and suspended, when the crisis hit. The current budget deficit rose to 7.6 per cent of GDP in 2009–10, while overall government borrowing hit more than 11 per cent of GDP. By mid-2011 government debt stood at £940 billion, or 61 per cent of GDP. Including the banks rescued by the government during the financial crisis pushed the debt up to a huge £2,266 billion, or 148 per cent of GDP.

Though Labour's fiscal rules proved ineffective when the economy fell into recession, the coalition government elected in 2010 both rejected further fiscal fine-tuning and adopted its own rules, to be assessed by the Office for Budget Responsibility (OBR). Its first fiscal rule was for the current budget to be in balance after five years. It would, in other words, always aim for a balanced budget, excluding capital spending and the effects of the economic cycle. The other rule, specific to the coalition's first term in office, was to have government debt falling as a percentage of GDP by 2015–16. The OBR's job was to regularly monitor the likelihood of these rules being met.

Taxes and behaviour

At its most basic the purpose of taxation is to raise the money governments need to finance their spending. The effects of taxation, however, go well beyond that. Adam Smith gave us the four 'canons' of taxation: that it should be based on ability to pay; that it should be 'certain' – taxpayers should know how much they have to pay and when; that it should be convenient to pay; and that taxes should be relatively cheap to collect relative to the amount of revenue they raise, they should be 'economical'. Ability to pay is perhaps the one that features most prominently in modern tax debates. 'Progressive' income tax regimes – where higher earners pay higher marginal rates (the rate of tax on the last pound of income) and therefore a greater proportion of their earnings in tax – exist in the majority of countries. In Britain there is a basic rate of income tax of 20 per cent and a top rate of 45 per cent (from April 2013). Such progressive regimes have faced a challenge, however, from advocates of a flat-rate income tax, in which the amount paid would simply rise in line with income. Under a flat tax of, say 30 per cent, the £100,000 earner would pay the same marginal rate as a £20,000 earner but would also, because of higher earnings, face a bigger tax bill. The ability to pay principle would be satisfied, although not to the same extent as with a progressive tax.

All taxes distort. Many people will have seen some of the windows of otherwise pristine old houses in Britain bricked up, a legacy of the infamous window tax, introduced in 1696 and abolished in 1851, under which properties with ten or more windows were subject to additional taxation. More recently the poll tax or community charge, brought in as a form of local government taxation in 1990 (and widely seen as a factor behind Margaret Thatcher's downfall), led many young people to remove themselves from the electoral register, thus depriving themselves of the opportunity of voting, rather than pay the tax.

The precise way in which income tax distorts will depend on circumstances – an increase in income tax rates could either make people work more to maintain their previous post-tax income, or work less because the incentive to earn more has been reduced. Taxes on employment, such as the National Insurance contributions employers have to pay will, by raising the cost of each worker, tend to reduce numbers employed. The high social security costs – the equivalent of NI – faced by employers in much of Europe are one reason for lower levels of employment, and higher unemployment, in some European economies. Indirect taxes such as VAT or excise duties on alcohol, tobacco and petrol will, other things being equal, have the effect of reducing the consumption of such products by raising their price. The extent to which changes in such taxes increase or reduce consumption will depend both on what is happening to income and whether demand for the product is 'elastic' (highly responsive to price changes) or inelastic. Indexation, merely increasing duties in line with inflation, is unlikely to have much impact on consumption. Indeed, if earnings are rising faster than prices, as is usually the case, the effects of indexation will be to make the product cheaper in relation to income. Say earnings are rising at 5 per cent a year and inflation is 2.5 per cent. Increasing duties by 2.5 per cent would still leave them cheaper relative to earnings. They need to rise by at least 5 per cent. This is one reason why duties on goods regarded as bad for health or the environment – tobacco, alcohol, petrol – are often 'over-indexed', raised by more than the inflation rate. The trouble with this is that, thanks to the EU Single Market and some well-organised smuggling operations, UK consumers of tobacco and alcohol have access to cheaper supplies. When the rules governing personal imports of cigarettes, wine, spirits and beer into Britain from the rest of the EU were relaxed, the tobacco and drinks lobby argued (with some conviction) that the more the British government taxed, the more incentive individuals and organised gangs of smugglers would have to exploit the 'Calais run'. Smuggling and legal imports cost the Treasury billions each year in lost revenues and for a time acted as a constraint on increases in duty in Britain. Legal and illegal imports of such products may mean that the unintended consequence of raising duties for health reasons is that increasing numbers of consumers seek access to them at lower prices than before. VAT, 20 per cent at time of writing, is not formally indexed but the revenue from it will tend to rise in line with the level of spending, reflecting both inflation and changes in the volume of purchases.

Laffer and the 'right' level of tax

Under Margaret Thatcher in Britain and Ronald Reagan in America, the supply-side revolution of the 1980s, there was a deliberate rejection of the idea that taxation should be used for fine-tuning purposes. An important part of that revolution was a powerful belief that high taxation in general, and high taxes on income in particular, distorts. Tax the rewards of success too heavily, it was argued, and people will have no incentive to take the risks necessary to achieve success. High tax rates on company directors will stifle enterprise. Ability to pay, in other words, can go only so far before it starts to do some damage. Moreover, if tax rates are set too high, their effect will be to *reduce* the amount of revenue the government receives.

In the late 1970s Arthur Laffer, an economics professor who held positions at the universities of both Chicago and Southern California, was having lunch in a Washington restaurant with Jude Wanniski of the *Wall Street Journal*. Laffer sketched out on a napkin the way in which high tax rates could cut revenue. If the income tax rate is zero, then the government gets no revenue. But if it is 100 per cent, the government is also penniless because there is no point anybody working for a zero post-tax income. Between those two points, Laffer demonstrated, there will be a rate of tax above which revenue starts to decline. Initially, say from zero to 50 per cent, higher rates swell government revenues. Somewhere around that point, however, the opposite will occur and the government will find itself, having raised tax, worse off. The Laffer curve is usually dome-shaped, with the optimum tax rate somewhere in the middle (although Thatcher, Reagan and the supply-siders would always think of anything like a 50 per cent income tax rate, even as the top marginal rate, as too high). When Britain's top rate of income tax was temporarily increased in 2010 to 50 per cent on earnings above £150,000 a fierce debate ensued about whether this would lead to a big enough exodus of high-earning people from the country to neutralise (or worse) any positive impact on government revenues – Her Majesty's Revenue and Customs was asked by Treasury ministers to adjudicate.

Earmarking or stealth?

When the Labour government took office in 1997, it immediately set about raising taxes. Mostly it did this in a subtle, or 'stealthy', way. It fulfilled an election promise by imposing a £5 billion one-off, or windfall, tax on former nationalised industries such as gas, electricity and water. It also announced a change that would be worth £5 billion a year by abolishing a tax credit on company dividends previously enjoyed by pension funds. This was a stealthy change because most individuals would not become aware of it until retirement. Stealth taxes can, however, backfire. One of the others the government used was to take advantage of weak world oil prices to sharply increase the duty on petrol. Because falling world prices were compensating for rising tax, nobody noticed. But in September 2000, when the world oil price surged higher, petrol prices also increased and the government got the blame. In a humiliating climb-down the Chancellor, Gordon Brown, was forced by widespread protests to cut the duties. Brown got caught out again with what he had hoped was another stealthy change. In his final Budget as Chancellor in March 2007 he abolished the 10 per cent starting rate of income tax he himself had introduced, under the cover of cutting the basic rate to 20 per cent. A political outcry followed, led by low earners and their political supporters.

The opposite of a stealth tax is one that is raised for a specific purpose – an earmarked or 'hypothecated' tax. When the Labour government embarked on a big increase in National Health Service spending in the early 2000s there was a debate about introducing a hypothecated health tax. The Treasury rejected it, saying it would be wrong to link health spending to the revenue from a tax that could vary from year to year, depending on economic conditions. The Treasury's real reason for caution about hypothecation, which is a long-standing objection, is that while people might be prepared to pay a health tax, they might object to a tax that had as its purpose raising the money to pay out welfare benefits. Even defence, a traditional public good, might struggle to raise money if it were given its own hypothecated tax.

Taxes, credits and reliefs

In the past two or three decades, in most countries, there has been a tendency to move from direct to indirect taxes, for supply-side or incentive reasons – the idea being that if people keep more of what they earn they will work harder. Even so, direct taxes are still more important in terms of raising revenue. The top marginal rate of income tax in Britain was reduced from 83 to 40 per cent between 1979 and 1988, and the basic rate from 33 to 20 per cent from 1979 to 2007, while the main rate of VAT increased from 8 per cent in 1979 to 20 per cent in 2011.

Another favoured shift has been to achieve lower tax rates by limiting tax reliefs. A tax relief is an amount that can be set against the amount of tax an individual or company pays. Taxpayers in Britain earning up to £100,000 had a personal allowance of £7,475 in 2011–12, the amount that can be earned before any tax is paid. Most households also benefited from tax relief on their mortgages until relatively recently but this relief was gradually pared down by the Conservatives before being abolished entirely by the Blair government, a rare example of cross-party consensus on tax policy. Another to be scrapped was the married couple's allowance, effectively an additional tax relief received by married men. The writing had been on the wall for that relief since the introduction, in the 1980s, of separate taxation for husbands and wives.

While tax reliefs have been scaled back, tax credits have come into vogue. What is a tax credit? For a long time the holy grail of tax reformers was a negative income tax. The idea was a smooth transition from low earners, who not only did not pay tax but also received money back from the tax authorities, to higher earners who paid tax. Tax credits work a little like that. The working families' tax credit, introduced in Britain by the 1997 Labour government and based on America's earned income tax credit, directly replaced a welfare benefit (family credit), the difference being that low earners received a top-up, not from the social security office but from their employer in their pay packet (the money being subsequently refunded by the Inland Revenue). This and other credits, while subject to reform on grounds of cost at time of writing, may have helped limit the rise in unemployment during the 2008–9 recession. Employees were able to stay in work, but on reduced hours, the difference in their income being made up by the tax credit.

That's probably enough about tax and public spending. As always, there is no shortage of information on this subject, nor limits to the scope for change. Chancellors have a Budget once a year and usually find a way of tinkering with the system, often by introducing new taxes. The best independent guide through the tax and spending maze is the Institute for Fiscal Studies (www.ifs.org.uk).

Its annual Green Budget, published a little in advance of the actual Budget, is an invaluable aid. The site also contains useful information on comparative tax systems. The Office for Budget Responsibility (http://budgetresponsibility.independent.gov.uk) is another great resource, as is the Congressional Budget Office (www.cbo.gov) in America.

And now – I have been hinting at his arrival for some time – the moment has arrived. Given that Adam Smith was Scottish, our next guest must rank as the greatest English economist, although David Ricardo has more than his fair share of supporters. Anyway, there can be no doubt that John Maynard Keynes was the greatest modern British economist, and one of the towering figures of the twentieth century.

10

Keynes gets cooking

If the title of this chapter makes Keynes sound like a master chef, a showy magician might be more appropriate. Keynes weaved his spell over economics at a time when the subject was growing up into a mainstream area of study in universities. *Time* magazine named him the greatest economist of the twentieth century and, in truth, there were no other serious candidates to challenge him. For the past 80–90 years the economic debate has been dominated by Keynes, both by those who followed and developed his ideas and, as importantly, by those who sought to challenge them. When, after the September 11 2001 terrorist attacks on America, the Bush administration pushed a programme of tax cuts and additional government spending to head off recession it was, said commentators, because Washington had rediscovered Keynes. Even more so, when the world was plunged into crisis in 2008, Keynes came to the fore and Keynesian economists pushed governments to follow what they believed were his remedies. Keynes was back or, perhaps more accurately, he had never really gone away.

Who was he? John Maynard Keynes, always known as Maynard by friends and colleagues, was born in 1883, the year of Marx's death. His father, John Neville Keynes, was a distinguished economics professor at Cambridge, although not as distinguished as Alfred Marshall (1842–1924), his contemporary. Marshall, who later taught the younger Keynes, is worth a brief digression. When we left English classical economics it was in a state of some disarray, Marx having emerged to challenge some of its cosy, and not-so-cosy, assumptions. Marshall's great contribution was to put classical economics into a coherent framework, recognisable to economics students today. His *Principles of Economics*, published in 1890, not only provided the first clear signal that economics was to develop as a science, rather than as the art of political economy, but it demonstrated how the 'marginals' – marginal cost, marginal revenue and marginal utility – that we have already encountered, fitted in. If Smith, Ricardo, Mill et al. were classical economists, Marshall's approach was 'neoclassical', adapting and setting their work in what was then a modern context. Keynes is sometimes said to have thrown back his teacher's work in his face by overturning some of its assumptions, but that is not really fair. Marshall was concerned mainly with microeconomics, the working of individual markets, Keynes's main area of influence was macroeconomics.

After studying at Eton, Keynes returned to Cambridge to read, not economics but mathematics, in which he took a degree. While there he became an Apostle, a member of the university's elite secret society and also, perhaps because of that society's belief in the superiority of homosexual love, became a practising homosexual. He did, however, apparently renounce homosexuality on his unlikely marriage in 1925 to the Russian ballerina Lydia Lopokova, who was to prove a great source of support during his later life, particularly after his first heart attack in 1937. Keynes entered the India Office (part of what is now the Foreign Office) in 1909, staying only two years before returning to Cambridge as a teaching fellow in economics, his skills in the subject having been noticed and encouraged by Marshall. Almost immediately he became editor of the prestigious *Economic Journal.*

The First World War and its aftermath was to be the making of Keynes, as we shall see, but even a brief account of his life cannot leave out his extraordinary renaissance man qualities. He was, of course, a member of the Bloomsbury group, which included Virginia Woolf and Lytton Strachey, and Keynes's own writing was much admired for its elegance. Indeed, some of his best sayings rival Oscar Wilde. 'I would rather be vaguely right, than precisely wrong,' he said, and: 'I do not know which makes a man more conservative – to know nothing but the present, or nothing but the past.' Most people will have heard, if not used, Keynes's justification for a shift of view: 'When the facts change, I change my mind. What do you do, sir?' He could also be wonderfully cutting. Of one senior Treasury mandarin, he wrote that 'he could stay silent in several languages'. Of another that 'caught young', he might have understood the elements of economics. He often attracted wit back. When, at the 1946 conference in Savannah, Georgia, that launched the International Monetary Fund, Keynes said he hoped no 'malicious fairy' would wreck the proceedings, Frederick

Vinson, head of the US delegation, said: 'I don't mind being called malicious, but I do mind being called a fairy.'

Keynes straddled the worlds of academic life, government, the City and the arts. He chaired National Mutual Life Assurance and the Cambridge Arts Theatre and, as a highly successful investor, made money for both himself and his beloved King's College, lost much of it in the 1929 crash, which he did not see coming, but made it back again, and some more, over the next few years. He was the first chairman of what became the Arts Council. Keynes was no ivory tower economist. He badgered and cajoled politicians and a Treasury that was generally resistant to his ideas. He often set out his views in the pages of *The Times* and publicly took on his critics. One of Keynes's most famous quotes is the one in which he takes to task politicians, 'madmen in authority', for being 'slaves of some defunct economist'. Keynes did his best to ensure his ideas were taken up before he was defunct. He lived until 1946, dying at the age of 62, a comparatively short life, and he was in poor health for the last ten years of it. Arguably, his influence was far greater after his death. Now let us see why.

The economic consequences of peace and Churchill

Keynes returned to government service early in 1915, once it became clear that the optimistic view of the First World War, that it would all be over by Christmas 1914, had proved to be badly mistaken. As a Treasury adviser, initially a junior, he rose rapidly and was put in charge of the key task of co-ordinating the country's foreign exchange expenditure on essential wartime imports. Keynes, as he was to demonstrate on many occasions, did not suffer fools gladly, however senior, on one occasion telling Lloyd George, the Prime Minister, that he was talking rubbish. Perhaps surprisingly, this brutal honesty did him little harm with political leaders. Despite being a young man of huge influence, he was evidently frustrated by his wartime service at the Treasury, writing to fellow Bloomsbury group member Duncan Grant in December 1917: 'I work for a government I despise for ends I think criminal.'

This frustration spilled over at the end of the war when, having been assigned to the UK delegation to the Versailles peace conference, he resigned in June 1919 over what he considered to be the dangerous direction it was taking. The issue was the amount of war reparations the defeated Germany should pay to the victorious allies. Keynes argued for no more than £2 billion, still a huge sum at the time, while others were pressing, it appeared successfully, for £24 billion. Although no figure appeared in the Versailles treaty, the implication was that reparations would be very substantial. After his resignation, Keynes wrote *The Economic Consequences of the Peace*, criticizing the approach of the allies at Versailles. 'If we aim deliberately at the impoverishment of Central Europe, vengeance, I dare predict, will not limp,' he wrote. Heavy reparations would result, initially, in a great inflation and eventually in a war 'which will destroy, whoever is victor, the civilisation and progress of our generation'.

Historians have long debated whether Keynes was right. After all, while the Versailles treaty sounded tough, the amount of reparations actually paid by Germany was under £2 billion. However, there was a great inflation, the hyperinflation of the Weimar era.

Inflation is when the general price level is rising. Hyperinflation is when it is rising very rapidly, by more than 50 per cent a month on one definition. Germany in the early 1920s certainly qualified. Between August 1922 and November 1923 prices rose by an average of 322 per cent a month. Thanks to the power of compound interest, this meant that prices at the end of the period were 10.2 billion times those at the start. To put that into perspective, a million marks at the start of the period would be worth less than a pfennig at the end of it. Versailles also established a climate in which the defeated German people felt angry and resentful because, it seemed, the victors were determined to extract full revenge. This was the perfect climate for the rise of Adolf Hitler.

The Economic Consequences of the Peace became a bestseller and Keynes a public figure in Britain and abroad, albeit one often at odds with the political establishment. This was compounded in 1923 when he published *A Tract on Monetary Reform*, in which he argued strongly against a return to the pre-war gold standard. The gold standard, whose heyday was from about 1880 to 1914, was, as its name suggests, a system in which currencies were tied to gold, for both domestic and international purposes. It appealed to 'sound money' bankers and had a certain theoretical simplicity. A country running a balance of payments deficit would in theory have to ship gold out to creditor nations (in practice it was usually moved between different parts of central bank vaults). This loss of gold would, in turn, reduce the supply of money and cut spending at home, thereby correcting the deficit. Keynes, however, had little time for gold, a 'barbarous relic', or for the system. When, against his advice, Britain returned to the gold standard in 1925, the then

Chancellor Winston Churchill having taken the decision, Keynes wrote *The Economic Consequences of Mr Churchill*. It predicted that the result would be a damagingly overvalued exchange rate and chronic unemployment. Again, he was right. Britain left the gold standard six years later, in 1931, but only after the damage was done.

Saving capitalism from itself

Keynes's criticisms of the conventional wisdom had given him fame, wealth and notoriety but his most constructive contribution was yet to come. The context was the high unemployment of the inter-war years, due to a series of events, including the mistaken desire of countries to return to the gold standard, the Wall Street crash of 1929, and the attempt by countries to protect themselves against global economic woes by putting up trade barriers (so-called 'beggar-my-neighbour' tariffs such as America's Smoot–Hawley Act of 1930, which pushed tariffs on US imports to more than 50 per cent). Staple industries such as coal, iron, steel and shipbuilding suffered from chronic overcapacity, hitting parts of Britain particularly hard. As Eric Hobsbawm put it in *Industry and Empire*:

> In 1913–14 about three per cent of the workers in Wales had
> been unemployed – rather less than the national average. In
> 1934 – after recovery had begun – thirty-seven per cent of the
> labour force in Glamorgan, thirty-six per cent of that in
> Monmouth, were out of work. Two thirds of the men in
> Ferndale, three quarters of those in Brynmawr, Dowlais and

*Blaina; seventy per cent of those in Merthyr, had nothing to do
except stand at street corners and curse the system which put
them there. The people of Jarrow, in Durham, lived by the
Palmer's shipyard. When it closed in 1933 Jarrow was derelict,
with eight out of ten of its workers jobless, and having like as
not lost all their savings in the crash of the yard, which had so
long been their harsh and noisy universe.*

In truth, however, nowhere was immune. In America, without
even Europe's limited pre-war welfare provision, the consequences
of mass unemployment were even more severe. The Great Depression, the mass movement of desperate people in search of work and
food chronicled in John Steinbeck's *The Grapes of Wrath* and the
failure of thousands of banks and therefore of the supply of credit
– on some explanations the cause of most of the trouble – spoke of
a global crisis for capitalism.

It is not true to say that the economists before Keynes had failed
to envisage mass unemployment. In general, though, they believed
that such episodes would be self-correcting. Temporary spells of
unemployment would result in falling wages, which would increase
the demand among employers for workers. The depression and
mass unemployment of the inter-war years appeared to mark capitalism's nadir. Arguably it was in its death throes. Many of the
intelligentsia in western capitalist societies saw the crisis as proof
that Marx was right, and many saw Marxism as the only solution
to it. Smith's 'invisible hand', it seemed, was either very shaky or
no longer worked at all.

Keynes did not. When he wrote *The Economic Consequences of*

Mr Churchill he advocated, as an alternative to returning to the gold standard, a programme of government spending, of deliberately running a budget deficit, in order to restore economic growth and reduce unemployment. He did so again when appointed to the Macmillan Committee on Finance and Industry in 1929, and whenever he was given the opportunity in his many writings for newspapers and magazines. He was, however, up against a powerful force, the so-called 'Treasury view'. For the guardians of Britain's public finances, Keynes's ideas were dangerously radical. The country, they believed, should run a balanced budget and, where possible, seek to repay debt, not deliberately allow it to build up. Gordon Brown, when Chancellor, spoke of finding a pamphlet by Keynes in the Treasury archive. Scrawled across it, by a senior official of the day, was the single word 'inflation'.

The General Theory

Keynes was not deterred. In 1935 he wrote thus to George Bernard Shaw, the playwright: 'I believe myself to be writing a book on economic theory, which will largely revolutionise – not, I suppose, at once but in the course of the next ten years – the way the world thinks about economic problems.' The book, published in 1936, was *The General Theory of Employment, Interest and Money*. Keynes persuaded Macmillan, his publisher, to put it on sale at five shillings (25 pence), believing that like his earlier works, it would be a bestseller. That was optimistic. Although tens of thousands of copies have been bought by economists and students over the years, the book was never one for the general reader. Even economists find it difficult and, in some respects, confused and contradictory. The great communicator, able to turn out highly readable op-ed articles for *The Times*, had produced a rather inaccessible book. That, however, was less important than its message which, as he predicted, did indeed make people think differently about economic problems and, as noted, made it one of the three most important economics books ever written, along with Smith's *Wealth of Nations* and Marx's *Capital*. We have yet to see a fourth to rank alongside these three, although this is not for want of trying on the part of publishers. When, at the end of the 1990s, the financier George Soros brought out a book on the 'crisis in global capitalism' (this was after Asia had hit economic and financial problems but ten years before the much bigger global financial crisis), his publishers claimed, optimistically, that he had produced the fourth in a quartet of greats.

To understand Keynes's breakthrough, without getting bogged down in the complexities of *The General Theory*, it is necessary to return to my 'most useful equation in economics'. This was the one that said: $GDP = C + G + I + X - M$, where C is consumer spending, G government spending, I investment, X exports and M imports. Let's ignore X and M for the moment and concentrate on the others. What happens when C is depressed because of high unemployment and I is weak because businesses cannot see any prospect of good times returning? Is it inevitable that GDP (gross domestic product – the economy as a whole) has to be weak, the more so because a government seeking to cut its cloth to suit its means would have to reduce spending in line with weaker tax revenues? Keynes said no. Governments should, in these circumstances, do precisely the opposite. They should increase spending, particularly on public works (which would mean, on modern definitions, pushing up I, because of higher government investment). By boosting G and the public sector's part of I, GDP would be automatically increased; economic growth would be restored.

Could it really be so simple? After all, governments do not create wealth, they merely redistribute the money they raise from taxation. Would not Keynes's solution result, if not in inflation, then in only a temporary fillip, after which the economy would be in even more trouble than before? Keynes came up with many memorable phrases to justify action to improve the lot of the people in the short-term, 'in the long-run we're all dead', being one of the most famous. Even more pertinent, in this context, is this one from *The General Theory*:

> *If the Treasury were to fill old bottles with banknotes, bury them at suitable depths in disused coalmines which are then filled up with town rubbish, and leave it to private enterprise on well-tried principles of laissez-faire to dig up the notes again (the rights to do so being obtained, of course, by tendering for leases of the note-bearing authority) there need be no more unemployment and, with the help of the repercussions, the real income of the community, and its capital wealth also, would probably become a good deal greater than it actually is.*

The point was that additional government spending, at the right time, would 'prime the pump', triggering higher growth elsewhere in the economy, and the mechanism by which this occurred was probably one of Keynes's most important contributions. The multiplier, already touched upon, ensured that this additional spending by government rippled through the economy. Suppose a public works programme employs 100,000 previously unemployed people at £500 a week. That means an extra £50 million of income. Not all of that will be spent, but if 90 per cent of it is (the workers have an average propensity to consume nine-tenths of their income), there is £45 million of extra spending which generates wages for factory workers, lorry drivers, shop workers and others. The multiplier, the size and strength of which will be determined by the propensity to consume, also ensures that at least part of the initial injection of public money feeds back to the Treasury in higher tax revenues. The size of that fiscal multiplier is, as discussed in the previous chapter, a matter of considerable debate. Enthusiasts for Keynesian remedies will argue that fiscal multipliers are large, particularly when certain government spending is boosted. Opponents will tend to argue that these multipliers are very small. This debate aside, the multiplier also offers a potentially strong reason why the 'classical' remedy to unemployment, reducing wages to price workers back into jobs, would not work. Apart from the fact that it is hard to get workers to accept wage cuts, even when prices are falling, wage cuts would, by reducing income, also mean lower spending power, or 'aggregate demand'.

This all sounds fine but was there not a more direct route to stimulating the economy, through cutting interest rates? The next chapter will go into some detail about how this process usually works but Keynes's essential point was that, at the time he was writing, interest rates had lost their potency. In his view a situation could develop where interest rates were as low as the authorities could push them but still too high to stimulate investment, because businesses were too gloomy about prospects – in Keynes's words, they lacked 'animal spirits'. It was possible, in other words, for the economy to be caught in what he called a liquidity trap. Even when interest rates were at their lowest practicable level, perhaps even zero, nobody wanted to borrow. In these circumstances, increasing money and credit would not help. All that would happen was that 'idle' balances would build up in banks. If all this sounds a bit far-fetched, there was a modern-day example even before the global financial crisis.

For almost two decades from 1990, until it was joined by most other advanced economies when the crisis hit, Japan was a living example of an economy caught in a liquidity trap, where interest rates were cut to zero without stimulating the economy, not least because of falling prices, or deflation. Interestingly, the Japanese government tried 'Keynesian' remedies on a number of occasions, with tax cuts and public works programmes. They did not work, mainly because the Japanese government was slow to tackle the problems in its banking system, because they were never followed through consistently – there were times when the authorities withdrew the fiscal stimulus prematurely – and because of a loss of public confidence in their political leaders. Japan's first 'lost decade' in the 1990s turned into a second decade of economic stagnation and deflation – falling prices – in the 2000s.

The global financial crisis provided what was widely seen as a second coming for Keynes, as described by his biographer Robert Skidelsky, in his book *The Return of the Master*, published in 2009:

The economist John Maynard Keynes is back in fashion. That guardian of free-market orthodoxy the Wall Street Journal *devoted a full page spread to him on 8 January 2009. The reason is obvious. The global economy is slumping; 'stimulus packages' are all the rage. But Keynes's importance is not just as a progenitor of 'stimulus' packages. Governments have known how to 'stimulate' sickly economies – usually by war – as long as they have known anything. Keynes's importance was to provide a 'general theory' which explains how economies fall into slumps, and to indicate the policies and institutions needed to avoid them. In the current situation no theory is better than bad theory, but good theory is better than no theory. Good theory can help us avoid panic responses, and give us insights into the limitations of both markets and governments. Keynes, in my view, provides the right kind of theory, even though his is clearly not the last word on events happening sixty-three years after his death.*

Keynes did not have it all his own way. Though most governments did introduce fiscal stimulus packages, the majority also put in place plans to repair their public finances – by withdrawing the stimulus – over the medium-term. A fierce debate ensued, with Keynesians insisting that it was necessary to maintain the stimulus well beyond the immediate crisis. Nobody, unfortunately, could say for sure which side the master would have come down on.

There is a lot more to Keynes and *The General Theory* than this brief summary has allowed. Students who delve a little deeper will quickly encounter the so-called 'IS and LM framework', developed by Keynes's followers Sir John Hicks and Alvin Hansen. They will get used to dealing with aggregate demand and aggregate supply. Further reading will reveal a fierce debate about whether Keynes's *General Theory* was in fact general, or merely applied to the special case of the inter-war years. They will also find that he is villain to as many people as he is hero. Keynes may have saved capitalism from itself in the 1930s but to his critics he also ushered in the era of big government and inflationary deficit financing (the Treasury view did not die completely). General readers with the time and interest should read Robert Skidelsky's excellent three-volume biography of Keynes.

Bretton Woods

Before leaving Keynes, it is worth touching briefly on what he did after *The General Theory*. Apart from harrying politicians and debating vigorously with his critics, to ensure his ideas were taken up he was soon, despite a heart attack in 1937, back in active government service. In 1940 he published *How to Pay for the War*, an ingenious plan involving temporary taxation (to prevent a wartime inflation because of the pressure on resources), with a refund to taxpayers once the war was over. There were hints of this in Kingsley Wood's 1941 budget, but it was more explicitly Keynesian in other respects. Keynes's bigger role was in international negotiations, mainly with the Americans. Rightly, he saw America's wartime ambition as supporting its old ally militarily but when it came to financial assistance, to do so on terms that would ensure Britain's displacement by the United States as an economic superpower. Keynes saw it coming, both in America's Lend-Lease assistance to wartime Britain and in the US loan that was to tide the economy over in the post-war period. Ironically the defeated European powers, which received Marshall aid, ended up as the stronger economies in the post-war period. Some say that Keynes's failure to change America's approach contributed to his early death in April 1946.

Before that, he had been Britain's chief negotiator at the Bretton Woods conference of the summer of 1944. Bretton Woods, a sprawling and now once more elegant hotel in the White Mountain National Park in New Hampshire, was chosen as the location for a conference that would shape the world's financial system in the post-war period. It was clear by then that Germany would be defeated, although it was to take nearly a year for the task to be completed, so it was necessary to create a framework that would avoid the problems of the inter-war years. Again, Keynes had a radical plan, the establishment of a world central bank, which would create credit and settle payments between countries in its own currency, to be called 'bancor'. Once again, he was ahead of his time, too far ahead for the American team and its Treasury secretary, Harry Dexter White. Bretton Woods gave birth to a bank of sorts, the World Bank, and to the International Monetary Fund. It also gave the world the fixed-but-adjustable exchange rate system that was successful for twenty-five years after the war. Currencies were fixed against others, within narrow bands, but could be adjusted in exceptional circumstances. Britain had two such adjustments under the system, devaluing the pound in both 1949 (from $4.00 to $2.80) and 1967 (from $2.80 to $2.40). Gallingly for Keynes, this system had echoes of the gold standard he so despised.

Called the gold exchange standard, it survived until America, under Richard Nixon, suspended the convertibility of dollars into gold in 1971.

Although Keynes did not get his way at Bretton Woods his contribution was immense. Some say the international monetary system he envisaged would still be in place today, and some leading Chinese figures have taken to quoting his plan approvingly, and preferable to the dollar-based system the world ended up with. As with everything else he did, he was impossible to ignore.

And now, as Keynes leaves us with a flourish, it is time to come right back up to date. The economic picture is almost complete and the guests are feeling rather full. It is time to talk about something that often comes up at the dinner table, and can be the cause of indigestion – bread in common parlance, money to you and me.

11

Bread and money

Sooner or later, vulgar though it may be, most dinner-table conversation gets round to money. It is perhaps surprising that we have come so far without talking about it explicitly, although we have explored those other favourite topics – mortgages and house prices. Without money, after all, what would we be, mere primitives exchanging half a dozen cows for a new wife? Cattle, in fact, played an important part in the development of money. They were widely exchanged, particularly for wives. Chattels, as in 'wife and chattels', and capital, as in capital investment, or even the name of Marx's most famous work, come from the same Old English roots as cattle. Actually, some apparently primitive societies used money in a highly sophisticated way, even if their money was rather different to ours. On the island of Yap in the South Pacific, very heavy stones were used as money, which had the virtue of making them hard to steal; while in the New Hebrides they used feather money, and what could be easier to carry around? In Borneo, by tradition, human skulls were used as money, and if this sounds gruesome to us, it was because they happened to be their most prized possessions. Whales' teeth were used in Fiji. Manillas, forms of ornamental metal jewellery, were used in West Africa as recently as 1949. Even in modern economies, in particular circumstances, other things have replaced conventional money. Cigarettes, or perhaps these days drugs, are the main currency within prisons, where cash is of limited use. Cigarettes also became the currency of choice during the great European hyperinflations of the twentieth century, particularly in Germany. Cigarettes, it seemed, held their value better than money.

It can be fun, if only on a rainy afternoon, to trace the way in which currencies came to have their names. A pound was called a pound for fairly obvious reasons – it was the amount of silver that weighed a Roman pound, or *libra* (hence lira as well, and the fact that the letter 'l' was used to denote both). A mark was also a measurement of weight – two-thirds of a pound. A drachma, now in Greece subsumed into the euro (at time of writing at least), meant a handful of grain. The unit of currency in medieval Britain was the penny, whose symbol until decimalisation in 1971 was the letter 'd', from the Latin *denarius*, which spawned many currency names, notably the dinar. Quite why the pound became the pound sterling from about the twelfth century, maybe a little earlier, is less certain. We know that sterling originally described a penny, so £1 sterling, was actually a pound of sterlings. Why sterling? One suggestion is that it was a corruption of starling, another that it derived from 'easterlings', north-eastern European merchants. Nicholas

Mayhew, professor of numismatics and monetary history and deputy director of the Ashmolean Museum at Oxford, who has written widely on the subject, favours the explanation that it derives from 'ster' a Middle English word implying strength and stability.

What does money do? We may wonder. Carl Menger, in his classic 1892 article 'On the Origins of Money', conceded that the fact that every individual and every business 'should be ready to exchange his goods for little metal discs, or for documents representing the latter', appeared to be 'downright mysterious'. The paragraph above tells most of the story. Money's primary purpose is as a medium of exchange. It therefore has to be generally acceptable. Cigarette money would not be much use in a nation of 95 per cent non-smokers. Acceptability is more important, in general, than something many people get hung up on – whether a particular form of money is legal tender. Legal tender simply means what people are required to accept, under the law, in payment of debts. That can vary. A penny is legal tender in most uses but anybody trying to settle a £1,000 bill in pennies could legitimately be refused. For generations, kilt-wearing Scotsmen, down for the rugby, have been outraged when London taxi drivers have refused to accept their Scottish banknotes. The cabbies are perfectly within their rights. While generally accepted north of the border, Scottish banknotes are not legal tender even in Scotland.

Money must also be a store of value, which is one reason why durable metals were used as money, and why it took time for paper money to be trusted. There are plenty of examples of food being used as money but, like any perishable good, it suffers from a certain basic disadvantage. Money should also be a unit of account. As long as people are able to assess the value of things in terms of the number of cigarettes they would cost, there is nothing to stop cigarette money acting as a unit of account. Menger, however, in his 1892 article, also explained why precious metals were peculiarly suited to act as money. They were, he pointed out, widely coveted and scarce in relation to the demand for them. You might turn up your nose at accepting a plastic token as payment, but never gold or silver.

From money to Mastercard

The story of banking is older than that of money itself, or at least coinage. In Mesopotamia or ancient Egypt, banks were storehouses for grain or other commodities. Receipts, promises to pay, issued for the deposit or transfer of grain became used as currency. Paper money, for that is what it was, therefore goes back a long way. Ancient civilisations had relatively sophisticated banking systems. We know from the Greek and Roman coinage that has survived that the amount of money in circulation was considerable. We also know that the coinage was only part of a more extensive monetary framework, including banks. The history of money is not, however, a smooth one. Paper money appears to have died out when the Roman Empire crumbled and was not revived, at least in Europe, until about the twelfth century, given an impetus by the crusades – when a way had to be found to make payments for supplies, equipment and paying allies. Banking services, already developing rapidly in Italian city-states such as Rome and Genoa, became international. If we now fast forward to England in the seventeenth century, and the Civil War (1642–51), wealthy people stored their jewellery, bullion and other valuables in the secure strongboxes or safes of goldsmiths. As in ancient Egypt, paper money was the consequence of such deposits. A cheque – an instruction to the goldsmith to pay – could effect a transfer of money from one person to another. Receipts given on the deposit of valuables could be exchanged. By about 1660 these receipts had become banknotes. Similar developments occurred in other countries.

So far, however, there is nothing about paper money, apart from the fact that it is lighter and more convenient to carry, that distinguishes it from the gold and other valuables that it represents. That difference began to occur when the goldsmiths began to realise that most of the valuables in their safes never left the premises. As long as people were confident that when the time came they would be able to withdraw their gold, they were happy to conduct their business in gold's paper form. And as long as the goldsmiths could be confident that not everybody was going to want to take out their gold at the same time, they could issue many more banknotes – drawn on gold – than there were quantities of the precious metal in their vaults. It sounds like trickery but it is the basis of modern banking. The Scotsman John Law, at one time described as the richest man in the world, took this process forward in the early eighteenth century by persuading the French royal court to adopt what was then the most sophisticated paper money system in the world. Because the scheme was linked to shares in the Mississippi Company, a highly speculative venture, the experiment ended disastrously. But the paper money era was born.

Except in circumstances like these, the issue of paper money should not be confused with the fact that banks still have to ensure that their deposits and loans are in rough balance. The same applies, of course, to cash now. I remember being quite shocked as a child when I discovered that if everybody wanted to take his or her notes and coin out of the bank at the same time there would not be nearly enough to go round. Sometimes, of course, depositors test that process to the limit, when there is a run on the bank of the kind that hit Northern Rock, a British bank, in September 2007 (the first such run since the 1860s), which is when the central bank has to step in as lender of last resort, often supported by other banks keen to maintain confidence in the system. When there is a run on the system as a whole, the central bank can respond by printing more money. The result of that is likely to be inflation, of which more below.

The process by which banks expand the amount of 'money' in the economy by building on a relatively small monetary base is known as 'credit creation'. The type of banking we are talking about is known as 'fractional reserve banking' and some people, admittedly a small minority, argue that the rot set in when this form of banking became the norm. Either way, the amount of money in circulation is determined by what is known as the 'money multiplier'. If, by custom and practice, banks find that they need to hold 10 per cent of loans and deposits in the form of cash, the money multiplier is 10 – there is ten times the amount of money in circulation, cheques drawn on the bank for example, as there is hard cash. In practice, most countries operate on the basis of an even smaller proportion of cash – certainly less than 10 per cent

– and on money multipliers of between 10 and 20. A central bank that wanted to slow lending in the economy, perhaps because the economy was in danger of overheating, growing too fast, and running into an inflation problem, could impose tighter 'reserve requirements' – increasing the amount of cash (and deposits with the central bank) that the banks have to hold.

What about plastic money? Apart from the fact that debit and credit cards have led people to economise even further on the use of cash, they are just an extension of the earlier variations of non-cash money described above. A debit card is simply a plastic version of a cheque. A credit card is slightly different, being a loan, usually a short-term one, from the bank to its retail customer, while the store receiving a payment usually has to pay the bank a merchant's fee for the privilege of doing so (although they would also typically pay the bank for processing a cheque). The underlying principle is, however, no different from other forms of credit creation.

Money and monetary policy

That's enough history, and certainly enough ancient history. Everybody knows what money is, but what is monetary policy? Every month, for two days, nine men and women gather together in a special committee room deep inside the Bank of England overlooked by a portrait of Montagu Norman, one of its legendary Governors, who went a little peculiar towards the end of his twenty-four-year (1920–44) term. These nine are collectively known as the monetary policy committee (MPC). While the Chancellor of the Exchequer and his treasury team are sorting out fiscal policy in SW1 – Whitehall – the MPC is fixing monetary policy in EC3, the City. This now seems entirely natural but, as most people will be aware, is a very recent phenomenon. The Bank has existed since 1694 but was only granted independence, controversially, by Gordon Brown in 1997. It has the task of setting interest rates or using other means to achieve the government's target for consumer price inflation, currently 2 per cent. If the Bank was responsible for setting its own target, it would be fully independent. Because the government sets the target it is, in the jargon, 'operationally' independent. The Bank subsequently acquired other responsibilities, of which more later.

Why was independence such a big deal? After all, similar arrangements had worked in America, where the Federal Reserve System has a Federal Open Market Committee to set interest rates, and in Germany, where the Bundesbank, which came into being in the 1950s after the second of Germany's post-war hyperinflations, had established a deserved reputation for sound money and low inflation. The Bundesbank, in turn, provided the model for the European Central Bank. New Zealand and Australia had established broadly similar arrangements. South Africa was in the process of doing so. It was a big deal in Britain because no previous Prime Minister, even if urged to do it by his Chancellor, had considered that central bank independence was appropriate for Britain. Britain is a nation of homeowners: nearly 70 per cent of all property is owner-occupied. It is also a nation of small- and medium-sized firms. Most of both categories borrow on the basis of variable interest rates. If interest rates double, homeowners and small firms feel the impact immediately. Despite strong academic evidence that independent central banks were associated with better economic performance – low inflation, greater stability and somewhat faster economic growth – Britain's politicians had always considered interest rates too important to hand over to unelected bankers. To understand why it did happen, it is necessary to review briefly the catalogue of errors that preceded Bank of England independence.

The seven ages of monetary policy

There are the seven ages of man and there are the seven ages of modern UK monetary policy. It is a good way of looking at the trials and errors that got us to where we are today. Other countries have also groped for the ideal monetary policy, although few have done so as ineptly as Britain. If we go back a quarter of a century or so, to the 1970s, this was a time of enormous turbulence for the world economy and near-disaster for Britain. It is also my first age of modern UK monetary policy – reluctant monetarism. In 1976 a near-bankrupt government had to call in the International Monetary Fund. This was the occasion for the burying of Keynesian fine-tuning. Peter Jay, sometime British ambassador to Washington, and economics editor of *The Times* and the BBC, drafted a speech for his father-in-law James Callaghan for the 1976 Labour party conference, which contained the immortal words 'I tell you in all candour that you can't spend your way out of recession.' The IMF's prescription contained two main elements. It insisted on sharp cuts in public spending – the biggest by any government in the post-war period. And it forced the government to adopt monetary targets, to control the money supply or, more particularly, two measures of 'money', one called sterling M3 and the other domestic credit expansion. There is no need to worry about the detail of what these were. The essential point was a simple one. To stabilise the economy, and to control inflation (which had risen above 26 per cent during 1975) it was necessary to control the money supply. There will be more on this when we meet Milton Friedman in the next chapter but the basis of this policy was quite simple – just as you cannot drive a car without petrol, you cannot have inflation without money. The faster that money is printed, and credit allowed to grow, the higher will be inflation. Targeting the money supply was by no means trouble-free. The Labour government found, as many governments have, that it was not possible to control the money supply and the exchange rate at the same time. By the time it lost the 1979 election inflationary pressures were starting to build up strongly. Even so, this 'reluctant monetarism' helped to save the economy.

In 1979 we had the second age – willing monetarism – under a Thatcher government philosophically committed to controlling the money supply as a means of limiting inflation. Despite being willing acolytes of Friedman, the Conservatives chose a 'broad' monetary target, sterling M3, which he would not have recommended. They then proceeded to undertake other policy actions, notably the abolition of exchange controls (limits on the amount of currency and capital that could be taken in and out of the country) and of the Bank of England 'corset' (controls on the banks' lending), which made it impossible to hit the targets for sterling M3. To this day many people think monetarism has something to do with public spending cuts. This was because the Thatcher government's choice of money supply target was linked to the level of public borrowing, and therefore the amount of government spending. This phase of willing monetarism lasted two or three years, before giving way to the third age – pragmatic monetarism.

By the early 1980s Charles Goodhart, then chief monetary adviser to the Bank of England, had come up with Goodhart's Law, a kind of Murphy's Law for economics. This did not say that if you drop a piece of toast it is bound to fall buttered side down but, rather, that any measure of the money supply you try to target will automatically become subject to distortions that make it hard to control. So the Conservative government adopted a more relaxed approach, making it clear that they still believed in controlling the money supply but also choosing to target a range of measures and not losing too much sleep if one or more of them missed the target. This approach worked pretty well. From 1982 until 1985 Britain had reasonable economic growth, albeit alongside high unemployment, and low inflation.

Unfortunately, sterling, the traditional Achilles heel of the UK economy, was still subject to periodic crises. In January 1985, not long after I had joined *The Times* as economics correspondent, the month began with interest rates at 9.5 per cent and ended the month at 14 per cent, sterling having come within a whisker of one-to-one parity with the dollar in the process. These days, we get excited when interest rates change by a quarter of a percentage point in a month and at time of writing they had not changed at all for over three years. And so, in about 1985, Nigel Lawson, the then Chancellor, became rather keen on taking sterling into the European exchange rate mechanism – the system of 'fixed-but-adjustable' exchange rates in Europe that had come into being in 1979 as a forerunner to the single currency. When Thatcher rebuffed him, he developed an alternative. Under the cloak of international efforts to stabilise currencies, the so-called G5 (Group of Five) and G7 (Group of Seven) Plaza and Louvre accords, that alternative was unofficial exchange rate targeting – shadowing the Deutschmark (Germany's currency before the euro), my fourth age of monetary policy. How much was this responsible for the boom and bust of the late 1980s? Quite a lot, because interest rates were cut to try to hold the pound down. The earlier pragmatism was replaced by dogmatism, with dogma directed at preventing the pound from rising above three Deutschmarks.

My fifth age is official targeting of the exchange rate – the ERM period. John Major was more successful than Lawson in persuading Thatcher of the virtues of joining the ERM, partly because he persuaded her that it was the route to lower interest rates. And so, when in October 1990 it was announced that the pound would be joining the ERM at an exchange rate of DM2.95, it was also announced that interest rates would be reduced at the same time. The problem with ERM membership was, however, the opposite of the one Major suggested, Far from being a route to lower interest rates, it blocked interest rate cuts at the very time they were needed. The combination of what was seen as a high exchange rate and the persistence of high interest rates meant that the period of ERM membership coincided with the 1990–92 recession. There was an additional complication. As a result of the pressures created by the unification of East and West Germany, German interest rates were higher than usual, and they set the pattern for the rest of Europe including, at the time, Britain. By the summer of 1992, the Conservative government, having narrowly won re-election in April 1992 (this time with Major as Prime Minister), was hanging on for dear life in the ERM. On 16 September 1992 the game was up. 'Black' Wednesday to the headline writers, 'White' or 'Golden' Wednesday to others, this was the day the Bank of England ran out of the reserves needed to prop up the pound within the system (it bought large quantities of sterling with its own foreign currency) but, thanks to George Soros and other speculators, it was to no avail.

The sixth age came after Black Wednesday and sterling's departure from the ERM, and it can be called quasi Bank of England independence. In putting together a monetary policy framework out of the ruins of the ERM failure, and in doing it both quickly and in an environment where it seemed the government could fall at any moment, the Treasury and the then Chancellor, Norman Lamont, performed a minor miracle. That framework, adopting an inflation target instead of money supply or exchange rate targets, requiring the Bank of England to produce a quarterly inflation report, and getting the Bank to advise openly and regularly on interest rate changes (this became the 'Ken and Eddie show' after Kenneth Clarke, Lamont's successor and Eddie George, the Governor of the Bank), was enormously successful. It paved the way for the 1990s to be a period, after the disasters at the start, of non-inflationary growth, the holy grail of economic policy. From there it was a relatively short step to giving the Bank the job.

The seventh age is thus operational independence for the Bank in which the Bank sets rates to meet an inflation target, 2 per cent, set by the government. Is this the final resting place for monetary policy? One is tempted to say yes. The possibility of Britain embracing Europe's monetary union, the euro, under which the Governor of the Bank would simply become a voting member of a large European Central Bank council, seems very remote. A question may arise over the Bank's wider responsibilities, acquired in the wake of the crisis, for supervising the banks and the wider financial system. Errors made in this area could compound criticism of the Bank that emerged before, during and after the crisis. That criticism centred on the Bank's failure, during a period its Governor Mervyn King described as the 'Nice' decade (non-inflationary, consistently expansionary), to respond to sharply rising asset prices – mainly property – and rapid credit growth. This criticism, which was also directed at other central banks, and most notably the Federal Reserve, argued that an obsession with achieving low inflation meant that other dangerous developments were ignored. Had central banks adopted a more rounded approach, it was argued, they would have kept interest rates higher and used other methods to restrain credit growth, even if it meant measured inflation was below the official target. Such criticism persisted after the crisis, when soaring commodity prices and in Britain's case a weak pound, pushed inflation up sharply. The 'Nice' decade, more generally known as the 'Great Moderation', in which central banks seemed all-powerful, appeared to have benefited from considerable good fortune.

How does monetary policy work?

When the Bank of England's monetary policy committee meets

each month it is to make one of three decisions on interest rates: to raise them, to lower them, or to leave them the same. For all central banks, leaving interest rates unchanged is the most common decision. To raise them, or to lower them, requires the economists and bankers on the committee to be convinced that enough has changed since they last met to warrant a shift. That does not mean rate changes are a rarity. Most central banks, in normal times, prefer to operate on the principle of 'little and often' in altering rates, rather than go in for the big, bold gesture.

What is it about interest rates that gives them this influence on the economy? After all, the economy is made up of savers and borrowers, and their savings and borrowings roughly equal one another, so surely the net effect of a change in interest rates is zero. A rise in interest rates is good for savers but is a blow for borrowers, and vice versa for a fall. One man's meat is another man's poison. It is, in fact, a little more complicated than that, although not greatly so. The way in which interest rates affect the economy is called the 'transmission mechanism of monetary policy' and there is a very good paper on the Bank's website (www.bankofengland. co.uk) called 'How Monetary Policy Works'.

Let us consider, first, what happens when the MPC decides to raise interest rates. It would do this because it believed there was a real danger of inflation rising above the 2 per cent target – the inflation rate deemed by the government to be consistent with a stable economy. The first and most obvious effect on individuals would be to make saving more attractive, by increasing the interest rates on saving accounts; borrowing becomes less attractive because it has become more expensive. People with savings are happy because their income has risen. People with borrowings – and more than 80 per cent of personal borrowings in Britain are in the form of mortgages – find that their monthly payments have risen. The consequence for them is that they have less to spend on other things. Why is this not exactly offset by greater spending by the savers whose income has risen? Here, it is necessary to make an assumption that is fortunately supported by the facts. It is that savers have a lower tendency to spend any extra income, a lower marginal propensity to consume, than borrowers. Why should this be? Under the life-cycle hypothesis, which we have already encountered, people's lives divide naturally into periods of spending and periods of saving. In general, those aged forty-five and under are high spenders and low savers. From forty-five or so until retirement, people save relatively more and spend relatively less, they are also less likely to have heavy borrowings. On retirement, they start to draw down those savings. A cut in interest rates therefore has the neat effect of putting more money into the hands of those people who are most likely to spend it, those with high mortgages relative to income. A rise in rates has the opposite impact. There are other consequences for individuals. Higher interest rates will tend to make people think there are more difficult times on the way, and perhaps their job is at risk. They may also be associated with slower growth (or a fall) in house prices and the stock market, thereby affecting wealth. Wealth, and this distinction is not always made clear, particularly by journalists, is the *stock* of assets built up over time. Income is the *flow* of new money coming in. Roughly half of individual wealth in Britain is in housing, with most of the remainder held (often indirectly through pension funds) in stock market-related investments.

So, higher interest rates will, through these various routes, tend to slow consumer spending, while lower rates will tend to speed it up. Similar principles apply, although in a slightly different form, when it comes to firms. As the Bank of England itself puts it:

> An increase in the official interest rate will have a direct effect on all firms that rely on bank borrowing or on loans of any kind linked to short-term money-market interest rates. A rise in interest rates increases borrowing costs. The rise in interest rates reduces the profits of such firms and increases the return that firms will require from new investment projects, making it less likely they will start them. Interest costs affect the cost of holding inventories [stocks of components or finished goods], which are often financed by bank loans. Higher interest costs also make it less likely that the affected firms will hire more staff, and more likely that they will reduce employment or hours worked. In contrast, when interest rates are falling, it is cheaper for firms to finance investment in new plant and equipment, and more likely that they will expand their labour force.

From growth to inflation

This is all very well, but where does inflation come into it? So far, all we have seen is that interest rates affect the growth of the economy, either for good or bad. The essential requirement, therefore, is that growth and inflation are linked, and for this we need another couple of tools. The first is the notion of the economy's long run, or 'trend' growth rate, which in Britain's case is thought to be about

2.5 per cent (though this is a matter of great debate). The second is what is called the 'output gap'. This needs explanation. Suppose that, year in, year out, the UK economy grew by 2.5 per cent a year. The economy would be growing exactly on trend and the output gap would be zero. Now suppose there are three consecutive years of zero growth. The consequences of this would be rising unemployment and spare capacity. It would also be low inflation. The more slack there is in the economy the weaker, other things being equal, are the inflationary pressures. Output would have dropped significantly below trend. An output gap, economy-wide spare capacity, would have been created. In this case three years of growth at 5 per cent a year would be required to get the economy back on track, and the Bank need not worry too much about such a rapid rate of expansion. If we take another situation, however, when three years of 5 per cent growth started from the point when the economy was already on trend, it would be a different story. The effect would be a sharp drop in unemployment, probably serious skill shortages, and pressures on capacity elsewhere. A 'negative' output gap – in other words an economy operating well above trend – would have emerged. Higher inflation would be expected and the Bank's response would be to raise interest rates to get the economy back on trend as quickly as possible.

These things can never, of course, be purely mechanical. Following the financial crisis and recession of 2008–9, a big debate opened up about how much of Britain's supply-side capacity had been permanently destroyed in the downturn and how much remained. Certainly, the economy's ability to grow, its trend rate of expansion, appeared to have been affected. Successful monetary policy requires skill and touch, as well as an ability to interpret the economic numbers. But this, in a nutshell, is the way it works. A rapidly growing economy which is at or above trend is likely to be heading for higher inflation, and a hike in interest rates should be the policy response, and vice versa.

There is one other transmission route from interest rate changes to inflation to consider, and that is the exchange rate. In Britain's case, because of the openness of the economy (exports and imports are each the equivalent of just under a third of GDP), the pound's performance has traditionally been very important. Many of the best-laid plans of governments, as we saw in the seven ages of monetary policy, have been upset by sterling's unwillingness to behave. In normal circumstances, a rise in UK interest rates should push the pound higher, while a reduction will have the opposite effect. This is because, in theory, international investors are always scanning the world to look for the best returns. If the Bank of England pushes up rates, that is a signal to those investors to shift their money to London. It does not always work out like this. In September 1992, even 15 per cent interest rates did not push the pound higher because the international financial community was convinced sterling was about to be devalued (so holders of sterling would have been left much poorer). Leaving such circumstances aside, and assuming higher interest rates do indeed lead to a stronger pound, it is not hard to see why this should be associated with lower inflation. There is a direct link to prices because, when sterling rises against other currencies, the effect is to reduce the cost of imports, right through from commodities to cars. There is also an indirect effect, via growth. A higher pound makes exports more expensive and therefore hurts exporting companies, while benefiting firms in other countries (those selling to Britain or competing with UK exports in other markets). These effects can be powerful, although the size of them depends on circumstances.

This is where it can get very tricky. With sterling's 1992 departure from the ERM and its subsequent large depreciation, many feared a sharp rise in inflation. (A depreciation is when a currency slides lower until it finds its level, a devaluation is when it is moved by the authorities from one fixed rate to a lower one – the last formal devaluation in Britain was in 1967, when sterling was devalued from \$2.80 to \$2.40.) It did not happen because the economy was just recovering from a severe recession. There was, in other words, a large output gap. When the pound fell sharply towards the end of 2007 in response to the financial crisis, eventually settling some 25 per cent below where it started, the effect in this case was inflationary. The Bank, thinking back to the experience of the early 1990s, had expected the even larger output gap that resulted from the 2008–9 recession to keep a lid on inflation. Instead, the inflation rate pushed up to 5 per cent, well above the official target. Why was this? One reason may have been that the pound's fall was bigger, 25 per cent instead of the 14 per cent in the early 1990s. Another was that the recovery from the 'great' global recession of 2009 was led by commodity-hungry emerging economies such as China and India. In contrast to the 1990s, when commodity prices fell for years in the aftermath of the recession, they bounced back very strongly, creating a more inflationary global environment. Another factor, as noted above, was that the output gap may have been smaller than it seemed.

Printing money

I said above that when monetary policy setting bodies meet they have one of three options: to raise interest rates, to lower them or to leave them the same. In normal times that is true. It is also the case, however, that central banks have other weapons in their armoury. During the financial crisis and subsequently, they engaged in what came to be known as unconventional policy. Some of this was straight out of the central banking text book: supply liquidity to financial markets in desperate need of it, act as lender of last resort to troubled institutions, and so on. But some of it was new, in particular 'quantitative easing', otherwise known as central bank asset purchases – electronically creating money or, to its critics, simply printing money. The easiest way to explain this is by reference to what central banks normally do, which is to adjust interest rates. What happens, though, when they cannot adjust any more, because they have cut interest rates to as close to zero as practicable? Actually, there was a debate about whether they *could* go further, and move to negative interest rates – penalizing those who hold deposits at the central bank, mainly commercial banks, by charging them for keeping their funds there – but in the middle of a banking crisis that hardly seemed sensible. So, instead of trying to boost the amount of money flowing into the economy indirectly, they decided to do it directly, through quantitative easing, or electronically creating money.

Not all central banks adopted the same approach. Japan, in fact, had pioneered quantitative easing before the crisis, from 2001 to 2006, though with little consensus on whether it worked. The debate over whether it was effective when employed by other central banks, mainly from 2009 onwards, will go on for years. Quantitative easing, usually shortened to QE, was a gift to headline writers. 'Bank launches QE', or 'Fed launches QE2' (a second phase of the policy) were typical examples. How does it work? Again, that is a source of some debate but the following description, from the Bank of England, is as good as any. It is from a document called 'Quantitative Easing Explained':

The MPC's decision to inject money directly into the economy does not involve printing more banknotes. Instead, the Bank buys assets from private sector institutions – that could be insurance companies, pension funds, banks or non-financial firms – and credits the seller's bank account. So the seller has more money in their bank account, while their bank holds a corresponding claim against the Bank of England (known as reserves). The end result is more money out in the wider economy. The MPC can opt to buy a variety of assets. For example, in March 2009, it decided to buy two types of asset – UK government bonds (known as gilts) and high-quality debt issued by private companies … Direct injections of money into the economy, primarily by buying gilts, can have a number of effects. The sellers of the assets have more money so may go out and spend it. That will help to boost growth. Or they may buy other assets instead, such as shares or company bonds. That will push up the prices of those assets, making the people who own them, either directly or through their pension funds, better off. So they may go out and spend more. And higher asset prices mean lower yields, which brings down the cost of borrowing for

*businesses and households. That should provide a further boost
to spending.*

The QE debate will probably go on for years. It was another
example of highly unusual things happening in response to highly
unusual circumstances. An assessment by the Bank estimated that
the £200 billion of quantitative easing it undertook in 2009 was
equivalent in its effects to a reduction in interest rates of between
1.5 and 3 per cent. It had boosted GDP by 1.5 to 2 per cent and
inflation by between 0.75 and 1.5 per cent. The Bank launched a
second round of QE in 2011.

Whatever happened to monetarism?

There is plenty more that could be said about money but it is
nearly time to move on. There is one more set of guests to entertain
us, and we should not keep them waiting too long. Since one of
them is Milton Friedman, however, we should briefly address one
question. Why is monetarism, so much in vogue in the 1980s, now
mentioned far less? Although quantitative easing was introduced
because of concern about slow growth in the money supply, indeed
a fall in the money supply, during the financial crisis you were
much more likely to hear people saying that 'We are all Keynesians
now', than that everybody had gone back to monetarism.

The roots of monetarism go back to the birth of modern economics. Its central tenet is simplicity itself. The faster the growth in the
amount of money in circulation the more rapid, other things being
equal, the rate of price rises – inflation. David Hume, a contemporary of Adam Smith, wrote in his 1750 essay 'Of Money' about the

effects of an increase in the quantity of money in circulation: 'At first, no alteration is perceived, by degrees the price rises, first of one commodity, then of another, till the whole at last reaches a just proportion with the quantity of specie which is in the kingdom.' The language is a little archaic but the message is relatively clear, although Alfred Marshall, Keynes's Cambridge teacher, perhaps put it a little more succinctly 150 years later. 'If everything else remains the same,' he wrote, 'then there is this direct relation between the volume of currency and the level of prices, that if one is increased by 10 per cent, the other will also be increased by 10 per cent.'

Until 1914 few economists challenged the basis of monetarism, the quantity theory of money. The pre-First World War gold standard, under which paper money was backed up by and convertible into gold, both underlined money's pre-eminence as an economic lever and institutionalised monetarist type arrangements. Under the gold standard unreliable politicians and central bankers were constrained from expanding the money supply too rapidly. It was something of a monetarist paradise.

So what happened? Two things – Keynes and the Great Depression. Keynes emphasised the power of fiscal policy, and explained how monetary policy could lose its effectiveness; it could be as effective as 'pushing on a piece of string'. As importantly, there was a real-life example in America during the depression years. Actually, there was a good monetarist explanation for the depression and deflation (falling prices) of the 1930s. America's Federal Reserve, in a lesson imprinted indelibly on the minds of every subsequent Fed chairman, particularly Ben Bernanke, a keen student of the era, allowed too many banks to fail, producing a sharp contraction in the money supply. Interestingly, one reason why Japan resorted to quantitative easing in the 2000s came from the belief that, having tried the Keynesian remedy, with repeated public works programmes, it was time to experiment with a monetarist one – a big expansion of money and credit.

In some countries monetarism did not go away at all, in others it did so only temporarily. In the 1950s, when the legendary Bundesbank came into being, it used a combination of a monetarist approach and the German folk memory of two hyperinflations to achieve more than forty years of low inflation. Britain and America were much keener on the Keynesian approach and on 'fine-tuning'. It took until 1979 and the election of Margaret Thatcher, for a British government to willingly embrace monetarism and then, as noted above, with mixed results.

Was monetarism right or wrong? Few economists would dispute that there is a relationship between the money supply and inflation, although many would question whether that relationship could ever be precise. For one thing, the speed that money circulates around the economy (the technical term is 'velocity of circulation') will affect the pass-through from money to inflation. For another, the lags between changes in the money supply and inflation are, as monetarists concede, 'long and variable'. The link between money and inflation can also be affected by changes in the financial system and in the use of money. A rapid shift towards a cashless society would not mean there was no useful message in the rate at which cash is growing, but it would mean that such information would need to be interpreted with care. Others would argue that there is nothing magical about the link between money and inflation. When the economy is picking up, one of the first things to happen is that individuals and companies start to borrow more. Measures of the money supply therefore start rising, ahead of any increase in inflation. The driving force of inflation is faster growth in the economy, not faster money supply growth. Every year there is a big rise in the money supply in the autumn, the critics of monetarism say, which is followed by a frenetic bout of Christmas shopping. Nobody, however, would pretend that the increase in the money supply has 'caused' Christmas.

We'll leave them to argue this out. The point is that, in setting interest rates, most central banks these days take note of what is happening to the money supply but are not slaves to it. The idea that monetary policy could operate on automatic pilot – simply set targets for the money supply and make sure you stick to them – has been discredited. One thing about economics, however, is that ideas come in and out of fashion, so we should not write off monetarism. For now, though, money matters, but so do plenty of other things.

Time to move on. Readers may have noticed that, with the exception of the occasional sideways glance at the French and the bulky presence of the German-born Karl Marx, British economists have dominated. All that, sadly, is about to change. Britain in 1945 discovered that she had not just lost an empire. She also lost her dominance of economics to the new superpower, America.

12

Just desserts – the Americans

Why did economics come to be dominated by America, and Americans, after 1945? With Europe ravaged by war and oppression, America's universities became a haven for European intellectuals displaced from their homelands. This was not just true in economics, of course, but it provided a significant boost for the subject. America, too, had fewer hang-ups about economics, which perhaps has something to do with the nature of its society. In Britain economics had a long battle against intellectual snobs who insisted that it was not quite a proper subject. The late Eric Roll, in his *A History of Economic Thought*, saw it as a natural consequence of Britain's displacement as a global economic power:

It is not surprising that the relative preponderance of English economic thought should decline once England ceased to be the only important capitalist country. Nor is it surprising that the emergence of the United States as the leading capitalist country should have coincided with a very considerable increase of American theoretical activity. Today the accumulated and current output of American economic literature is vast; and it is only barely an exaggeration to say that the study of economics, as we have become accustomed to it over the last hundred years, has its most congenial home in the United States.

America's modern-day control of economics is not in doubt. The Nobel Prize for economics, strictly speaking the Sveriges Riksbank Prize in Economic Sciences in Memory of Alfred Nobel, was instituted in 1969. At time of writing, sixty-seven economists had won it (some sharing with others). America's dominance is underlined by the fact that forty-five of these were American (though some were dual nationality). Britain has had seven Nobel laureates in economics. America's prizewinners have included Milton Friedman, Paul Samuelson, Kenneth Arrow, Herbert Simon, Robert Solow, Gary Becker, John Nash, Robert Lucas, Edmund Phelps, Paul Krugman and Elinor Ostrom, the only female winner of the prize.

From an early stage in America there were few doubts about the value of economics, although the determination of many practitioners of the subject to turn it into a fully fledged, mathematically-based science also meant that it became very different from the 'political economy' of most of the classical British economists and even their twentieth-century successors. This is not to say America invented mathematical economics – Alfred Marshall's approach was highly mathematical – but American economists developed it. It is not to say, either, that there were no great American economists before 1945. One was John Bates Clark (1847–1938), whose work on wages and income distribution, and in other areas, followed the 'marginalist' approach of, for example, Britain's Marshall. Better known these days, however, is one of the greatest of all, Irving Fisher (1867–1947).

Fisher and money

Irving Fisher, to some the best American economist ever, was also a fascinating character. He became a millionaire, not through economics but through inventing for his own use, and patenting, the index card system we now know as the Rolodex. Fisher set up a company to manufacture it, sold it on, and by the 1920s was sitting on a fortune. Unfortunately, such was his belief in the 'new era' for the American economy of the 1920s – something like the new economy of information technology of the 1990s – he failed to see the 1929 crash coming. 'Stock prices have reached what looks like a permanently high plateau,' he wrote in mid-October 1929. His reputation and his fortune suffered when the market crashed, and he never really recovered.

Fisher's two big contributions were on the way we think about the rate of interest and, in particular, money. Two books, *The Rate of Interest* in 1907 and *The Theory of Interest* in 1930, established what became the conventional framework for thinking about interest, which as he put it in the earlier book 'is an index of the community's preference for a dollar of interest of present over a dollar of future income'. The higher the rate of interest, in other words, the more we will be prepared to forgo spending now in favour of spending later. This time aspect was crucial. It explained why, in normal circumstances, real (after-inflation) interest rates have to be positive – otherwise any money saved is eroded in value by inflation. The 'Fisher equation' showed that the level of interest rates at any one time was made up of the real interest rate plus expected inflation. Fisher also demonstrated the role of interest rates in investment decisions, and how different rates could alter the ranking of, say, competing projects, depending also partly on the payback period for such projects.

His most famous contribution was, however, what is known as the quantity theory of money (sometimes called the 'Fisher identity' or, confusingly, the 'Fisher equation of exchange'). This may be the point to relax the 'no equation' rule of this book just once more. Thinking back to the monetarism of the previous chapter, Fisher turned what had essentially been an often wordy and imprecise description of the relationship between money and prices into something modern economists can use. The quantity theory is simple enough: $MV = PT$. In it, M is the amount of money in circulation (the stock of money); V is the speed, or velocity, at which it circulates around the economy; P is the level of prices; and T the number of transactions. On the simplifying assumption that V is fairly constant and T does not change much either (assumptions, it should be said, that have caused monetarists a lot of trouble), a change in M – the stock of money – results in a change in P, prices. As Fisher himself put it: 'The level of prices varies in direct proportion with the quantity of money in circulation, provided that the velocity of money and the volume of trade which it is obliged to perform are not changed.' Control money and you will control inflation. This, of course, was the basis both of Margaret Thatcher's monetarism and the version pursued in America under Ronald Reagan in the early 1980s by Paul Volcker at the Federal Reserve Board. One of the aims of quantitative easing, described in the previous chapter, was to boost M, the money supply, and so prevent P, the price level, from falling.

The Keynesian economist as bestseller – Paul Samuelson

As any author does, I have high hopes for this book, but I can safely predict that it will not sell as many copies as Samuelson's *Economics*. It was first published in 1948, when he was thirty-three, and has been through numerous editions since. There can be few students of economics, business studies or other related subjects, who have not pored over a copy. '*Economics* was destined to become the most successful textbook ever published in any field,' writes Mark Skousen, in his *The Making of Modern Economics*.

> *Sixteen editions have sold more than four million copies and have been translated into over forty languages. No other textbook, including those of Jean-Baptiste Say, John Stuart Mill and Alfred Marshall, can compare. Samuelson's* Economics *survived a half-century of dramatic changes in the world economy and the economics profession: peace and war,*

boom and bust, inflation and deflation, Republicans and Democrats, and an array of new economic theories.

Other textbooks have come and gone. British students of my generation will recall Richard Lipsey's *An Introduction to Positive Economics*. Later students will have benefited from one of the many editions of Begg, Dornbusch and Fischer's *Economics*. Samuelson, however, provided the template. He may have been lucky with his bestseller. It emerged when there was a gap in the market, none of the existing textbooks of the time having caught up properly with Keynesian economics. It started life as course notes for students at Harvard and MIT (Massachusetts Institute of Technology), the latter institution being where Samuelson made his name. He was, however, much more than someone who just popularised Keynes. Like other eminent American economists such as Alvin Hansen, one of Samuelson's teachers, he gave us what became known as the Keynesian framework. This was not just a question of interpretation. Keynes, in his *General Theory* of 1936, was often imprecise and contradictory. The American Keynesians, in particular, made it coherent.

They also made it very mathematical. Samuelson was a noted mathematician, like most of the top post-war American economists, and made no secret of his view of the shortcomings of the British 'literary' tradition of economic exposition. If economics was to be regarded as a grown-up science, it had to start using the language of science. What this meant, of course, was that academic economics became a closed society with its own in-built restrictive practices – anybody who did not understand the language and code could not hope to enter. Articles in economic journals became impenetrable to even the intelligent layman, although Samuelson would argue, correctly, that this was not the case for his textbook.

Samuelson gave us in diagrammatical and equation form what most would recognise as standard Keynesian analysis, using the national income identity (otherwise known as the most useful equation in economics). This is the one from back in our main course that shows that gross domestic product consists of consumer spending, investment, government and net exports (exports less imports), in other words $Y = C + I + G + X - M$. He also developed the consumption function – consumer spending rises in proportion to income, and other underpinnings of Keynesian economic policy. Keynesian policy was, in essence, that on the many occasions when the market fails to generate full employment, the government should do so. He advised John F. Kennedy during his 1960–3 administration. A couple of examples of his contributions are worth pulling out. One is the paradox of thrift, referred to in Keynes's *General Theory* but only properly developed by Samuelson. This was that, while additional savings to fund productive investment would normally be regarded as unequivocally good, that extra saving, if it reduced consumption, and therefore aggregate demand, could be damaging, even to investment. If all businessmen see is a slowing economy because people are saving more and spending less, why should they invest?

Another of his contributions, the 'balanced budget multiplier', shows the subtlety of Keynesian economics at work. A balanced budget implies that the government is neither adding nor subtracting from demand in the economy. Government policy is neutral.

But Samuelson demonstrated that whether or not it was neutral depended on the detail of the government's fiscal policy. A government that introduced 'tax and spend' policies, raising tax to increase public spending by the same amount, would, while still sticking to a balanced budget, boost the economy. How so? Because government spending provides the economy with a greater stimulus – it goes directly into extra demand for goods, services and people. Tax, however, is subject to various 'leakages', for example into savings or imports. Thus £1 billion spent by government will, through the multiplier, have a bigger impact than £1 billion used for tax cuts. By implication, £1 billion raised through extra taxes and spent on public services will provide a net stimulus.

Such thinking was hugely influential in the 1950s, 1960s and 1970s, then fell out of fashion but has revived recently. Samuelson, who died at the end of 2009, lived long enough to see some of that revival.

Friedman and the backlash

There was a time, not so long ago, when the entire economic debate could be characterised as a battle between monetarists and Keynesians. As bitter as any religious dispute or deep-seated sporting rivalry, there was a schism that ran right through the economics profession. Pragmatism may have become the fashionable, and appropriate, position to adopt but in the 1980s that was not allowed. Either you were a monetarist or you were a Keynesian, and never the twain did meet. In 1981, famously, 364 Keynesian economists from British universities signed a round-robin letter claiming that Margaret Thatcher's monetarist policies would result in economic disaster. In America, the battle was just as bitter. The Keynesians were seen as smug, prosperous, Ivy Leaguers who did not care that the policies they were advocating would ultimately result in inflation. Critics argued that they were also, by promoting a bigger role for government, coloured with a pinkish political tinge. The monetarists, in contrast, came from outside the establishment. They fought a guerrilla campaign against the prevailing Keynesian orthodoxy, with their belief not only in sound money but also in free markets and small government. They were terrier-like, and none more so than Milton Friedman.

Friedman, born in Brooklyn in 1912 to poor, first-generation Jewish immigrant parents, nearly did not become an economist at all, lack of money threatening to cut short his studies. Fortunately he was able to persevere, and fortunately too, he found himself at the University of Chicago. The Chicago school of economics, like the Austrian school associated with important names such as Ludwig von Mises and Friedrich Hayek, kept the free market/sound money tradition going at a time when it was in danger of being snuffed out. Half the world was pursuing versions of Marxist economics, while the other half was, to free market thinkers, following a course that was nearly as dangerous, that of far-reaching government intervention. Chicago in the 1930s and 1940s, through economists such as Henry Simons, Lloyd Mints, Frank Knight and Jacob Viner, stood as a bastion against the Keynesian thinking sweeping the world of economics.

Friedman, who was to later feature in his own television series on economics, providing a graphic demonstration of the way inflation is created by switching on a banknote printing press, made three key contributions. The first, in 1956, was his revival of Fisher's quantity theory of money. His paper, 'The Quantity Theory of Money: A Restatement', did more than dust off Fisher's work. He also addressed one of the fundamental Keynesian criticisms of monetarism, that there could never be a stable and predictable relationship between M, money, and P, prices, because the amount of money people wished to hold – the demand for money – was inherently unstable. Friedman agreed that money was only one of a number of assets that people wanted, the others being anything from stocks and shares through to cars, consumer durables and houses. He also developed, as noted earlier, the concept of 'permanent' income. The permanent income hypothesis was simply the idea that people have a notion of what their long-run, or permanent, income is. In other words, they look beyond temporary windfalls and shortfalls. Tied to this, said Friedman, they also have a clear idea of how much money they want to hold, for precautionary and other purposes, in relation to that permanent income. So what happens when the money supply increases? Everybody finds that they have more money, in relation to those other assets and their permanent income, than they want. Their response is to get rid of the money by buying, not only other financial assets (saving), but cars, washing machines, anything. An increase in the money supply stimulates spending. Part of that results in higher economic growth but much of it, he argued, would spill over into inflation. Inflation, he said famously, was 'always and everywhere' a monetary phenomenon, and the relationship between money and prices was as robust as any in science.

His second big contribution, with Anna Schwarz, was a massive exercise, *A Monetary History of the United States*, published in 1963. This demonstrated, not only that the relationships he had postulated in his version of the quantity theory worked in practice (although others disputed that) but, more importantly, it provided a completely different take on America's Great Depression of 1929–33. It was, said Friedman and Schwarz, nothing to do with Keynes's liquidity trap, or a crisis in capitalism to which only public works programmes could provide the answer. Instead, there was a straightforward monetary explanation. The Federal Reserve, America's central bank, had become worried about the pace of economic expansion in 1928, when the roaring twenties were still roaring, and started to apply the monetary brakes. It applied them a little too hard and by the following year, when banks were failing across America as financial confidence ebbed, the money supply was dropping like a stone. The Great Depression was, said Friedman, testimony to the power of monetary policy. The economy 'fell because the Federal Reserve System forced or permitted a sharp reduction in the monetary base, because it failed to exercise the responsibilities assigned to it in the Federal Reserve Act to provide liquidity to the banking system.'

The natural rate
Finally, Friedman gave us a tool that economists and policymakers use extensively, with varying success. The 'natural rate of unemployment' sounds like a very clinical concept, which is perhaps why it is more usually expressed these days as the much clumsier 'non-accelerating inflation rate of unemployment' (Nairu). Horrible expression, it just means the unemployment rate at which

inflation is stable. Push unemployment too low, and upward pressures on wages – together with expectations of rising prices – will result in higher inflation. Allow unemployment to rise too high and the result should be falling inflation. It sounds more precise than it is. Economists waste a lot of time trying to work out what the Nairu is, only to find that in practice unemployment can fall below that level without triggering higher inflation. Anyway, back to the natural rate. In the late 1960s, in his presidential address to the American Economic Association, Friedman took on the Keynesian Phillips curve. The Phillips curve, which you may remember was invented at the London School of Economics by the same Bill Phillips who designed and built machines to display the workings of the economy, demonstrated the relationship between unemployment and wage inflation. When unemployment went up, inflation went down, and vice versa. For governments fine-tuning the economy through Keynesian demand management (small touches on the tiller by means of tax or public spending changes), the Phillips curve told them what to do. If inflation is too high, just apply the brakes by raising taxes and cutting spending – in other words create a bit of unemployment. If, instead, inflation is very low and unemployment high, then create a bit of growth, perhaps by boosting public spending. To Friedman this represented a fundamental misunderstanding of the way inflation worked, and he developed the natural rate to demonstrate why.

Let us say the natural rate of unemployment in the economy is 5 per cent of the workforce. It is at this level because, perhaps, there is always a certain amount of 'frictional' unemployment – people moving between jobs – but also because some people lack the necessary skills, and others are stuck in regions where there is little work available and it is difficult for them to move elsewhere. Now suppose a government is elected on a promise of halving unemployment. It tries to do so by expanding the economy, both through fiscal and monetary policy (increasing the money supply). Initially it works. Faced with greater demand firms take on even those workers whose skills are not quite right and expand output. They also raise prices, confident about doing so because they see demand in the economy as strong, not least because of all those extra people in jobs. Lower unemployment results in higher inflation. Perhaps the inflation rate goes up from 2 to 4 per cent. So far this is just the Phillips curve. But Friedman then examined the next round. What would happen if the government tried to keep unemployment below its natural rate by keeping its foot on the accelerator? Next time round, workers would remember the higher inflation of the previous episode and would want compensating for it in higher wages. Their 'expectations' have changed. They now expect inflation to be 2 per cent higher than its current rate, in other words 6 per cent, and so it goes on. The key point was that trying to keep unemployment below its natural rate did not just mean accepting a one-off rise in inflation. It meant accepting an accelerating rate of inflation (hence the Nairu). So is there nothing policymakers can do about unemployment, if its natural rate or Nairu happens to be high? Not at all. But policymakers must act on the supply-side of the economy, for example by making labour markets more flexible and reducing restrictive practices, rather than by simply boosting demand.

Lucas and the rationalists

Friedman's introduction of the natural rate of unemployment emphasised the role of expectations in influencing behaviour and the effectiveness of policy. Friedman's version of the Phillips curve is sometimes known as the 'expectations-augmented' Phillips curve. In the 1970s, a group of American economists took this a stage further. Robert Lucas, Thomas Sargent and John Muth, particularly Lucas, gave us 'rational' expectations. Rational expectations was, like all big breakthroughs, very simple. The Lucas critique of conventional Keynesian economics was that it assumed people were stupid. Take a typical situation in British electoral politics. The governing party, seeking re-election, has a spring Budget ahead of a summer election. It cuts taxes and ensures interest rates are falling (not so easy now with an independent Bank of England). Voters feel good, happily give their support, but a few months later, as sure as night follows day, taxes and interest rates are going back up again. If voters are stupid that might happen over and over again. Rational expectations proposed that, just like laboratory rats or mice, we learn from our mistakes. If we get stung once, we won't go there again. This applied, of course, not just to pre-election economic policy but also to policy in general. Keynesian demand management worked because people responded to the initial economic stimulus, the tax cuts or extra public spending, by spending more themselves, blissfully unaware of the higher inflation that would follow. The Lucas critique said this would not happen. People would immediately look through to the higher inflation, and not respond to the inducements of policymakers. They would beware governments bearing gifts.

Are people rational in this way? It is hard to say. The mere fact that governments have persisted with election economics for very many years would suggest that it is possible to fool some of the people at least some of the time. There are plenty of examples where people continue doing things long after it appears to be rational. The boom in technology shares in the second half of the 1990s resulted in a peak for the Nasdaq (the US index of mainly technology stocks) of over 5,000 in March 2000. Within a year or so the index had plunged to less than a third of that peak. Well before shares had reached the peak Alan Greenspan, the Federal Reserve chairman, had warned of 'irrational' exuberance. What about the long, credit-driven boom in the 2000s in the run-up to the global financial crisis? As we shall see in the final chapter, some critics blame rational expectations, and its embodiment in so much economic thinking, for the crisis.

There is another interesting idea attached to the behaviour of, for example, share markets. The 'efficient market hypothesis' says in essence that a market will settle at a level that efficiently reflects the current state of information available to investors. How can a market be efficient which is over 5,000 one year and 1,500 the next? The answer, which may not be entirely helpful to anybody wanting to determine in a scientific way whether stocks are cheap or dear, may be that part of the information being used efficiently by investors at the peak was that there were plenty of suckers out there apparently willing to buy, whatever the price. Again, the efficient market hypothesis has had its fair share of critics lately.

Anyway, back to rational expectations. The Lucas critique suggested that there was no point in governments trying to prevent cyclical variations in the economy – boom and bust – because people and businesses would always, by operating rationally, be able to second-guess policy decisions. Lucas had another reason for rejecting such a policy approach. He is also a proponent of what is called 'real business cycle theory'. The Keynesians believed that the business cycle (the tendency of the economy to have periods of boom followed by slow growth or recession) was caused by variations in demand, in other words in investment and consumer demand. The real business cycle theorists argue, in contrast, that the cycle is due to variations in supply caused by positive and negative economic shocks. In particular, periods of boom are caused by the discovery or spread of new technology – such as America's information and communications technology (ICT) boom of the 1990s – while recessions happen when the positive shocks have worn off and, for example, productivity (output per worker) growth is low. The traditional Keynesian solution of trying to prevent recession by increasing government spending is misplaced. Some would go so far as to claim that any kind of stabilisation policy, for example the Bank of England cutting interest rates in a slowdown, is inappropriate. Booms and recessions are part of the natural order of things, they would argue, and trying to prevent them may do more harm than good. Few policymakers, it should be said, subscribe to this view, although one argument that emerged after the long boom turned to bust in 2008 and 2009 was that a small recession or two along the way would have reduced the severity of the eventual downturn.

Laffer and the supply-siders

Every era brings to the fore economists who seem particularly attuned to the political mood. In the 1980s, when under Ronald Reagan in America and Margaret Thatcher in Britain, there was an emphasis on tax cuts as a way to restore incentives and boost long-run growth, it was the supply-siders. In the late 1970s, Arthur Laffer, then an economics professor at the University of California, gave us the Laffer curve. This showed that there are tax rates, zero and 100 per cent, when the government gets no revenue at all. When the tax rate is zero, it is self-evident that no revenue comes in. But none comes in either with a 100 per cent tax rate because there is no point anybody working. Between those two points, there will be a range of combinations of tax rates and revenue. As drawn by Laffer, tax revenue would rise in line with increases in tax rates up to a certain point but then revenue would fall, because high tax rates provide a disincentive for people to work. If the country was already beyond that point, it could even be the case that cutting tax rates would bring in extra revenue. The supply-siders, who included Paul Craig Roberts and Robert Mundell, provided intellectual support for tax cuts.

Supply-side economics goes beyond tax cuts, however, and it is no longer associated just with the American right and their bible, the *Wall Street Journal*. Supply-side economics embraces anything that raises the economy's long-run, or sustainable, growth rate. This might be tax cuts, or it might be increasing competition by breaking up cartels, attacking the restrictive practices of trade unions, improving the climate for business start-ups, or making it easier to hire and fire workers. Supply-side economics means taking action to enable the economy to achieve its potential, and increasing that potential.

The Behaviouralists

Perhaps one of the liveliest economic debates of recent years has been between the 'rationalists' and the 'behaviouralists'. The rationalists assume that individuals, and markets, behave rationally. Behaviouralists do not. Behavioural economics, and behavioural finance, assumes at the very least that people adapt their behaviour in response to their circumstances and surroundings. Behavioural economics is not new. In the 1940s Herbert Simon, then of Carnegie Mellon University, questioned the idea of rational economic man. He said that a better description was 'bounded rationality' – people can act only as rationally as the information available to them allows and reflects their own ability to work things out. In 1979 Daniel Kahneman of Princeton and Amos Tversky of Stanford published a hugely influential paper, 'Prospect Theory: An Analysis of Decision Making under Risk', which examined how people take decisions when confronted with uncertainty and risk. One of its key insights was that people's decisions will differ according to how the alternatives are framed. People are not, in other words, rational calculating machines; they can be influenced, often quite easily. This may be why behavioural economics has been taken up enthusiastically by many in the advertising industry. Both Simon and Kahneman won Nobel prizes in economics (Tversky had died by the time of Kahneman's award).

A good example of the framing idea is provided by Richard Thaler, co-author with Cass Sunstein of the best-selling book,

Nudge. Thaler, a prominent behavioural economist – whose ideas have been adopted widely, including by the coalition government in Britain – cites a number of instances in which people can be influenced. One of his favourites is that 'spillage' problems can be solved in, say, airports and other public buildings by the simple device of painting a fly on the porcelain of the male urinals. The aim of the users apparently improves significantly. A more important example was the 'Save More Tomorrow' programme. Thaler, along with Shlomo Benartzi of UCLA looked at the thorny issue of how to increase retirement saving. Instead of asking people to save more for retirement out of their current income, they were invited instead to pre-commit to increasing their pension contributions out of future salary increases. Because the pain was deferred (as are the benefits from additional pension contributions), take-up improved considerably. One experiment within a firm showed that while just a few per cent of people were prepared to increase contributions out of current income, nearly 80 per cent were prepared to do so out of future salary rises. There are many other such examples.

Britain's New Economics Foundation (NEF), in a 2005 paper, 'Behavioural Economics: Seven Principles for Policy Makers', provided a useful description of how behavioural economics differs from the 'neoclassical' rational model. The NEF's seven principles were:

- Other people's behaviour matters: people do many things by observing others and copying; people are encouraged to continue to do things when they feel other people approve of their behaviour.

- Habits are important: people do many things without consciously thinking about them. These habits are hard to change – even though people might want to change their behaviour, it is not easy for them.
- People are motivated to 'do the right thing': there are cases where money is de-motivating as it undermines people's intrinsic motivation, for example, you would quickly stop inviting friends to dinner if they insisted on paying you.
- People's self-expectations influence how they behave: they want their actions to be in line with their values and their commitments.
- People are loss-averse and hang on to what they consider 'theirs'.
- People are bad at computation when making decisions: they put undue weight on recent events and too little on far-off ones; they cannot calculate probabilities well and worry too much about unlikely events; and they are strongly influenced by how the problem/information is presented to them.
- People need to feel involved and effective to make a change: just giving people the incentives and information is not necessarily enough.

Behavioural economics has provided an exciting new branch of the subject. Economists debate whether it has changed economics fundamentally or merely explained what most knew anyway, that rationality was always just a simplifying assumption. As explained right at the start of this book, it is possible to put most behaviour, including altruism, into a fairly rational economic context. The behaviouralists have, at the very least, explained why we do things in certain ways.

American miscellany

America has produced many great economists in the post-war period. There is neither time nor space to mention them all. Many will know Paul Krugman, awarded the Nobel in 2009 for his work on international trade but better known these days as a polemicist. Joseph Stiglitz, another well-known commentator, won his Nobel in 2001, along with George Akerlof and Michael Spence, for work on the economics of asymmetric information, as in the 'market for lemons' described earlier in the book. The great thing about economists in America is that they have had the time and the resources to take the subject into new areas. Gary Becker has applied economics to pretty well everything, including crime, drug addiction and racial discrimination. The 'behavioural' label fits much of his work pretty well. James Tobin, who died in 2002, twenty-one years after winning the Nobel Prize, was another. His 'Tobin tax' – a tax on speculative foreign exchange transactions to be used to help the world's poor – became a totem for poverty pressure groups and anti-globalisation protestors. A financial transactions tax, not restricted to foreign exchange deals, was being hotly debated in Europe at time of writing. Tobin served in the US Navy in the Second World War, alongside Herman Wouk, who was later to write *The Caine Mutiny* and feature Tobin in it, thinly disguised as a character named Tobit. Tobin's work was wide-ranging. He demonstrated how financial markets fitted into a Keynesian economic framework with his work on portfolio selection. He showed how the characteristics of households affect their economic behaviour (this was called the 'Tobit analysis'). He also provided financial market analysts with a tool, called Tobin's 'q' – the relationship between a company's stock market valuation and its underlying net worth – for calculating whether a share, and the stock market as a whole, is overvalued or undervalued.

Another fascinating branch of economic theory developed by American economists, particularly those such as James Buchanan and Gordon Tullock, is public choice theory. Public choice theory applies economic principles to the behaviour of voters, political leaders and bureaucrats. The behaviour of bureaucrats, for example, may be governed by self-interest, not a desire to selflessly serve the community. So they are driven by salary, position, the perks of office, reputation and power. Elected politicians, meanwhile, are driven by the desire to be re-elected but are prey to powerful interest groups. Voters, who should check and balance the behaviour of politicians, are not particularly efficient at doing so. Public choice theory suggests that, unless controlled, government will tend to grow bigger and bigger. Its proponents argue for such controls. Tax rises, for example, should only be permitted if two-thirds or three-quarters of the legislature approve, and bureaucrats should only be allowed to hold office for a limited time.

With so many Nobel prizes under their belt, a chapter on American economists could have filled a book. It is worth looking on www. nobelprize.org. In most cases the Nobel winners' acceptance lectures give a fuller flavour of their work than space here has allowed.

13

Arguing over coffee

All good meals, and all books, must come to an end. It would be wrong, however, to disappear into the night without a chat, perhaps even a little debate. Economists argue all the time. The subject advances, or sometimes goes back a little, by means of constructive engagement. To some, economists disagree a little too much. Churchill famously said that if you had two economists in a room you were guaranteed two different points of view, 'and three if one of them is Mr Keynes'. That may be a little too harsh. Where would we be without controversy? The comforting thing about economics, indeed, is that it is often possible for both sides to be right. With this in mind, let us have a look at some long-standing controversies.

Why are some countries richer than others?
In the end, there are perhaps only two economic questions that

matter – how much wealth is created and how it is distributed between people and countries. Since Adam Smith's day the world has created wealth at an exponential rate. Its distribution has, however, become more uneven as time has gone on. The disparities in income and wealth between rich and poor are striking. Estimates by Branko Milanovic of the World Bank in 2009 showed that the richest 10 per cent of the world's population, just under 700 million people at time of writing, received 57 per cent of the world's income. Milanovic, in a paper 'Global Inequality and the Global Inequality Extraction Ratio: The Story of the Past Two Centuries', also published in 2009, found that inequality had increased sharply from the early nineteenth century until around 1950, and then roughly stabilised. There was, however, one important difference. Two hundred years ago, most inequality was due to differences within countries. Now it is between countries. David Landes, the economic historian, estimated that the income gap between one of the richest countries, Switzerland, and one of the poorest, Mozambique, is 400 to one. Prior to the Industrial Revolution of the middle of the eighteenth century, he suggests, the biggest such gap would have been about five to one.

Why such disparities? There are three broad explanations. The first is the 'late developer' thesis. Political correctness requires that we call poor countries 'developing countries' even when some of them are not developing at all. On this view, prosperity and success eventually comes to everybody but for some it takes longer than others. Many African countries, for example, have a level of income per head about the same as that of Europe two centuries ago. Though living standards are improving in much of Africa, catching up will take time. Perhaps in two centuries they may be only a hundred years behind Europe, and thus above present European living standards. It is a big perhaps. It is true that changes have taken place in the global economic rankings. Britain had first mover advantage – by starting first she managed to stay ahead of the pack – as the cradle of the Industrial Revolution and reigned supreme for a hundred years or so after it. The writing was on the wall, however, as early as the Great Exhibition of 1851, when people began to notice the superiority of the products being exhibited by German companies. Britain was caught and surpassed, not just by other European economies, but also more particularly by America. Japan, an economy closed to the outside world until late in the nineteenth century, was another to come through rapidly, both before and even more impressively after the devastation of the Second World War, until it too succumbed to problems at the end of the twentieth century. China could have had an Industrial Revolution at the time of the European renaissance but chose a different path. Now China is on course to be the most powerful economy of the twenty-first century, although nothing is preordained.

The fact that countries have changed position in the rankings does not, however, offer comfort. Anti-globalisation critics would argue that the rich countries, and their corporations, have organised things in such a way that they have effectively kicked the ladder away. Poor countries, in other words, are there to exploit, not to provide with a helping-hand. This criticism cannot be dismissed out of hand, and certainly richer countries have tended to control the rules of global trade and have done so in a way that excludes the products of poor countries. That, we hope, is changing. As for corporations, their main interest is in creating new markets of prosperous customers, not in preserving poverty. We must look for another explanation for persistent poverty.

The second explanation has to do with location. The eminent Canadian-born (but American-adopted) economist J. K. Galbraith noted years ago that if you were to mark a line around the globe a thousand miles either side of the equator, there would be no developed, in other words 'rich', countries there. Poor countries tend to be in tropical and semi-tropical zones. There, disease tends to be rife, including traditional diseases such as malaria and modern ones like AIDS, and thus life expectancy is low. Agriculture is more difficult and less productive, so producing a relatively small amount of food absorbs a great deal of labour. Many poor countries, particularly those in Africa, are poorly placed geographically to benefit from trade. Landlocked countries, in particular, struggle, most notably if they are in dispute with the neighbours they need to traverse to get to the sea. A study by Jeffrey Sachs and others attributed Africa's economic failure to climate, disease, geography and poor policies. Non-tropical South Africa is about five times as wealthy, per capita, as tropical Africa, and not just because of gold and diamonds.

The third explanation, put forward by David Landes in his fine book *The Wealth and Poverty of Nations*, is that it all comes down to culture. Landes's title deliberately echoes Adam Smith's *Wealth of Nations*. Smith, you will recall, explained the route to prosperity through the division of labour. Organisation was the key to harnessing and advancing the powerful forces of industrialisation. Britain, as the first modern industrial country, was ideally placed to take advantage of it. There was a powerful desire for economic advancement, a willingness to embrace new technology, an already well-developed capital market (the City), a rule of law and a respect for property rights. Other countries, often with similar societies – Germany, America, Australia and others – either possessed or were able to emulate this work ethic.

Whether that work ethic was Protestant in origin can be debated, but that would certainly not explain Japan's success. In other parts of the world, however, religion, whether it is Roman Catholicism or Islam, appears to have inhibited economic development. 'If we learn anything from the history of economic development it is that culture makes all the difference,' Landes wrote.

Witness the enterprise of expatriate communities – the Chinese in East and Southeast Asia, Indians in East Africa, Lebanese in West Africa, Jews and Calvinists throughout much of Europe, and on and on. Yet culture, in the sense of the inner values and attitudes that guide a population, frightens scholars. It has a sulphuric odour of race and inheritance, an air of immutability.

His message should be an optimistic one. Cultures can change, adapt. Many countries have a tradition of enterprise even if their most entrepreneurial people tend to express themselves elsewhere. In a sense most development programmes follow his line of thinking. The tools of development are as much the establishment of the rule of law, of property rights, of efficient government, as the granting of foreign aid. Lord Bauer, the distinguished British economist who died in 2002, pointed out that over decades indiscriminate aid did poor countries more harm than good. Douglass North, the American economic historian and joint winner of the Nobel Prize for economics in 1993, has studied the role of institutions in economic development. According to him: 'Institutions provide the basic structure by which human beings throughout history have created order and attempted to reduce uncertainty in exchange.' The inability to enter into binding contracts and the prevalence of bribery and corruption hold back development. Get the institutions right and you have a chance. And yet the message is also a depressing one. People have known for years that there are cultural barriers to economic development. There are good examples of where those barriers have been lowered but plenty of others where those advocating such reforms have been knocking their heads against a brick wall, not least because the fruits of even small-scale development have gone to corrupt rulers, rather than the general population.

Paul Collier, the Oxford economist, in his book *The Bottom Billion*, noted that while most of the world's poorer people were in countries which could properly be regarded as developing, it was also the case that many others, Collier's 'bottom billion', were not. Collier identified a range of explanations. They included the 'conflict trap': civil wars can be the enemy of economic development. And the 'resource curse': natural resources, the source of Chinese-led prosperity in Africa at time of writing, can lead to conflicts and a lack of competitiveness (because of a high exchange rate or high wage levels) for other industries. People living in landlocked countries with poor neighbours suffer, according to Collier, as do those in small countries with corrupt governments. The problem is not just that people in these countries are stuck in poverty. It is that their situation and prospects diverge so dramatically from the rest of the world. As he put it:

The point is that they are stagnant, and because they are stagnant, they are diverging from the rest of mankind. Just amongst the 5 billion of the developing world, before we think about the billion of us – just amongst that 5 billion, the bottom billion, the countries that are now the poorest, diverged at an accelerating rate. By the 1980s and 1990s, they were diverging at 5 per cent a year, and by the millennium the gap between the average citizen in the bottom billion and the average citizen in the next 1 billion was five to one. Five to one, and widening at 5 per cent a year. That's the challenge for development. It is not to reduce global poverty; it's to replace divergence with convergence. The billion at the bottom have not just got to have a reduction in poverty; they have to catch up with the rest of mankind. Continued divergence is the road to global social unsustainability. It is both a human tragedy for the billion people stuck there and a nightmare for everybody else. So there is no alternative but to replace divergence with convergence. And that is a much tougher problem than reducing global poverty, and it is a different problem ... The bottom billion are not defined as the countries that have not grown. They are defined as being caught in one or other of a set of problems.

Is globalisation a good or a bad thing?

Closely related to the existence of huge inequalities between countries is the role of globalisation. It is a term much bandied around, but what does it mean? According to a definition used by Britain's Department for International Development (DfID), globalisation is

> *the growing interdependence and interconnectedness of the modern world through increased flows of goods, services, capital, people and information. The process is driven by technological advances and reductions in the costs of international transactions, which speed technology and ideas, raise the share of trade in world production and increase the mobility of capital.*

It is not, in other words, just Coca Colonisation – the dominance of the world by a few large companies and brands – although the global corporation is clearly an aspect of it. It is the movement of vast amounts of money around the international financial system, the fact that the toy in your child's Christmas stocking was probably made in China, or that the call centre you are required to ring (or that cold calls you) is based in India. It is the breakdown of barriers. It is the fact that, more than ever, no country is an island unto itself in economic terms. The old chaos theory cliché, that a butterfly flapping its wings in the Amazon jungle could cause a hurricane thousands of miles away, has its parallels in our globalised world. Globalisation was controversial, even before the global financial crisis that began in 2007, which was widely described as the first crisis of the globalisation era.

Beginning at the World Trade Organisation (WTO) ministerial meeting in Seattle in November 1999, and at many gatherings of political and business leaders since, anti-globalisation protestors came out in force. Later protests switched tack, attacking the austerity programmes that the financial crisis had ushered in. The anti-globalisation campaign, however, provided the template. As a campaign, whether you agreed with it and its methods or not, it was a considerable success in making politicians, businessmen and economists think. It also has high-profile supporters. 'For millions of people globalisation has not worked,' wrote Joseph Stiglitz, former chief economist at the World Bank, in his book *Globalization and its Discontents*. 'Many have actually been made worse off, as they have seen their jobs destroyed and their lives become more insecure. They have felt increasingly powerless against forces beyond their control. They have seen their democracies undermined, their cultures eroded.' The new world trade round launched in Qatar in November 2001 was called the 'Doha development agenda', an explicit recognition that the future opening-up of world trade must explicitly be geared towards the needs of poor countries. Ten years later it had still not been completed.

Economists, as a rule, have little difficulty in agreeing that free trade is highly beneficial. A crucial element in post-1945 global prosperity, out of the ashes of the protectionism of the inter-war years, was trade liberalisation – the removal of barriers to trade, both formal and informal – under the auspices of first the General Agreement on Tariffs and Trade (GATT) and then the World Trade Organisation (WTO). Successive trade rounds, in places as diverse as Tokyo, Uruguay and Torquay, liberalised the global economy. Free trade has had a powerful effect. Countries have become more open and have mainly benefited hugely from it. World trade growth has, over time, averaged two or three times the rate of growth of national output. Developing countries that have adopted free trade rules, according to one study, experienced growth rates averaging 4.5 per cent a year in the last three decades of the twentieth century, compared with 0.7 per cent for the limited number of closed economies.

So where is the debate? One powerful critique is that free trade, far from being of mutual benefit, has been a means of exploiting the world's poor. An Oxfam report entitled *Rigged Rules and Double Standards*, estimated that for every $100 generated by world exports, only $3 goes to poor countries; and for every dollar given to developing countries in aid, $2 is lost because of unfair trade rules. It found that tariffs and taxes on imports levied by rich countries are four times as high when the imports are from poor countries as from other industrial countries. Perhaps the worst examples of where trade acts against the interests of poor countries are in agriculture, where rich countries spend $1 billion a day on farm subsidies, exporting surpluses on world markets in a way that drives down prices for farmers in developing countries. None of this suggests that the world should abandon the quest for free trade, or that poor countries would be better off by opting out of the global system. What it does say is that a meaningful drive for free trade would target the cosy little deals that enable rich countries to scratch each others' backs, and which protect their domestic industries and farmers.

Those deals create one of the paradoxes about free trade, which is that creation of free trade areas, such as the European Union's single market or the North American Free Trade Agreement involving the United States, Mexico and Canada, can actually be damaging to free trade, if the existence of these 'preferential trading agreements' have the effect of excluding other countries. According to Jagdish Bhagwati, one of the world's leading experts on trade, in his book *Free Trade Today*:

> *We are thus reproducing in the world trading system, in the name of free trade but through free trade areas that spread discrimination against producers in non-member countries, the chaos that was created in the 1930s through similar uncoordinated pursuit of protectionism that discriminated in favour of domestic producers. In both cases, the preferred solution would have been non-discriminatory pursuit of freer trade.*

There is a more fundamental criticism of globalisation, which is that it was allowed to go too far, and certainly beyond the ability of democracies to control it. Even before the worst of the global financial crisis had occurred, Harvard's Dani Rodrik, author of *The Globalization Paradox: Democracy and the Future of the World Economy*, highlighted the dangers in a world that had moved beyond the 'shallow multilateralism' of the three decades after 1945 and replaced it with something more far-reaching. Now, that new model of globalisation in which countries big and small lost their economic independence, was itself under threat. He wrote in mid-2008:

The world economy has seen globalisation collapse once already. The gold standard era – with its free capital mobility and open trade – came to an abrupt end in 1914 and could not be resuscitated after the First World War. Are we about to witness a similar global economic breakdown? The question is not fanciful. Although economic globalisation has enabled unprecedented levels of prosperity in advanced countries and has been a boon to hundreds of millions of poor workers in China and elsewhere in Asia, it rests on shaky pillars. Unlike national markets, which tend to be supported by domestic regulatory and political institutions, global markets are only 'weakly embedded'. There is no global anti-trust authority, no global lender of last resort, no global regulator, no global safety nets, and, of course, no global democracy. In other words, global markets suffer from weak governance, and therefore from weak popular legitimacy … That model, we have learned, is unsustainable. If globalisation is to survive, it will need a new intellectual consensus to underpin it.

Globalisation appeared to have survived the financial crisis and the 'Great Recession' of 2008–9. The debate, however, will go on.

Are high taxes good or bad for you?

In 2011 an unusual thing happened. Warren Buffett, one of the richest men in America, complained that he was paying too little tax. 'My friends and I have been coddled long enough by a billionaire-friendly Congress,' he wrote in the *New York Times*. 'It's time for our government to get serious about shared sacrifice.' The billionaire investor complained that while he was paying a tax rate of 17.4 per cent, the more junior people in his office paid tax rates of between 33 and 41 per cent. It appeared to be catching. Liliane Bettencourt, France's richest woman, joined a group of top businessmen and wealthy people in demanding to be taxed more. 'We, chairmen of companies and business leaders, business men and women, finance professionals or wealthy citizens, call for an exceptional levy that would target France's richest taxpayers,' they wrote. In Britain, the debate was rather different. After twenty-two years in which the top rate of income tax had been 40 per cent, it was raised to 50 per cent on earnings above £150,000 in April 2010. The move was partly political, a means of punishing the bankers who had got the economy into so much trouble, and partly to close the record budget deficit. Critics said the tax would not raise any net revenue but instead lead to an exodus of high earners. There was no parallel in Britain to the Buffett article and the Bettencourt letter. A reduction in the rate to 45 per cent was announced in the March 2012 Budget.

One of the most enduring debates in economics is over the level of tax and government spending, and whether high taxes depress economic growth. We have encountered the American supply-siders, and the view that after a point high taxation not only did economic damage but was counter-productive in terms of its main purpose, that of raising revenue. It was an article of faith when the Conservatives were in power in the 1980s that lowering taxes on income boosted incentives (mainly for the better-off) and led to stronger sustained growth, for supply-side reasons. In relatively recent history in Britain, the overwhelming majority of working people paid no income tax. Now the vast majority do so.

Yet the rise and rise of government spending, and therefore taxation, has been associated with more prosperity, not less. Where has the damage occurred, when real disposable incomes (after allowing for inflation and tax) have generally risen in spite of a rise in the government's share of GDP? The puzzle becomes even greater when we look at comparisons between countries. Australia, Japan and America have levels of tax of around a third of GDP. Yet at time of writing Japan has endured a two-decade struggle since the early 1990s while America, having enjoyed much stronger growth, is suffering a huge economic hangover from the financial crisis. Australia suffered much less in the crisis and appears to have much better prospects. Sweden has taxes equivalent to more than 50 per cent of GDP but has enjoyed strong growth since the mid-1990s. It suffered along with everybody else in the crisis but bounced back strongly. Certainly in the early 2010s, Sweden was doing better than Britain, where taxes are just over 40 per cent of GDP, and crisis-hit Ireland, where they are about 35 per cent (but rising). On the face of it, there is no relationship between the level of tax and public spending and economic performance. How would an economist go about trying to solve this puzzle?

The answer is firstly to deconstruct some of the data. Yes, prosperity has risen strongly during a period in which the size of government has increased. It may be, however, that it would have risen a lot more if tax and public spending had remained lower, as some studies have shown. The second point is to recognise that the size of government is not the only factor at work at any time. If we take the Japan–America–Australia comparison, for example, one argument would be that Japan's low tax advantage was swamped by other factors, most notably the prolonged effects of the abrupt ending of a huge speculative boom (the 'bubble' economy) and an ageing population. Not only that, but the response of the Japanese government to the difficulties of the 1990s was to increase public spending sharply, which could have added to the problem. Government debt in Japan rose to more than 200 per cent of gross domestic product after twenty years of slow growth. Modern interpreters of David Ricardo, one of our trio of classical economists, would argue that debt on this scale points clearly to the need for higher taxes in the future. In what is known as 'Ricardian equivalence' the prospect of future increases in taxes has the effect of constraining growth and consumption now. As for America, it remains to be seen how permanent its difficulties are. Many would argue, however, that they would be made worse by big increases in taxation.

At the root of the tax-and-spending question is the motto of this book, there being no such thing as a free lunch. There is a cost to raising tax, for it means, in the case of individuals, that they will tend to have less incentive to work and less money to spend. Against this have to be set the benefits of government spending. A government that spends wisely and efficiently on health, education and other public services, with the full support of taxpayers, may do so in a way that not only offsets the economic costs incurred in taxation but also sometimes exceeds them. There is a net benefit, in other words, from raising taxes to increase government spending. Countries that spend taxpayers' money efficiently can, in other words, prosper with higher taxes than others. The settled societies of the Scandinavian countries, with government spending equivalent to between 50 and 60 per cent of GDP, appear to be examples of this. Appropriately enough it was a Swedish economist, Knut Wicksell, who gave us the notion of the 'Wicksellian equilibrium', the level of tax and government spending that most closely reflected society's preferences.

There are no easy answers. In 2009, a book by Richard Wilkinson and Kate Pickett, *The Spirit Level: Why More Equal Societies Almost Always Do Better*, claimed to prove that more equal societies perform significantly better on a range of economic and social measures, including physical health, mental health, drug abuse, education, prison population, obesity, social mobility, trust, community life, violence, teenage pregnancies and child welfare. Their work, however, was widely criticised for its statistical methods and was contradicted by other studies. It may be a question of horses for courses. There are some societies that are naturally more equal and naturally more successful. It is not hard to envisage many circumstances in which attempts to force equality through taxation lead to an overall loss of welfare in society.

All this still leaves some economists uneasy. Surely there must be some kind of rule that can be laid down about optimal size of government, the level of taxation, even if there will always be exceptions to that rule. In general, studies show that government spending is quite efficient when it starts from a low level and, for example, introduces universal education, healthcare and a pension safety net. These things, particularly better education and health, contribute to economic growth. A major study by Vito Tanzi and Ludger Schuknecht, *Public Spending in the 20th Century: A Global Perspective*, as well as work by Robert Barro, conclude that the gains between 1870, when public spending in industrial countries averaged 11 per cent of GDP, to 1960, by which time it was nearly 30 per cent, were well worth having for those reasons. Beyond that, however, any gains are questionable. 'We have argued that most of the important social and economic gains can be achieved with a drastically lower level of public spending than prevails today,' Tanzi and Schuknecht wrote. 'Perhaps, the level of public spending does not need to be much higher than 30 per cent of GDP to achieve most of the important social and economic objectives that justify government interventions. However, this would require radical reforms, a well-working private market, and an efficient regulatory role for government.' As it is, few advanced economies have spending and taxation as low as 30 per cent of GDP.

Is the euro a good idea?
There was a time when the answer to this question was very closely balanced, even in Britain. When *Free Lunch* was first published, the issue of UK membership of the euro was a hot one. Tony Blair's Labour government set five *economic* tests for entry – whether it would be good for jobs, the City, investment, and whether Britain was sufficiently converged with Europe, as well as being flexible enough, to make a success of membership. An initial assessment, in the autumn of 1997, concluded that the time was not right for Britain to be part of the first wave of euro members. A second assessment, in 2003, concluded that Britain was still not ready but that progress was being made. Entry would be good for Britain's financial services industry, it said, but the other tests had not been

met. It held out the hope of later entry, however, concluding: 'The assessment sets out the real benefits to Britain of membership of the single currency, shows that with the achievement of sustainable convergence and flexibility all five tests could and can be met, and lays down the concrete and practical steps which the Government will follow – radical steps which set out a new direction for reform, steps which set out the clear path ahead for Britain.' Despite this positive interpretation, Gordon Brown, Chancellor at the time, was later to claim credit for keeping Britain out of the single currency.

Why credit? Because in the aftermath of the global financial crisis the euro area became, for a time at least, a zone of extreme financial instability. In May 2010, other European governments, together with the International Monetary Fund, had to put a rescue package together for Greece. Other rescues followed in sub-sequent months, for Ireland, Portugal and Greece again, and for Spain's banking system in June 2012, as financial markets questioned the ability of the euro, which had come into existence at the beginning of 1999, to survive. The problem was central to the single currency. Member countries, operating under the 'one size fits all' interest rate of monetary union, had diverged in their economic performance and, more particularly, in keeping their public finances under control. There was, however, no formal mechanism within the euro for dealing with the problem.

Before returning to that, what was the case for the euro anyway? Let us look at the arguments for and against, a cost–benefit analysis, seen from Britain's perspective, starting with the benefits:

- Joining the euro means certainty and stability for business, particularly exporters. In Britain, where firms have had to cope over the years with a highly volatile exchange rate, this could be a significant plus. Firms could plan long-term strategies for export markets on the basis of currency certainty, and invest accordingly.

- It could lead to an increase in trade. Europe's single market, free movement of goods, services, capital and people, officially commenced at the end of 1992, although it has yet to be completed in some of these areas. One argument is that having different currencies is itself a significant barrier to trade and until all twenty-seven (at time of writing) EU members have adopted it Europe can never be a true single market, on the scale of, say, America. A single currency, in other words, is needed for a single market.

- It lowers and in many cases removes transaction costs. Everybody knows the story, perhaps apocryphal, of somebody who starts in Dover with £100, changing into local currency each time he visits a different EU country (this is a pre-euro story). By the time he gets back, the £100 has gone, not because it has been spent but because each time commission has had to be paid for changing the cash. As I said, this is a pre-euro story. Even so, UK individuals and companies dealing with Europe still have to go through the hassle and expense of changing currency. These costs are not high – removing them was calculated by the European Commission to be worth 0.3 to 0.4 per cent of EU GDP annually – but they are not negligible either.

- Interest rates are lower in the euro area, 'euroland', or at least they were. For a long time, not least when interest rates of 10 or 12 per cent or higher were common in Britain, one of the most powerful attractions of the euro was that it would offer significantly lower interest rates. Britain, in a sense, could buy into Germany's low-inflation credibility. Economists would say that Britain's interest rates were high for a reason, notably because the economy was prone to high inflation, but to the extent that rates were high because of sterling's recurrent vulnerability, there was a point. Joining the euro provided a huge boom for some countries. Italy, for example, found that it could fund its government debt at significantly lower interest rates, removing its budget deficit problem at a stroke. For Britain the argument diminished when interest rates came down with Bank of England independence and disappeared during the financial crisis. In March 2009 the Bank reduced interest rates to a record low of 0.5 per cent, while the low in Europe was 1 per cent (though the practical difference was negligible). By the summer of 2011 the European Central Bank had begun to increase its rates, to 1.5 per cent, while Bank Rate in Britain was still at 0.5 per cent. Time will tell what the relationship between interest rates in Britain and the eurozone will be, and also whether euro members will ever return to the position – lost during the crisis – in which they can all hope to pay a similar interest rate on their government debt as Germany.
- The euro also creates price transparency. When everything is priced in euros, it becomes easier to compare prices, not just

between different firms, but between different countries. Some, not all, large multinationals have adopted identical pricing across the eurozone. Others have continued to vary prices between countries, not least because rates of VAT differ.

Some of the euro's supposed advantages can, however, be seriously questioned. Yes, the euro would remove currency instability within Europe, which is where over half of Britain's visible exports (goods) go, but under 50 per cent of total trade. It would, however, do nothing about instability with regard, say, to the dollar. The single market, as noted, needs a lot more than a single currency to complete it. Transaction costs are small, and arguably getting smaller in an era of electronic money. The interest rate gains are not significant any more. As for price transparency, as long as there are tax differences between EU members, and as long as product differences persist (something manufacturers are keen to preserve), it may not happen.

There is a bigger argument against the euro, however, and it has to do with that 'one size fits all' problem. Countries in the euro have to adopt the same exchange rate. A single currency means just that. No longer can France alter its exchange rate vis-à-vis Germany, or any of the other euro member countries. A euro is a euro, the currency shared by people from Berlin to Barcelona, Lisbon to Leipzig. They also, however, have to live with the same interest rate, set by the European Central Bank. Each country, admittedly, has a voting representative on the ECB's rate-setting council but each, too, is implicitly accepting that they can live with the interest rate set by others. The easiest kind of monetary union would be between two identical countries, each with similar industries and similar vulnerability to economic shocks. If oil prices go up, or the price of steel goes down, they are affected in the same way. Sharing a currency, and an interest rate, poses no dangers, as long as they started with roughly the same economic performance. There would clearly be trouble if, at the outset, one country had zero inflation, the other a 100 per cent rate. This was why, when the decision was taken to proceed with the euro at Maastricht in 1991, conditions, or criteria, were set down, requiring countries wishing to take part to have broadly similar inflation, long-term interest rates, budget deficits and debt. The criteria, it should be said, were not observed to the letter, particularly in the case of budget deficits and debt, leading to some of the later problems. Suppose, though, that unlike our two similar countries euro participants are very different, which comes closer to reflecting reality. The members of the EU differ in size, in industrial structure, in dependence on oil, in the proportion of GDP they export to non-EU countries, and so on. As individual countries, with their own central banks, they could compensate when such differences began to tell by adjusting interest rates. In euroland that is not possible. Thus a standard piece of economics is the theory of optimal currency areas, most associated with Robert Mundell, the Canadian-born Nobel prize-winning economist. It was the basis of a 1999 book of mine, *Will Europe Work?*, which cast serious doubts on whether the euro would work.

An optimal currency area requires all participants to be not only closely interlinked through trade, but also broadly similar in structure. A single currency area that consisted of two economies, one whose sole product was wheat, the other cars, would be unlikely to work. A slump in world wheat prices would hurt one badly while leaving the other unaffected. Looked at another way, countries have to have the ability to respond to economic shocks, an example of which might be a sharp rise in world oil prices. There are three conditions for an optimal currency area. The first is 'geographical mobility' of labour. If people are made unemployed in one part of the euro area, they have to be willing to move to where the jobs are. The second requirement, either in tandem with or instead of geographical mobility, is wage flexibility. Suppose there is a shock that is threatening big job losses in one region. They have to be prepared to accept a cut in wages to persuade the employer not to pull out. The third requirement is a large enough central budget, so that fiscal policy can be used to provide help where monetary policy – which is set for the whole area – cannot. In America's single currency (dollar) area, the federal budget works in precisely this way. When there is a downturn in California, Washington can provide direct help, not least through larger assistance payments. At the same time a phenomenon known by economists as the 'automatic stabilisers' operates. California, during its downturn, pays fewer taxes into the federal budget, helping the state get through its difficulty. Is Europe an optimal currency area? Prior to the launch of the euro some economists believed that a small group of countries at the heart of Europe – France, Germany, Belgium, Luxembourg and the Netherlands – fitted that description. Few believed that it was true for the eleven who made it to the starting gate (Austria, Finland, Ireland, Italy, Portugal and Spain joined too), or the seventeen 'euroland' consists of at time of writing. Even the smallest of these groups, lacking sufficient geographical mobility of labour and wage flexibility, did not satisfy pure optimal currency area requirements. The EU as a whole, with a tiny central budget of just over 1 per cent of GDP, is well below the 25 per cent of GDP level generally reckoned to be needed to provide a proper offset to monetary policy.

Mundell, curiously, became an advocate of the euro because, equally curiously, he decided that there were never any optimal currency areas in real life but that it was worth pressing ahead with monetary unions anyway. For Britain, there was another consideration. Previous monetary arrangements between Britain and Europe had ended in disaster. In 1972 sterling stayed in the 'snake' a forerunner of the European Monetary System (EMS) for just six weeks. Between 1990 and 1992 Britain spent twenty-three agonizing months inside the exchange rate mechanism of the EMS, before a humiliating exit on 16 September 1992. thanks to huge selling of sterling, led by George Soros and others, which overwhelmed the authorities.

This was why, when the euro got into difficulties in 2010, there was a certain amount of smug satisfaction in Britain. The eurozone's problems arose directly out of the fact that it was not, and never had been, an optimal currency area. The assumption had been that, even if countries were not economically converged when they joined, the discipline of membership would bring it about. It did not happen. In essence, nobody could keep up with Germany, Europe's benchmark economy. Ten years after the euro came into being several economies, including Greece, Ireland and Portugal, had lost between 20 and 30 per cent competitiveness, vis-à-vis Germany. Combine that with large budget deficits for these economies in the wake of the crisis and it became a recipe for serious problems. Investors began to speculate on the previously unthinkable, a default – reneging on debts owed – by a eurozone member. The exit of some countries, even a complete break-up, was predicted. By the time you read this, things may be clearer. The first tentative steps towards bolstering the fiscal side of the euro began with the establishment of a European Financial Stability Facility (EFSF). Whether countries are prepared to go as far as a Mundell-style fiscal union and other measures to ensure the survival of the euro (after all, the world's second biggest currency), time will tell.

Economics and happiness

Economics and happiness may seem like an odd marriage, particularly when the subject has been known on and off since the nineteenth century as the dismal science, and when you do not have to look too hard to find some pretty gloomy economists. The economics of happiness is, however, one of the subject's growth areas. 'The extent to which people are happy or unhappy is an essential quality of the economy and society,' wrote Bruno Frey and Alois Stutzer in their book *Happiness and Economics*. 'The state of the economy strongly affects people's happiness.' The LSE economist and Labour peer Lord (Richard) Layard was so influenced by his own research on happiness that he established a movement, Action for Happiness. 'For fifty years we've aimed relentlessly at higher incomes,' he claimed. 'But despite being much wealthier, we're no happier than we were five decades ago. At the same time we've seen an increase in wider social issues, including a worrying rise in anxiety and depression in young people. It's time for a positive change in what we mean by progress.'

How do you measure something as subjective as happiness? Mainly through surveys that ask people how satisfied they are with life, or with their job. One difficulty, of course, is that people's expectations change. Consumers come to expect product improvements, employees better working conditions. It is hard to compare two very different situations. A Victorian factory worker teleported to a modern industrial plant would think he had arrived in heaven. So would a Model T driver handed the keys of a modern car. Most improvements are, however, incremental. Whether or not people are happy or not depends on whether those improvements exceed, keep pace with, or fall behind the rise in expectations. This also applies to areas of public service delivery such as the National Health Service, as successive British governments have discovered. This both supports and challenges the Action for Happiness argument: it supports it by conceding that material improvements have probably not made us any happier; it challenges it by suggesting that, without those material improvements, we would have become a lot less happy. In other words, unless expectations change dramatically, higher living standards will be needed to maintain a constant level of happiness. Despite this, the effort is being made. In November 2010 the UK's Office for National Statistics launched a consultation on measuring national well-being, with the specific aim of moving beyond purely economic data.

So what do we know about happiness? Andrew Oswald of Warwick University, with a number of co-researchers, has tirelessly researched the issue, over many years. His work with Jonathan Gardner on job satisfaction suggested that it declined during the 1990s, particularly among women and public sector workers. Of more interest, perhaps, is that the happiest workers in Britain are those with no educational qualifications (and lower job expectations), while the least satisfied are those with a degree. This may suggest that many people are over-qualified for their jobs, particularly those with degrees. People with postgraduate degrees, interestingly, are happier at work than graduates. People in non-profit organisations have the most job satisfaction, probably because they feel they are doing most good for society. By age, the happiest workers are those in their sixties, with retirement just around the corner, the least happy are in their twenties. Oswald, along with David Blanchflower of Dartmouth College in America, also compared job satisfaction across nations. They found, in a survey of twenty-seven different countries, Britain came seventeenth in terms of workers being satisfied with their lot at work. Denmark topped the rankings, while Cyprus, Israel, the Netherlands, the Philippines, Spain, Switzerland, the United States and even Russia had higher levels of job satisfaction than Britain.

Does money buy you happiness? Oswald and Gardner tested this by looking at the psychological health and happiness of a randomly chosen sample of 9,000 people. Some of those in the sample had been lucky enough to receive financial windfalls, such as lottery or football pools wins, or unexpected inheritances. On the basis of this information they were able to calculate the impact of money on happiness. A windfall of £50,000, or around $80,000, was sufficient to give people a significant lift in terms of happiness. But how much did it need to make a really miserable person happy? According to the study, a windfall of £1 million (about $1.6 million) was required to do this, to 'move someone from close to the bottom of a happiness frequency distribution to close to the top'. Oswald and Blanchflower also studied the effects of marriage. Apart from married people tending to be wealthier and live longer, they used their US data to calculate that a happy marriage was worth £65,000 (just over $100,000) a year.

Does happiness bought by extra money last? Probably not. Further study is needed but intuitively it seems that windfall effects wear off over time. The effect of money, in addition, can be relative. The same amount of wealth could make you feel as rich as Croesus in most parts of the world but a relative pauper in Monte Carlo or the Bahamas. Three Swedish economists, Olof Johansson-Stenman, Fredrik Carlsson and Dinky Daruvala, found that people's happiness depended, not just on absolute income, but also on their relative position in the income ladder. Not only that, but when a sample of people was surveyed, using a series of scenario-based questions – they were asked to choose between two imaginary future societies – most expressed a preference for a more equitable distribution of income, largely because of the fear that they would end up at the bottom of the heap in an unequal society. Lots of conflicting factors come into the equation. People are competitive, driven by a desire to 'keep up with the Joneses', and their tastes and desires are conditioned by what others are doing. As Marx put it: 'A house may be large or small; as long as the neighbouring houses are likewise small, it satisfies all the social requirements for a residence. But let there arise next to the little house a palace, and the little house shrinks to a hut.'

There is no limit to the potential for happiness research. A study by Betsey Stevenson and Justin Wolfers looked at the happiness of American women since the 1970s and found that it had declined both in absolute terms and relative to men over three decades. This was, on the face of it, odd. Over a period in which the pay and social and economic status of women had improved in relation to men, their happiness had declined. Separately, in a huge country-wide study, Oswald and Blanchflower found conclusive evidence of mid-life crises, or at least middle-age blues. People feel happier when they are younger and older than when they are in middle age, making for a U-shaped happiness curve over people's lifetimes. But the low point for happiness can vary widely between countries. As Nick Powdthavee pointed out in his book *The Happiness Equation*, the low point for Swiss happiness was at the age of just 35.2 years, while in France, geographically very close, it was as late as 61.9 years.

Are we getting better off?

The economics of happiness is closely tied to another question, that of economic progress. When John Major was Prime Minister of Britain in the 1990s he made what to many seemed like a rash promise – that of doubling living standards over twenty-five years. Actually it was a rather safe pledge. By the time anybody was able to check, Major would be long gone from politics (he soon was anyway). Moreover, the power of compound numbers is a wonderful thing. Growth in per capita real incomes of a shade over 2.5 per cent a year will produce a doubling of living standards every twenty-five years, just as growth of 4 per cent annually would produce that in fifteen years. Major, in fact, was echoing an earlier prominent Conservative, R. A. 'Rab' Butler, who made a similar pledge in 1954. Both appear to have been stretching things somewhat. For the twentieth century as a whole in Britain real income per head rose by about 300 per cent, thus at the end of the century they were four times the level at which they started – doubling every fifty years rather than every twenty-five. Most of that rise, however, happened in the second half of the century. Even then, real income per head trebled over fifty years rather than quadrupled, as the 'doubling over twenty-five years' pledge would have required. The big debate in the wake of the global financial crisis is whether Britain and other advanced economies are entering a period more like the first half of the twentieth century, with very subdued increases in real income, and therefore living standards. For people who grew up in an age of strongly rising prosperity that would be a difficult adjustment.

Some would question setting a target for living standards in terms of doubling gross domestic product or real income per head. Is it the same as a doubling of living standards? Many people would argue that while they are materially better off, the downside of modern life – crime, congestion, stress, even declining moral standards – means GDP or real income per capita is a poor measure of progress. Some economists favour other measures, which try to take into account other factors. The United Nations' human development index, which is particularly useful for measuring progress in poorer countries, takes into account factors such as life expectancy and educational provision. Some people favour a measure known as the Index of Sustainable Economic Welfare and claim that it shows a decline in living standards in Britain from the 1970s. However, Professor Nick Crafts of Warwick University, a noted expert on long-term growth and income trends, strongly challenged that. His research suggested that adding additional factors, most notably rising life expectancy, demonstrated clearly that living standards were rising and, if anything, by more than the raw real income data suggested.

The fact is that, in the absence of recessions, which tend to be short-lived, we do become better off each year. In both 2010 and 2011, when real household disposable incomes fell in the UK, the effect was notable because it was rare for there to be a single year of declining real incomes, let alone two in a row. Harold Macmillan, one of Major's Tory predecessors, became associated with the phrase 'You've never had it so good', when he said in 1957: 'Let us be frank about it: most of our people have never had it so good.' Few Prime Ministers, in fact, would have been unable to make that boast. Lord Young, an adviser to David Cameron, got into trouble and resigned in 2010 for repeating the Macmillan claim. He was right, at least until 2009, but made his 'never had it so good' comments at a time when real incomes were falling. So living standards tend to improve, but at what rate? The answer to this, fairly obviously, is that it depends on circumstances. Nick Crafts has tracked Britain's growth rate, on a per capita basis, back to the nineteenth century. Dividing the period into four, 1870–1913, 1913–50, 1950–73 and 1973–2000, the results show rising GDP per capita in all four periods, but at different rates. In the first period, 1870–1913 (which included the so-called great depression of the late nineteenth century), GDP per capita rose by an average of 1 per cent a year. The second period, 1913–50, included two world wars and the more familiar Great Depression, and growth did well to average 0.9 per cent a year. The period 1950–73, known by economic historians as the 'golden age' of healthy growth, low inflation and full employment, saw GDP per capita rise by 2.4 per cent a year (Major was clearly thinking of a new golden age), while from 1973 onwards, as the economy hit oil crises, financial market instability, regular recessions and generally greater turbulence, growth slipped to 1.8 per cent a year.

More interesting than these bald figures is what was happening elsewhere. In the earliest period Britain's 1 per cent growth rate was by no means high, but it was in the same broad area as other countries. Already, however, with American per capita GDP rising by 1.8 per cent a year in the 1870–1913 period, the writing was on the wall. Again, in the period 1913–50, Britain held her own in comparison with other European countries but was well behind America's 1.6 per cent growth rate (think of the power of compound numbers). It was in the golden age, however, that a gap really opened up. Britain's 2.4 per cent growth rate over the 1950–73 period sounds respectable, and in fact matched that of America, but it was well behind France, 4 per cent, Germany and Italy, each 5 per cent, and Japan, 8 per cent.

What causes economic growth?

Economies grow, and so generally do living standards, but why? Adam Smith gave us one important route – the gains from trade and from the division of labour mean that productivity, output per worker, increases from one year to the next. Karl Marx gave us another clue, in his observation that what all capitalists are interested in is investing, accumulating capital. A rise in the amount of capital equipment per worker will also tend to be associated with rising output per worker. Growth theory is an entire branch of economics in its own right. One interesting, but difficult, exercise is to try to account for economic growth by splitting it into its component parts. Angus Maddison, a specialist in this so-called 'growth account-ing', has produced results that suggest investment other than in housing is the most important source of growth, with significant contributions also made by rising educational standards, trade and, for most countries, a 'catch-up' effect as they adopt the technology or methods used by countries with higher productivity levels.

Extra investment, the main source of growth, does not always flow smoothly. It is subject to – indeed is one of the primary causes – of the business cycle. It is also subject to more pronounced fluc-tuations, as new technologies become available. When people spoke of the 'new economy' of the ICT (information and com-munications technology) revolution of the 1990s, they were fol-lowing a long tradition. There have been many 'new' economies over the ages, from the transformation of the cotton industry by the spinning jenny of James Hargreaves, Thomas Arkwright's water frame and Samuel Crompton's mule. Steam, canals, railways, elec-tricity, radio in the 1920s and television in the 1950s – all have provided spurts of large-scale investment activity and an apparent move up to a new and higher plane of economic growth. In each case, the initial effect is to produce a sharp rise in productivity in the sector concerned, whether it is transport (canals and railways), energy production (electricity), media or ICT. Then, as this increase in productivity is passed on, falling prices lead to a boom in investment. There is also, typically, a restructuring of the economy around the new technology.

Why, if we have had all these 'new' economies over the decades has productivity not grown even faster over time? To an extent, the story of the twentieth century, and in particular its second half, was about not just the invention of new technology but also the realisation of its potential. There is also a sense, however, in which maintaining economic growth requires these bouts of what the Austrian economist Joseph Schumpeter called 'creative destruction'. He saw capitalist economies leading to episodes that 'incessantly revolutionise the economic structure from within, incessantly destroying the old one, incessantly creating a new one'. Put another way, when the effects of a technological revolution wear off, it is time for another one, otherwise growth will slow. Fortunately, capitalism has been reasonably good at coming up with periodic breakthroughs. There is one other lesson from 'new' economies, both ancient and modern. It is that in each case there is usually a stock market boom that anticipates the mass application of the new technology. The railway mania in Britain in the 1840s, when the shares of railway firms soared to sky-high levels before crashing back down to earth, was very similar in character to the Nasdaq boom of the 1990s. The lesson, in all cases, is that while some lucky investors do well, many have their fingers burned, both by the ups and downs of the share prices of even the successful innovating firms, and because there is inevitably a winnowing out process as the majority fall by the wayside. For every Microsoft that makes it, there are thousands of others that do not. New technology usually helps the economy more than it does the bank balances of investors.

One big question concerns the sustainability of economic growth. By this I mean not just whether growth damages the environment thus making expansion ultimately unsustainable but, rather, economic sustainability itself. Before he was appointed Governor of the Central Bank of Ireland in September 2009, the economist Patrick Honohan wrote of the two phases of Ireland's 'Celtic Tiger' period. The good phase, up until about 2000, was based on export-led growth and competitiveness underpinned by wage restraint. Then, it became unsustainable. 'From about 2000 the character of the growth changed: a property price and construction bubble took hold,' Honohan wrote. 'This boom sustained employment and output growth until 2007 despite a loss of wage competitiveness. The banks fuelled the boom, especially from 2003, exposing themselves both to funding and solvency pressures.' A similar diagnosis was provided for Britain by George Osborne, Chancellor in the coalition government elected in May 2010. In a speech in September 2011, he said:

Globally we are living through a painful and fundamental re-adjustment of a model of global growth that was badly broken; a model of growth fuelled by unbalanced global demand and amplified by poorly regulated financial markets. In short, a model of growth built on unsustainable debt. Here in Britain our model of growth was the most badly broken of any major economy, our debt burden one of the biggest, and the necessary re-adjustment correspondingly difficult. As the

*research presented recently by the Bank for International
Settlements at Jackson Hole, Wyoming, confirmed, of all the
world's major economies the UK saw the biggest expansion in
debt over the past decade. That is because the UK had the
biggest housing boom, the most indebted families, the most
leveraged banks and the biggest structural budget deficit. All
the evidence from economic history suggests that, thanks to this
overhang of debt, recoveries from financial crises are slower and
choppier than recoveries from other kinds of recession.*

So there is economic growth based on the fundamentals of productivity and investment – the rise in the economy's productive potential – and there is much more rapid growth which, by its nature, cannot last. In the long run, of course, the unsustainable cannot last. So assessing how an economy is really doing should properly be done over quite a long period, not a year or two.

Why do we need low inflation?
This is the kind of question you do not ask in the company of central bankers. It is also less commonly asked than it used to be in general conversation but you still hear it from time to time. When the Bank of England's monetary policy committee meets to set interest rates each month, there is often a trade union leader or Labour MP on hand to question its 'anti-inflation obsession', even though the government, not the Bank itself, sets the 2 per cent inflation target. The European Central Bank, which to some is afflicted by an even greater obsession (it sets its own target, an inflation 'ceiling' of 2 per cent), was long held by its critics to be responsible for Europe's low

growth and high unemployment. If only central bankers would loosen up a bit, the argument goes, the economy would do a lot better. Such criticism should not be dismissed out of hand. It is not as if when countries have had significantly higher inflation than now, growth suddenly grinds to a halt. Britain's inflation rate averaged nearly 7.5 per cent during the 1980s and yet the economy enjoyed one of its longest upswings on record, lasting from the spring of 1981 to the summer of 1990. Trumping this, perhaps, was the fact that the longest UK upswing on record, from the spring of 1992 to early 2008, occurred alongside low inflation.

The other question is one of degree. Suppose a central bank is determined to achieve 1 per cent inflation through thick and thin, whether oil prices surge to $150 a barrel or there is some other inflationary shock. Would that be at the expense of growth and jobs? Certainly, although most central bankers would argue that they would never interpret their remit so inflexibly. Many showed flexibility in the period from 2008 to 2011. Commodity prices rose to record levels in the summer of 2008, with the oil price reaching $147 a barrel. Inflation rose everywhere, particularly in emerging economies such as China but also in the UK and other advanced economies. They then slumped, as did inflation, when the financial crisis hit. But by 2010 the Bank of England and other central banks were again struggling to cope with high inflation brought about mainly by a rebound in commodity prices. Most had very low interest rates, 0.5 per cent in the case of the Bank of England. This is what Sir Mervyn King, Governor of the Bank of England, said in 2011 in response to critics when inflation pushed closer to 5 per cent than 2 per cent:

*We could have made a different judgment. We could have
raised Bank Rate significantly so that inflation today would be
closer to the target. But that would not have prevented the
squeeze on living standards arising from higher oil and
commodity prices and the measures necessary to reduce our twin
deficits. And it would have meant a weaker recovery, or even
further falls in output, despite our having experienced the worst
downturn in output and spending since the Great Depression.
To force nominal wages below their already depressed level
would have meant much higher unemployment, a greater
erosion of living standards, a marked degree of 'undesirable
volatility in output' (contrary to our remit), and a risk of
inflation falling well below the target in the medium term.*

The circumstances between 2008 and 2011 were, one hopes, abnormal. The argument that just a little bit more inflation, in normal circumstances, would give us more economic growth dates back to the era of the simple Phillips curve trade-off. Under this, it appeared that there was indeed a choice between unemployment and inflation. As we now know, and as a Labour government discovered as long ago as the 1970s, it does not work like that. Countries that try to buy growth by permitting a little more inflation usually end up with a lot more inflation and little to show for their faster growth. Policies that permit higher inflation may provide a temporary boost – Friedman likened the effects to that of a drug – but eventually make things worse. When expectations enter the equation – people cannot be fooled over and over again – inflationary policies are doomed to failure. In the jargon, there is no long-run trade-off between inflation and growth. Low-inflation economic stability is the best environment for growth. But what is the right inflation rate to aim for? Alan Greenspan, the former Federal Reserve Board chairman, subsequently criticised for keeping interest rates too low, defined the right level of inflation as one that does not interfere with economic decisions. At 10 per cent inflation, people and businesses start to behave in a way in which at least some of their actions are conditioned by the need to protect themselves against inflation, perhaps by buying index-linked bonds or investing in property. At 2 per cent (the UK target) that is probably not the case. There is also some persuasive evidence, because of the role of expectations, that higher inflation rates are unstable. A country trying to run a 10 per cent inflation target would, according to some research, find itself unable to hold it there, and would face the risk of the disaster of hyperinflation.

All this sounds like carte blanche for the central bankers' club and, indeed, research by Albert Alesina and Larry Summers and others suggests that the more independent the central bank, the better the unemployment–inflation trade-off, though by the early 2010s all countries seemed to have suffered a deterioration in that trade-off. Before then, it seemed that with the right policy framework you could have it all – low unemployment and low inflation. There is always a risk, though, that central bankers will try a little too hard. Mistakes by the Bank of Japan, emanating from excessive worries about inflation, helped give the country its deflation of the 1990s, with damaging consequences. Deflation, when the real value of debt increases and monetary policy can become ineffective, is a more dangerous condition than inflation. Why is this?

Suppose you take out a mortgage of £100,000 that has to be paid back after twenty-five years. If there is no inflation, then £100,000 is the amount that has to be paid back in real terms. At a 2.5 per cent inflation rate, however, the real value of that debt would halve, so the equivalent of £50,000 would have to be paid back. The knowledge that inflation tends to erode debt's real value is one reason why people and businesses are willing to borrow. Suppose, though, we had deflation – prices falling by 2.5 per cent a year. The real value of the debt would rise, to the equivalent of £200,000, even as the property on which the mortgage was taken out fell in value. In a period of deflation, few would want to take on new debts, and defaults would be common. The economy would start to grind to a halt. That is why deflation is to be avoided. Central banks, to be fair, were fully alive to this possibility when the financial crisis hit and responded aggressively with lower interest rates and quantitative easing to head off the danger.

Does manufacturing matter?

Finally, let me turn to a perennial question. At a time when three-quarters of the new cars sold in Britain are imported, and the country's factories have long ago ceased to make many of the things sold in our shops, does it matter? Would we be worse off if there was no UK car industry? After all, it does not seem to matter that the big car manufacturers are not British-owned. In other words, does manufacturing matter? The conventional economic answer to this is no. The decline in manufacturing's share of the UK economy to barely more than 10 per cent went alongside rising, not falling prosperity. Richard Scase pointed out in the early 2000s that more people in Britain worked in Indian restaurants than in shipbuilding, steel-making and coal mining combined, and that there were more public relations consultants than miners. Out of workforce jobs of more than 31 million in 2011, only just over 2.5 million were in manufacturing. If Britain's comparative advantage lies elsewhere than in manufacturing, say in tourism or financial services (the City), the theory goes, then the optimal position could be to have no manufacturing industry at all. In fact, there is a long-standing debate between, on one side, those who say the City has never benefited British industry, and, on the other, those in the Square Mile who say that if only UK manufacturing was as internationally competitive as financial services, the economy would be hugely successful. The arguments for retaining manufacturing become strategic, not economic. Would we really want to have no domestic defence equipment manufacturers? Or, thinking back to the Second World War, would we really, in admittedly very different circumstances, want to be in a position where there would be no domestic manufacturing capacity to convert to producing the modern equivalent of Spitfires?

Real life, of course, is more complicated than that. While manufacturing in Britain is less than a quarter of the size of the private services sector and just over a tenth of the economy, it punches above its weight. Manufacturers, for example, contribute more than their fair share of export earnings – manufactured goods account for nearly half of UK exports of goods and services. The economy could not manage without these. Britain has also been successful in attracting inward investment from outside the European Union, particularly Japan and America, much of it into manufacturing. This is hardly the mark of a country that has lost its

277

comparative advantage in making things. Not only that, say advocates of manufacturing, other European countries with larger manufacturing sectors than Britain tend also to have higher living standards, higher per capita GDP, most notably Germany. Even in 2010, on the strength of its manufacturing sector, Germany was vying with China as the world's biggest exporter. The UK would do better, in other words, with an expanded manufacturing sector. It is also the case, in Britain and elsewhere, that manufacturing firms tend to be more innovative, introducing more technologically driven products and processes than their service-sector counterparts. Innovation, as we have seen, is one of the drivers of economic growth. It may even be that the bald figures understate the importance of manufacturing. The Engineering Employers' Federation and others have pointed out the substantial linkages between industry and other parts of the economy, notably service industries. Without manufacturing as a driver of demand, other parts of the economy would soon suffer. The broad picture is that while it is possible to discuss in the abstract the idea of Britain without a manufacturing sector, the reality is rather different.

That reality became very different in the aftermath of the global financial crisis. The coalition government elected in May 2010 embarked on a strategy of 'rebalancing' the economy, with an emphasis on reviving the role of manufacturing. In his March 2011 Budget, George Osborne, the Chancellor, called for 'a Britain carried aloft by the march of the makers'. He said:

Over the last decade, the share of the economy accounted for by financial services increased by over two thirds – while

manufacturing's share fell by almost a half ... Yes, we want the
City of London to remain the world's leading centre for
financial services, but we should resolve that the rest of the
country becomes a world leader in advanced manufacturing,
life sciences, creative industries, business services, green energy
and so much more.

That leads on to a further debate: if we need a vibrant and successful manufacturing sector, how do we go about creating one? Pretty well every government gets around, at some stage, to launching a manufacturing strategy. None has yet been notable for its success. A stable economic environment is one essential ingredient, as are a ready supply of skilled workers and a change in the attitudes that have put industry at the bottom of the pecking order when it comes to, for example, graduate career choices. A full answer, however, would require another book.

There are many more arguments we could have about economics and I hope you will have been stimulated to have some. This has been a fairly rich diet of economics. I hope that it has given the lie to the perception that economics is impenetrable and scary. In economics, as in so many things, there is usually nothing to fear except fear itself. Having read this book, nobody need have any fear of economics. But now, to finish, let me deal with an episode that was very scary indeed, called into question many people's belief in economics, and left most of us suffering at least some discomfort.

14

A nasty bout of indigestion

Economies are prone to periodic, often hugely damaging crises. Normally that sentence is preceded by the word 'capitalist' as a nod to Karl Marx, though all economies, whether capitalist or not, are prone to crises. Moreover, many non-Marxist economists have sought to explain why such crises occur. The biggest of them all, in terms of crises most of us have experienced, began in 2007. Generally, people were not expecting it, just as you do not expect an adverse reaction after dining in a fine restaurant. Perhaps the title of this chapter understates how bad it was and more serious medical analogies might have been more appropriate. Certainly in the autumn of 2008, the global banking system had something more akin to a heart attack. I don't want to make readers feel unnecessarily queasy, nor make this chapter a re-run of the crisis – with every sweaty brow, expletive and takeaway pizza lovingly retold. You can find that, with the exception of the expletives, in my 2010 book *The Age of Instability: The Global Financial Crisis and What Comes Next*. Rather, I will talk about the impact of the crisis on economics and on economic policy. After all, before the world was plunged into crisis, many people thought macroeconomics had become very boring and all the interest was in microeconomics – and the wackier the better. So, how much of what you have read so far remains relevant? Did the crisis represent such a challenge to conventional thinking that it will never recover? I shall try to answer these questions at the end of the chapter. First, though, it is necessary to say a little about the crisis and its causes.

Out of a cloudy August sky

Some dates are etched permanently on the memory and can properly be called world-changing. September 11 2001, the tenth anniversary of which had been marked just before I wrote this, is one. The terrorist attacks on the United States that day were to cast a long shadow and had far-reaching geopolitical implications. They also probably had an economic effect, such was the determination of the US authorities to avoid letting Al-Qaeda win by inflicting lasting economic damage. For a few years, at least, growth became the priority, maybe at the expense of prudence. When it comes to the Great Financial Crisis, which in turn gave us the Great Recession (apologies for all these 'greats' but the episode was preceded by the Great Moderation or the Great Stability), there is as yet no agreement on the start date, let alone when it finished. Even well into the 2010s, it is much too early to declare the crisis over – perhaps by the time you read this, it will be. Some would say the crisis began in 2006, when house prices in America began to fall. Others date it to mid-September 2008, and the collapse of Lehman Brothers, the US investment bank.

I think as good a candidate as any is 9 August 2007. A month earlier, two hedge funds owned by the Wall Street investment bank Bear Stearns (later taken over as a result of the crisis) collapsed. This was not the first sign of difficulties in the markets or in America's sub-prime mortgage market, essentially loans to borrowers who were poor credit risks. Such mortgages were sometimes disparagingly called 'Ninja' mortgages – for people with 'no income', 'no job' and 'no assets', though one US mortgage firm was so proud of its Ninja product that it copyrighted the name. In early 2007, HSBC told investors it was setting aside more than $10 billion for losses by Household, its US mortgage subsidiary; and in April New Century Financial, one of the biggest sub-prime lenders, filed for Chapter 11 bankruptcy. The significance of the two collapsed Bear Stearns' hedge funds was that it showed that sub-prime mortgages were creating losses beyond the mortgage market itself. The two hedge funds, the High-Grade Fund and the Enhanced Fund, were both heavily invested in financial instruments, which were sliced, diced and bundled together out of these low-quality mortgages.

Perhaps the simplest explanation for why this was important was the one I gave in the *Sunday Times* on 5 August 2007:

> *Problems in the American sub-prime mortgage market – loans to borrowers with dodgy credit histories – have been apparent*

*for months. But the defaults have been getting bigger and more
frequent. Think of it as an inverted pyramid, resting on these
dodgy, sub-prime loans, which were sliced and diced and
turned into a range of sophisticated financial derivatives,
notably collateralised debt obligations (CDOs). If the base is
rotten, the pyramid risks collapse, and fears of this have grown,
widening spreads (increasing the cost of borrowing) across a
range of markets. Deals that looked good when spreads were
narrow, such as leveraged buyouts, are no longer viable.*

Problems and tensions occur regularly in financial markets.
Most pass by without having a serious impact. In 1998, for example, three big crises came together at once: the Asian financial
crisis, a default by Russia and the failure of Long-Term Capital
Management, a big hedge fund. Yet the impact on western economies was minimal. So why was what happened in 2007 so prob-
lematical? The answer is that the potential losses for the banking
system from holdings of dodgy mortgage-backed securities and
their derivatives were unknown, thus compounding the uncertainty, but potentially very large indeed. We may never know how
big the losses attributable to such bad investments were – separat-
ing them from 'normal' recession-related losses is difficult – but
one International Monetary Fund estimate in 2009 suggested an
eyewatering $4 trillion.

The reason 9 August 2007 is a good candidate for the start of
the crisis is because that was the day when the problems clearly
moved beyond America's sub-prime market, beyond its economy,
and on to the world stage. One of the duties of a central bank is to

act as 'lender of last resort' usually to an individual institution that is in difficulty. When a central bank provides liquidity to the market as a whole, it is only at times of intense strain, of panic. Walter Bagehot, the nineteenth-century renaissance man – editor of the *Economist* and author of the foremost text on the British Constitution – described it in his 1873 book *Lombard Street*: 'Any notion that money is not to be had, or that it may not be had at any price, only raises alarm to panic and enhances panic to madness … A panic grows by what it feeds on; if it devours these second-class men shall we, the first-class, be safe?' So, 9 August 2007 was the day the European Central Bank, many miles away from Wall Street or the Florida towns where sub-prime mortgages had been handed out far too easily, responded. It flooded the European markets with liquidity after discovering that banks in Europe, and in particular those in France, were caught up in the turmoil and were losing the trust of the markets.

Rocked to its foundations

It did not end there, of course. What followed was a kind of domino effect, with banks regarded as weak or excessively dependent on wholesale money markets – those borrowing from other banks or financial institutions rather than relying on savers' deposits – being the most heavily exposed. When, on 13 September 2007, it was revealed that Northern Rock, Britain's fifth largest mortgage lender, was being supported by 'lender of last resort' assistance from the Bank of England, it was clear that something was up. The following day saw a run on Northern Rock's branches (and over the Internet), the first run on a British bank since Overend & Gurney in 1866.

There was much more to come. Northern Rock was eventually nationalised by Britain's Labour government after a five-month attempt to find a viable private-sector buyer. There were hopes, after the excitement of August and September when money markets froze from a lack of banks' confidence in each other, that the worst might be over. It was, however, a vain hope. After months in which Wall Street investment banks and America's other large banks had announced ever-larger writedowns (losses) on their sub-prime-related investments, one of their number, Bear Stearns, was forced to sell itself at a knockdown price to J. P. Morgan, the deal only being possible because it was accompanied by $30 billion of loans from the Federal Reserve, America's central bank. Bear Stearns, founded in 1923, had been part of Wall Street's aristocracy, surviving the 1929 Crash but not the credit crunch of 2007–8. It had first exposed that crunch with the problems at its hedge funds eight months earlier. Now it was a victim. Soon afterwards the International Monetary Fund said that the world was facing the biggest financial shock since the Great Depression of the 1930s.

In September and much of October of 2008 it seemed that each weekend brought a new crisis that threatened to bring the financial system to its knees. The crisis that had begun more than a year earlier entered a new and more deadly phase. Suddenly, the fear of losses and counterparty risks (banks and other institutions not trusting counterparts they had previously been comfortable dealing with) reached exaggerated levels. For investment banks in particular, reliant on raising funds in the wholesale markets – unlike commercial banks they lacked retail customers – this lack of confidence was dangerous in the extreme. The drama began on the weekend of 6–7 September with an announcement from the US Treasury of a taxpayer-funded bailout of Fannie Mae (the Federal National Mortgage Association) and Freddie Mac (the Federal Home Loan Mortgage Corporation), the bulwarks of America's mortgage market. Though owned by shareholders, both Fannie Mae and Freddie Mac were so-called government sponsored enterprises, with access to lower-cost funds than commercial rivals and chartered by Congress to increase home ownership. The fact that they had to be rescued was testimony to the scale of the problem.

However, it was the non-rescue the following weekend of Lehman Brothers, the blue-blooded Wall Street investment bank, that really sent financial markets into a spin and almost produced what for once it was not an exaggeration to call 'financial melt-down'. As Sir Mervyn King, Governor of the Bank of England, described it a few weeks later:

Since August 2007, the industrialised world has been engulfed by financial turmoil. And, following the failure of Lehman Brothers on 15 September, an extraordinary, almost unimaginable, sequence of events began which culminated a week or so ago in the announcements around the world of a recapitalisation of the banking system. It is difficult to exaggerate the severity and importance of those events. Not since the beginning of the First World War has our banking system been so close to collapse. In the second half of September, companies and non-bank financial institutions accelerated their withdrawal from even short-term funding of banks, and banks increasingly lost confidence in the safety of lending to

each other. Funding costs rose sharply and for many institutions
it was possible to borrow only overnight. Credit to the real
economy almost stopped flowing.

The 'almost unimaginable' sequence of events described by King included a $700 billion bailout of the US banking system by America's Treasury Department, a plan approved only after a tough battle with Congress. George W. Bush, pleading with Congressional leaders to back the White House's banking bail-out package two weeks after the Lehman collapse, was typically blunt: 'If money isn't loosened up, this sucker could go down.' Rescuing the banks cost governments hundreds of billions in providing capital, liquidity support and guarantees for the banking system. In Britain the response included the nationalisation of much of Bradford & Bingley, a mortgage bank, and the emergency merger of Lloyds TSB and Halifax Bank of Scotland (HBOS), with the government waiving competition rules to allow the deal to go through. Banks were in trouble and had to be rescued. Merrill Lynch, another Wall Street giant, was forced into a merger with Bank of America. AIG, America's biggest insurer, had to be rescued by the US government. Several European banks, including the Belgian-Dutch Fortis Bank and Germany's Hypo Real Estate Bank, got into trouble. It was a dangerous contagion.

Alphabet soup
The banking crisis was similar but different to that described by Walter Bagehot in the nineteenth century. It was similar because financial panics follow a similar pattern across the ages. It was

different because of the nature of the investments causing all the trouble. A mortgage-backed security was just a pool of mortgages bundled together – or 'securitised'. Investors would get their return from the regular monthly payments of mortgage borrowers. There were other forms of asset-backed security (ABS). Collateralised debt obligations (CDOs) were more sophisticated, splitting the 'debt', or borrowing – most split it into tranches reflecting the different risks of default. It got even more complicated. The notorious CDO-squared (CDO^2) instruments were CDOs consisting of other CDOs. This alphabet soup had two more acronyms: CDSs (credit default swaps) and SIVs (structured investment vehicles). Credit default swaps are a type of insurance contract. A firm wishing to minimise its credit risk gets somebody else to take on that risk, the risk of default, and pays a premium to it to do so. It buys a CDS from another firm, in some cases an insurance company (AIG, the American insurance giant, was very big in CDSs). The CDS market grew and grew. When the global financial crisis broke in 2007 they were worth $55 trillion, almost equivalent to the world's gross domestic product, though this was only a fraction of the $500 trillion trade in all so-called derivatives. Structured investment vehicles were used extensively by the banks. SIVs would parcel up and issue debt and in return receive a flow of income on that debt. Most of their credit was supplied by the banks themselves but they stayed off their balance sheets.

These derivatives and other financial instruments were important not just because they were responsible for many of the losses in the banking system, but because they provide a striking example of intelligent people getting it wrong. While investors like Warren

Buffett of Berkshire Hathaway – otherwise known as the Sage of Omaha – were sceptical of these derivatives, many policymakers were sold on them, none more so than Alan Greenspan, former chairman of America's Federal Reserve Board. 'What we have found over the years in the marketplace is that derivatives have been an extraordinarily useful vehicle to transfer risk from those who shouldn't be taking it to those who are willing to and are capable of doing so,' he told a Congressional committee in 2003. 'Prior to the advent of derivatives on a large scale, we did not have that capability. And we often had, for example, financial institutions, like banks, taking on undue risk and running into real, serious problems.' The question of whether economists and policymakers were too willing to believe in the financial markets is one I shall return to.

The worst recession

In March 2007, Gordon Brown gave his final Budget speech to the House of Commons as Chancellor of the Exchequer, before becoming Prime Minister. Everything, it seemed, was going well. 'I can report the British economy is today growing faster than all the other G7 economies – growth stronger this year than the euro area, stronger than Japan and stronger even than America,' he said, 'and that after ten years of sustained growth, Britain's growth will continue into its 59th quarter … and then into its 60th and 61st quarter and beyond.' The British economy, often a watchword for instability, was now outperforming others and growing strongly 'on the foundation of the longest period of economic stability and sustained growth in our country's history'. Just in case anybody had forgotten it, he repeated the New Labour mantra that he and Tony Blair had used repeatedly since 1997: 'And we will never return to the old boom and bust.'

The economic, or business, cycle is as old as economics itself. Gordon Brown and Tony Blair must have known this, not least because the fiscal rules they adopted on taking office were cyclically adjusted. In other words, they allowed for the fact that over a period of years the economy will fluctuate between strong and weak growth, and between falling and rising unemployment. Surely they must have recognised the danger of a more pronounced cycle – in other words, boom and bust? As it turned out, Blair left office before the bust, though Brown occupied Downing Street for all of it – and it was a corker. Official figures for gross domestic product (GDP) and its components are prone to significant revision over time. However, the recession that began in early 2008 and formally ended in late 2009 saw, on statistics available at time of writing, GDP drop by over 7 per cent from the pre-recession peak to its recessionary low point, the trough. This compared with nearly 3.5 per cent in the 1973–4 'OPEC' recession, just over 4.5 per cent in the first Thatcher recession of the early 1980s and just 2.5 per cent in the early 1990s. It was, therefore, the worst recession in the post-war era, and not just in Britain. Before 2008–9, global recessions in the post-war era had been 'growth' recessions, sharp slowdowns in world growth but not outright contractions. But in 2009 the world economy shrank for the first time since 1945.

Why did the world economy suffer its steepest dive in living memory? It may have been the cumulative effect of a financial crisis that by the autumn of 2008 had been going on for more than a year. Modern economies run on credit, so cutting off the supply of credit was bound to have an impact. Some blamed the oil price which in the summer of 2008, helped by an investor shift into commodities, rose to $147 a barrel, an extraordinarily high level at that time. However, until autumn 2008, most economies appeared to be coping pretty well with record oil prices. So the trigger had to be September 2008, the collapse of Lehman Brothers, and the collapse of confidence in the banking and financial system. The question is: what was the economic explanation for that collapse?

The royal question

Apart from the impact on her own investments, you would not expect the Queen to have much relevance to the global financial crisis. Yet a throwaway remark she made on a visit to the London School of Economics (LSE) in November 2008 has entered the folklore. The crisis was raging and, in conversation with Professor Luis Garicano, director of research at the LSE's management department, she described the global financial crisis as 'awful' and asked: 'If these things were so large how come everyone missed it?' Garicano referred to declining lending standards, particularly in America's housing market, and the herd instinct in financial markets. But he also admitted that the warnings should have been louder. 'We economists and academics should have been louder in our warnings and more proactive in suggesting solutions,' he wrote later. 'Particularly problematic and subject to a serious rethink are the short-term and one-sided incentives prevalent in the financial industry – and the failure by those who took the risks to bear the risks. The public is right to be outraged.'

The Queen's question, simple and innocent enough, provoked many responses. In June 2009, the British Academy assembled a meeting of economic and financial experts, including seven people who were either serving or had served on the Bank of England's monetary policy committee (MPC): Tim Besley, David Miles, Paul Tucker, Sir Alan Budd, Sir John Gieve, Professor Charles Goodhart and Sushil Wadhwani. Sir Nicholas Macpherson, Permanent Secretary to the Treasury, and two of his predecessors, Sir Douglas Wass and Sir Gus O'Donnell, then Cabinet Secretary, were there, along with many others. Tim Besley and Peter Hennessy, both professors and fellows of the British Academy, summed up the forum's conclusions in a letter to the Queen. Though some had foreseen a crisis of some sort, it said, 'the exact form it would take and the timing of its onset and ferocity were foreseen by nobody'. On the important question of risk, and the pricing of it in financial markets, the letter noted that plenty of people had engaged themselves in the assessment of risk, including 4,000 risk managers in one of Britain's big banks alone. 'But the difficulty was seeing the risk to the system as a whole rather to any specific financial instrument or loan,' they wrote. 'Risk calculations were most often confined to slices of financial activity, using some of the best mathematical models in our country and abroad. But they frequently lost sight of the bigger picture.'

Even economists who were concerned about the rapid pace of credit growth were swept along with the new mood. If they believed the emperor had no clothes, they were too embarrassed to say so, or thought they must be getting it wrong while the banks and financial markets were getting it right.

'Most were convinced that banks knew what they were doing,' the British Academy said. It continued:

They believed that the financial wizards had found new and clever ways of managing risks. Indeed, some claimed to have so dispersed them through an array of novel financial instruments that they had virtually removed them. It is difficult to recall a greater example of wishful thinking combined with hubris. There was a firm belief, too, that financial markets had changed. And politicians of all types were charmed by the market. These views were abetted by financial and economic models that were good at predicting the short-term and small risks, but few were equipped to say what would happen when things went as wrong as they have. People trusted the banks whose boards and senior executives were packed with globally recruited talent and their non-executive directors included those with proven records in public life. Nobody wanted to believe that their judgment could be faulty or that they were unable competently to scrutinise the risks in the organisations that they managed. A generation of bankers and financiers deceived themselves and those who thought that they were the pace-making engineers of advanced economies.

Another reason the crisis was so bad was that the build-up was so long. There is a case for tracing the events that unfolded so damagingly back as far as 1980 and the beginnings of the 'shadow' banking system in America (which by the time of the crisis was as big as the formal banking sector). Shadow banks are either separate entities such as money market funds, or bank-owned off-balance sheet subsidiaries. Former Bank of England monetary policy committee member Andrew Sentance and his colleague Michael Hume were certainly able to track the global credit boom back to the early 1990s. It began in America, with a sharp increase in lending to businesses, partly associated with the dot.com boom. Then, rather than tailing off, it spread, to business lending elsewhere in the world but more particularly to consumers. For the three or four years before the crisis, if not longer, consumers in Britain and America maintained their spending by borrowing. Though the biggest increase in debt in Britain from the early 1990s was in the financial sector itself, household debt rose from £390 billion at the end of the 1990–92 recession to £1,430 billion at the start of the 2008–9 downturn.

Imbalances and irrationality

So most economists, unlike the Queen, were asking the wrong questions, or not questioning enough. But there was a long tradition of economists warning of one particular danger, that of global imbalances. These imbalances – essentially current account deficits in economies such as America and surpluses in countries such as China and Japan – were at the very least, a contributory factor. Nouriel Roubini, who made his reputation as the 'Dr Doom' of the crisis, warned repeatedly that America's current account deficit was an accident waiting to happen. He likened the US situation to that of an emerging market economy facing a balance of payments crisis. On a global scale, the world economy had been unbalanced for so long that at some point it had to tip over.

Economists had been waiting for a crisis on which to pin global imbalances since the collapse of the Bretton Woods system of fixed-but-adjustable exchange rates in the early 1970s, and certainly since America's twin deficits – budget and balance of payments – of the 'Reaganomics' era in the 1980s. Global imbalances suffered from the problem of crying wolf. Nobody was unaware of them, though the world appeared capable of living with them. Part of the reason for the crisis may have been that they were stretched to breaking point. One symptom of the imbalances was what was known as the 'global savings glut'. Countries like China, where consumer spending was low and savings high, were generating surpluses that washed around the world economy. This surplus of savings kept interest rates low – think of interest rates as the price at which the supply and demand of funds is equalised – fuelling a powerful and sustained credit boom. It also led to the curious by-product of China being the biggest international holder of US 'treasuries' – American government bonds.

Some economists could rightly claim to have spotted other problems early. Robert Shiller, the Yale professor described by his publishers as 'the Sage of New Haven', wrote a book, *Irrational Exuberance*, in 2000 which took its title from a phrase used by Alan Greenspan in 1996. In it he warned that stock market euphoria based on the idea of a 'new era' or 'new paradigm' built on technology was misplaced. Just as in past episodes of irrational exuberance, such as the railway mania of Victorian Britain, the markets were building false hopes. Shiller was right, and became regarded as a prophet when his book anticipated the bursting of the dot.com bubble, with the consequent collapse in technology shares. When a second edition of *Irrational Exuberance* appeared in 2005, warning of a real estate bubble in America as pronounced as the one in the stock market a few years earlier, people should have taken more notice. He warned that the consequence of real estate values continuing to rise and then falling back sharply would be a steep increase in personal bankruptcies. This could lead to failures for financial institutions, hitting personal and business confidence hard and threatening a recession, possibly a worldwide one. Again, he was right, although those with responsibility for running the economy took a different view. Soon after he had been appointed to head the Federal Reserve (succeeding Greenspan), Ben Bernanke, then chairman of George W. Bush's Council of Economic Advisers, offered instead reassurance about housing. In the autumn of 2005, after Shiller's warnings, he said:

House prices have risen by nearly 25 per cent over the past two years. Although speculative activity has increased in some areas, at a national level these price increases largely reflect strong economic fundamentals, including robust growth in jobs and incomes, low mortgage rates, steady rates of household formation, and factors that limit the expansion of housing supply in some areas. House prices are unlikely to continue rising at current rates. However, as reflected in many private-sector forecasts ... a moderate cooling in the housing market, should one occur, would not be inconsistent with the economy continuing to grow at or near its potential next year.

Bubbles and booms

What is the difference between a 'bubble' and a 'boom'? Though the two are used interchangeably, they are different. It is possible, for example, to have a boom that lasts for many years and is not followed by a bust. Periods of rapid economic development are booms. At time of writing, China has been in a boom, broken by occasional periods of slower growth, since the late 1970s. So booms can be sustainable, or at least long-lasting. Bubbles, from the South Sea Bubble of 1720 onwards, if not before, are never sustainable. Robert Shiller, in a later book, *The Subprime Solution*, described the phenomenon of bubbles, likening them to a kind of disease:

> *Every disease has a contagion rate (the rate at which it is spread from person to person) and a removal rate (the rate at which individuals recover from or succumb to the illness and so are no longer contagious). If the contagion rate exceeds the removal rate by a necessary amount, an epidemic begins ... So it is in the economic and social environment. Sooner or later, some factor boosts the infection rate sufficiently above the removal rate for an optimistic view of the market to become widespread. There is an escalation in public knowledge of the arguments that would seem to support that view, and soon the epidemic spirals up and out of control. Almost everyone appears to think – if they notice at all that certain economic arguments are more in evidence – that the arguments are increasingly heard only because of their true intellectual merit. The idea that the prominence of the arguments is in fact due to a social contagion is hardly ever broached, at least outside university sociology departments.*

Blaming economists

Economists often get judged, perhaps unfairly, on their predictive abilities. Any economist who had perfect foresight of the crisis could, however, have kept quiet and made a great deal of money out of it. Though some hedge funds did indeed profit hugely from the global financial crisis, there is little evidence that economists, collectively, were hiding their lights under a bushel. To be fair to them, even two days before it happened, it would have been impossible to predict the single most damaging event in the autumn of 2008, the failure to rescue Lehman Brothers. The crisis, in other words, could have turned out differently. The criticism of economics, however, went deeper than mere forecasting failures and some of the harshest criticism came from within economics itself. Paul Krugman, after being awarded the 2008 Nobel Prize for economics, said in June 2009 that most of the macroeconomic thinking of the past three decades had been 'spectacularly useless at best, and positively harmful at worst'. We had, he said, been living through a 'Dark Age of macroeconomics', in which essential truths learned decades before, and in particular in the age of Keynes in the 1920s, 1930s and 1940s, had been forgotten.

Willem Buiter, a founder member of the Bank of England's monetary policy committee (MPC), posted a blog entry under the headline 'The unfortunate uselessness of most "state of the art" academic monetary economics'. Many of those working at the Bank of England were well equipped with such training, but such economics, he said, 'turned out to be a severe handicap when the central bank had to switch gears and change from being an inflation-targeting central bank under conditions of orderly financial markets to a financial stability-oriented central bank under conditions of widespread market illiquidity and funding illiquidity. Indeed, the typical graduate macroeconomics and monetary economics training received at Anglo-American universities during the past thirty years or so may have set back by decades serious investigations of aggregate economic behaviour and economic policy-relevant understanding. It was a privately and socially costly waste of time and resources. Most mainstream macroeconomic theoretical innovations since the 1970s ... have turned out to be self-referential, inward-looking distractions at best.'

Buiter spared nobody in his criticisms. Everybody, it seemed, was guilty, at least in part: the 'New Classical' rational expectations revolution associated with Robert Lucas, Edward Prescott, Thomas Sargent, Robert Barro and others (who we have encountered), and the 'New Keynesians' such as Michael Woodford (who we have not). Both failed dismally, Buiter said. The theoretical models developed since the 1970s assumed that a crisis of illiquidity, which is how the global financial crisis began in 2007, could not occur; such a crisis could not feature in their version of the world. Their 'constraining assumptions' were that systemic crises of illiquidity and insolvency did not happen. I will return at the end of the chapter to the response to these criticisms.

Shooting at the target

Those who have stayed the course through this meal will recall the importance of inflation targeting in changing the nature of monetary policy in Britain. Normally it takes a setback to produce a change of course. The crisis was rather more than a setback. Will it mean that inflation targeting will not be the final resting place for monetary policy, and merely an interlude? The Bank of England was caught unawares by the crisis. Was the policy it had followed before it directly responsible? Lord Saatchi, the Conservative peer and Chairman of the Centre for Policy Studies (CPS), provided the most extreme critique, in a CPS paper, 'The Myth of Inflation Targeting'. The crisis was not the fault of bankers, regulators or borrowers but of misguided faith in inflation targeting, he argued. 'Their mistake was to believe what they were told,' wrote Saatchi. They were lulled, he said:

> *into a false sense of security by an idea – that if policy makers could maintain low inflation (and more important, low inflation expectations), then all good things would follow – growth, employment, prosperity, stability. Unfortunately, the idea turned out to be a myth – the largest policy failure of our generation. The Myth of Inflation Targeting created the illusion of the New Jerusalem, the new paradigm – the end of the economic cycle … the inflation targeting policy encouraged the view that it was safe to borrow, safe to invest. The Myth led bankers to lend more, traders to risk more, homeowners to borrow more, regulators to relax more, and politicians to boast more – about the end of boom and bust. When the Myth collapsed, it took all of us down with it.*

Though Saatchi's was an extreme version of events, the Bank was also criticised by others. Some said its problems were as a result of having an inflation target imposed on it by Gordon Brown in

2003 which did not include house prices. (The original target, based on the retail prices index, had a house-price element; its successor, the consumer prices index did not.) The boom in asset prices, including house prices, told a story of very rapid credit growth, which the MPC was said to have turned a blind eye to. The Bank, it was said, should have paid much more attention to the house-price boom, either by raising interest rates even when its target measure of inflation was comfortably under control – a strategy known as 'leaning against the wind', or by 'verbal intervention', tough statements to try and talk down the market. Some central banks did this, notably the Reserve Bank of Australia (RBA).

Raising interest rates when there is no apparent danger to the inflation target is easier said than done. Spencer Dale, the Bank's chief economist in 2009, talked of 'the practical difficulty of implementing a policy of "leaning against the wind", where the main policy instrument is short-term interest rates'. 'If, as policymakers, we were successful in preventing a bubble from inflating, it might appear as if we were responding to phantom concerns,' he said. 'The bubble or imbalance would be nowhere to be seen, but interest rates would be higher, inflation would undershoot the inflation target and we would appear to have inflicted unnecessary economic hardship.'

For central banks, two big lessons were learned in responding to the crisis. The first was that even ultra-low interest rates – in the Bank of England's case the lowest since it was founded in 1694 – might not be enough. So, as already described, central banks had to go further. On the face of it a central bank policy of buying the bonds of its own government, particularly when that government is running a huge budget deficit, looks questionable, the kind of thing that happens in banana republics. But that is exactly what happened in Britain in 2009, when the Bank bought £200 billion of assets, mainly government bonds (gilts). Members of the MPC, who made the decision, were keen to emphasise how this benefited the wider economy. Professor David Miles described in September 2009 the ways in which he claimed the policy was working. The policy of buying gilts pushed up their price, thus pushing down yields (the interest rate on them), an effect that was replicated in the market for corporate bonds. That, together with an accompanying rise in the stock market, had made it easier for companies to finance themselves on the markets and was helping to move the economy from deep recession into recovery. 'Conventional monetary and fiscal policy are doing a lot – but have reached the limits of effectiveness,' he said. 'Less conventional policy is also playing a role: and for monetary policy that means quantitative easing (or QE), the rather arcane term used for the central bank policy of buying assets from the private sector financed by the creation of reserves, or central bank money … I believe the evidence is that QE is having an impact and that it is relevant to economic conditions right across the country. And not just in financial markets in London but in high streets and factories and homes throughout the UK.' A later assessment by Bank staff suggested QE boosted GDP by between 1.5 and 3 percentage points relative to what it would have been in the absence of the policy.

The other lesson, according to Miles's MPC colleague Spencer Dale, was 'the need to expand the range of instruments available to policymakers'. If the aim of quantitative easing was to boost the amount of money in the economy, there might be future occasions when the central bank would wish to limit the growth of money and credit. A crude instrument for controlling house prices might be restricting the amount people can borrow, either in relation to their income or the value of the property they are buying. A more sophisticated approach – though there would be no point implementing it until bank lending returned to something like normality – would be to set aggregate lending limits; controlling the overall flow of credit into the economy. This would be a return to the practices of the past. In the 1970s Britain's banks were subject to what was known as 'the corset' (its proper name was the Supplementary Special Deposit Scheme), which imposed penalties on banks whose deposits exceeded pre-set limits. It was abandoned in 1980. As it turned out, the coalition government elected in May 2010 chose to persist with the inflation target but also to transfer financial regulation from the Financial Services Authority back to the Bank of England. According to the Bank, its new financial policy committee, which would operate in parallel with the MPC, would have the role of 'identifying, monitoring, and taking action to remove or reduce, systemic risks with a view to protecting and enhancing the resilience of the UK financial system'. As well as the 'micro-prudential' regulation of individual firms, the new committee – which would draw on the work of regulators in the Bank – would have responsibility for 'macro-prudential' regulation; ensuring the system as a whole was safe. The apparent simplicity of policy in the run-up to the crisis was giving way to something more complex. Other countries also took steps to beef up their regulation of the banking and financial systems.

Are markets efficient?

Inflation-targeting, according to its critics, established a mood of complacency and missed what was really going on. Was there a more direct culprit? The efficient market hypothesis had been around in various forms for much of the twentieth century. It was defined by Professor Eugene Fama of Chicago University, in a 1970 article, 'Efficient Capital Markets: A Review of Theory and Empirical Work', published in the *Journal of Finance*. Fama's idea was very simple: financial markets are efficient in the sense that the price of a company's shares reflects all the known information at the time. There were, he said, various degrees of 'strength' with which the proposition could be stated. In the weakest version, the current price reflected only past information on prices. In the 'semi-strong' version, it reflects all publicly available information affecting the company; while in the strongest version, the price reflected all publicly and privately available information. It immediately won many fans. 'There is no other proposition in economics which has more solid empirical evidence supporting it than the efficient market hypothesis,' said Michael Jensen, the Harvard financial economist, in 1978. It implied that it was hard for investors to claim to consistently beat the market. Today's price reflected all known information today. Tomorrow's price would reflect the state of information tomorrow, which might be different but which nobody could hope to anticipate without possessing that information in advance.

Simple though it was, it was widely blamed for contributing to the crisis. In a review published in March 2009 Lord Turner, chairman of Britain's Financial Services Authority, wrote that 'the predominant assumption behind financial market regulation – in the US, the UK and increasingly across the world – has been that financial markets are capable of being both efficient and rational and that a key goal of financial market regulation is to remove the impediments which might produce inefficient and illiquid markets'. The reality, he wrote, was rather different: 'Policymakers have to recognise that all liquid traded markets are capable of acting irrationally, and can be susceptible to self-reinforcing herd and momentum effects.' Other critics weighed in. 'Most of the economics profession continued to swallow the efficient market hypothesis hook, line and sinker,' wrote Willem Buiter. Lord (Robert) Skidelsky, the biographer of Keynes, said 'it led bankers into blind faith in their mathematical forecasting models. It led governments and regulators to discount the possibility that financial markets could implode.'

It seemed Fama's theory was responsible for untold economic and financial damage. Maybe, however, the damage was done by those who tested it to destruction. The idea that the price of a stock or security is the best distillation of all available relevant information does not exclude what critics of the hypothesis describe as 'momentum', or 'herd' effects. The knowledge that other investors are buying and intend to buy more is part of the available information that helps set the price. The hypothesis does not say anything about what the price will be tomorrow, or even in a few minutes' time. The information affecting the price can change quickly and dramatically. The most important implication of the efficient market hypothesis, moreover, was that professionals could not legitimately claim consistently to beat the markets. There really is no such thing as a free lunch. Those claiming consistently above-normal returns – whether fraudsters such as Bernie Madoff, or investment banks claiming new ways of making high returns in a low-yield world – were saying they could beat the market. The efficient market hypothesis should have told regulators there was something suspicious about this. If they believed the markets were always right and that the markets always priced in risks and dangers accurately, then perhaps more fool them.

Maths and models

This book, as you know, is almost an equation-free zone. That is not true of economics in general. Throughout its history economics has become more mathematical, increasingly reliant on algebraic formulae and econometric 'proofs'. For some, the rot set in when political economy, which was largely descriptive, evolved into economics. In April 2009 *Business Week* magazine published a cover article under the headline 'What Good Are Economists Anyway?' It quoted a number of critics, including Nassim Nicholas Taleb, the author of *Fooled by Randomness* and *The Black Swan*. Economists, he said, had deluded themselves and everyone else into believing their mathematical models could predict the future. Economic models can range from the very simple to the highly complex. Among the complex are so-called DSGE models, widely used by central banks, governments, private sector forecasters and consultancies. DSGE stands for 'dynamic stochastic general equilibrium' and these models embodied modern macroeconomic thinking. All the major central banks had them, including the European Central Bank, the Federal Reserve and the Bank of England. The latter's model was known as the Bank of England quarterly model, the BEQM – or if you preferred, 'the Beckham', after the footballer. These models were all 'dynamic', incorporating change, unlike the old static models. They demonstrated the impact of shocks and changes, which was the stochastic element, and they were based on 'general equilibrium', essentially the idea that all markets in the economy will move towards a position where supply and demand are in balance.

Such models appeared to work pretty well during the Great Moderation or Great Stability when, perhaps, forecasting was straightforward. But they failed when they were needed most, in the crisis. Professor Charles Goodhart, the former monetary policy committee member best known for Goodhart's Law (any money supply measure you target will automatically become distorted), spotted one obvious flaw: 'Generalised problems with liquidity almost always go hand in hand with concerns about solvency, as in 2007. If you could assume that I can certainly repay you, you would always lend to me unsecured at a risk free rate, an invalid assumption that alas is incorporated into most macro-economic DSGE models.' In fact, these models, by either excluding the financial sector or by assuming that finance, or bank lending, was always on tap, could not have foreseen the crisis. That and the in-built tendency of models to return to equilibrium meant that they were inappropriate for addressing the situation that plunged the world into crisis. Some policymakers were aware of the problem.

David Blanchflower, another former Bank MPC member, spotted some of the impending problems of 2008 even when the model was painting a benign picture of the outlook. 'Our macroeconomic models have little to tell us when the tipping point may come …' he said later. 'With no financial sector within macro models, there was little room to assess the macroeconomic implications of financial instability. This may be one reason central bankers were slow to realise the severity of the credit crunch until a full-blown crisis had emerged.'

So, will economists tear up their equations and abandon their models? No. Policymakers, even the rare ones who admit they relied too much on their models, will always stress the role of judgment and common sense in decisions. As I write this, a frantic effort is under way to improve the models by incorporating the financial sector into them. It will be some time, however, before models recover their reputation.

The return of Keynes
For followers of John Maynard Keynes, the global financial crisis was important not just because of its scale, it also restored their man to what they saw as his rightful place at the heart of the economic debate and the policy response to the crisis. Though Keynes had never gone away, 'Keynesian' fiscal policy had for some time taken a back seat. Monetary policy – interest rates – had become the main lever for influencing short-term economic activity. Sure enough, when the crisis hit, central banks reduced interest rates aggressively to near-zero levels. Keynes had warned in the 1930s, however, that even very low interest rates might not be enough.

They could become as ineffective, as he memorably put it, as 'pushing on a piece of string'. If monetary policy was ineffective (though central banks tried to make it more effective with 'unconventional' measures such as quantitative easing), the scene was set for a large-scale fiscal stimulus. Keynes was back.

In November 2008, the International Monetary Fund called for a global fiscal stimulus equivalent to around 2 per cent of GDP, some $1.3 trillion, though that was based on the prediction that the world economy would merely slow to 2 per cent growth in 2009. The Washington based body later revised its prediction for the global economy in 2009 to a fall of nearly 2 per cent. The G20 (as in Group of Twenty) was a grouping that included, as well as the advanced industrial countries, the big emerging economies: including China, India, Brazil, Indonesia, Mexico, Turkey and Saudi Arabia. It became the key body during the global financial crisis and, at a meeting in Washington in November 2008, endorsed fiscal measures to stimulate demand 'with rapid effect', while pledging also to take steps to ensure that 'fiscal sustainability' would be achieved again when the crisis was over. So bigger budget deficits would be the response to the crisis and its economic impact but they would be temporary. Around the world, governments introduced stimulus packages, including $586 billion in China, €50 billion in Germany (despite the apparent scepticism of Angela Merkel, the country's Chancellor), €26 billion in France, ¥12 trillion in Japan and £25 billion in Britain. The latter, necessarily small because of the poor state of the country's public finances, was mainly centred on a temporary reduction in VAT from 17.5 to 15 per cent, to run from 1 December 2008 to the end of 2009.

The revival of Keynes seemed complete. 'I guess everyone is a Keynesian in a foxhole,' said Robert Lucas, the University of Chicago new classical economist, only half-jokingly. When Barack Obama was elected President late in 2008, one of his first acts, in February 2009, was to announce a $789 billion stimulus in the face of Republican opposition. Two months later, in April 2009, Gordon Brown hosted another G20 summit, in London's Docklands, where G20 leaders boasted of 'a concerted and unprecedented fiscal expansion' amounting to $5 trillion, which they said would boost the global economy by 4 per cent. Though the $5 trillion included a large element of the combined deterioration in budget deficits in the global economy (because of the recession's impact on tax revenues and government spending), it also included deliberate fiscal measures to ease the crisis's impact. There was, in other words, a Keynesian response. The story might have ended there but it did not.

Non-Keynesians were uneasy about all these fiscal stimuluses flying around. Robert Barro, professor of economics at Harvard, attacked President Obama's fiscal stimulus plan. 'As we all know, we are in the middle of what will likely be the worst US economic contraction since the 1930s,' he wrote. And he continued:

In this context and from the history of the Great Depression, I can understand various attempts to prop up the financial system. These efforts, akin to avoiding bank runs in prior periods, recognise that the social consequences of credit-market decisions extend well beyond the individuals and businesses making the decisions. But, in terms of fiscal-stimulus proposals,

it would be unfortunate if the best Team Obama can offer is
an unvarnished version of Keynes's 1936 General Theory of
Employment, Interest and Money. *The financial crisis and*
possible depression do not invalidate everything we have
learned about macroeconomics since 1936. Much more focus
should be on incentives for people and businesses to invest,
produce and work. On the tax side, we should avoid programs
that throw money at people and emphasise instead reductions
in marginal income-tax rates – especially where these rates are
already high and fall on capital income. Eliminating the
federal corporate income tax would be brilliant. On the
spending side, the main point is that we should not be
considering massive public-works programs that do not pass
muster from the perspective of cost–benefit analysis.

Barro was backed up by 250 conservative economists who signed
a letter criticizing the stimulus plan which appeared in leading US
newspapers.

Keynesians, for their part, divided their time between attacking
people they regarded as flat earth theorists – those who would
return the world to what Paul Krugman described as 'a Dark Age
of macroeconomics' – and despairing of the government response.
Keynesians thought the lesson had been learned in the 1930s, when
a premature policy tightening had pushed America back into recession in 1937. They could also point to modern-day Japan, whose
government had also, in their view, erred by putting the fiscal
brakes on too early. Despite this, most governments stuck to the
second part of the G20's November 2008 pledge, by taking steps

to bring their public finances back to health once the immediate crisis was over. Keynesians argued that with the private sector 'deleveraging' – reducing its debt – the worst thing governments could do was to try to cut both their debt and deficits at the same time. It was one of those intractable disputes. At a practical level, governments appeared to have no option but to cut their budget deficits to try to head off a dangerous sovereign debt crisis – the risk of national insolvency and default – particularly in the troubled eurozone. There, beginning with the bailout of Greece in May 2010, governments tried – often in vain – to convince the markets that they were getting to grips with their budget deficits. Even America, which saw its sovereign debt downgraded from AAA (Triple A) status in August 2011, was not immune from these pressures. Keynesians argued that what the world needed was growth and that all this fiscal tightening was the best way to ensure it did not get it. Most agreed that we could have done with the wisdom of Keynes himself.

Hayek and the Austrians
The first edition of *Free Lunch* did not have enough on the Austrian School of economics. The crisis opened up an opportunity for me to rectify that omission, and I am not the only one to do so. In 2011, the BBC broadcast a 'Keynes versus Hayek' debate held at the London School of Economics. The two men themselves were, of course, long gone, so their followers did battle. The Austrian School is a branch of economics dating back to nineteenth-century Vienna and its founders, Carl Menger, Eugen Böhm-Bawerk and Ludwig von Mises. The School is also associated with the

twentieth-century economist Friedrich Hayek, Keynes's great rival, as well as Joseph Schumpeter and, in America, Murray Rothbard and others. Its followers argue that the run-up to the crisis and its denouement followed the pattern of the classic Austrian credit cycle. Just as the Great Depression was the consequence of the credit boom of the 1920s, so the global financial crisis that began in 2007 was the logical outcome of the big expansion of credit and debt in the 2000s. Low interest rates resulted in a sharp rise in borrowing from the banking system and a shift into ever more risky and unsustainable investments. The process of credit growth and credit creation is stimulated by what the Austrians saw as an essentially unstable system brought about by the interaction of central banks setting inappropriately loose policy (most Austrians oppose the idea of central banks) and fractional reserve banking, which we encountered in the chapter on money. The longer the process goes on, the more this process of over-investment on the back of bank borrowing becomes unsustainable. This eventually results in a sharp reversal of the cycle, a credit crunch.

According to Roger Garrison, professor of economics at Auburn University in Alabama, and a modern US follower of the School, Austrian theory was 'tailor-made' for understanding the mess the economy got into. 'The central bank is central to our understanding of the current crisis,' he wrote. And:

> *The Federal Reserve under the leadership of Alan Greenspan*
> *kept interest rates too low during 2003 and 2004 and then*
> *ratcheted the rates steeply upward. Time-consuming*
> *investments that were initiated while cheap credit made them*

*artificially attractive were then made prohibitively costly to
carry through. Macroeconomically, that sequence translates
into an Austrian-style boom and bust. The background against
which the story unfolded was a long-running, politically
motivated sequence of housing policies whose dubious goal was
to increase home ownership beyond what mortgage markets
themselves would allow. The actual effect of the various policies
was to desensitise both lenders and borrowers to the risk of
default, causing mortgage markets and hence housing markets
to play leading roles in this particular boom–bust episode.*

As an account of the conditions leading up to the crisis, the
Austrian credit cycle does reasonably well, although many people
who were not fully signed-up members of the Austrian School
were also worried about the growth of credit and the build-up of
debt. William White, former chief economist at the Bank for
International Settlements, who warned more than most of the
impending crisis, quoted approvingly Ludwig von Mises and other
early Austrian economists. One problem for Austrian theory, however, was that while it was favoured by some investors, it operated
on the fringes of the mainstream. When most economists in America are debating what the Federal Reserve should do, the Austrian
position, that it should not exist at all, is easy to dismiss as cranky.

Those who did not accept the Austrian explanation argued that
it did not fit a world characterised less by over-investment than by
an explosion in unconventional financial instruments and an
under-pricing of risk. The other problem for followers of the Austrian School, which is where they further parted company from the

mainstream, was that they were so horrified by the response of the authorities in America and other countries – large-scale bank bailouts and big 'Keynesian' fiscal stimulus packages – that many denied the existence of the crisis. Austrians hated central banks and government intervention even in the good times. They hated it even more when the authorities took centre stage in the bad times. The most popular forum for Austrian economists is the website of the Ludwig von Mises Institute. Through 2008 and 2009 the most common postings on its blog railed against bank bailouts and even bigger government. With apologies for introducing another 'Great', some referred to the crisis as 'The Great Hoax of 2008', invented with the aim of increasing the power of the state. Others argued that, instead of bailing out the banks, governments should have stood aside, whatever the consequences. No bank, in other words, should be 'too big to fail'. Failure, even on a massive, recessionary scale, was part of the process economies had to go through before they could purge themselves of the excesses and recover.

Minsky and his moment
Before leaving the crisis – though I suspect it will be some time before it leaves us – there is one more economist to mention. Hyman Minsky, born in Chicago in 1919, studied at the Universities of Chicago and Harvard. At Harvard he was a teaching assistant to Alvin Hansen, one of the leading disciples of Keynes in America. His own research and teaching career took in periods at various universities, including Carnegie Mellon, Brown, the University of California at Berkeley and, for twenty-five years from 1965, as professor of economics at Washington University in St

Louis. Minsky regarded himself as a Keynesian but was uncomfortable with conventional interpretations of Keynes. He also rejected the efficient market hypothesis. He was no ivory tower theoretician: at Berkeley he studied the behaviour of Bank of America executives, and he was a director of the Mark Twain Bank in St Louis. By the time of his death in 1996 he had a small but devoted following, which grew hugely with the onset of the financial crisis in the summer of 2007, because he had given us a template for understanding the crisis and what he saw as capitalism's inherent tendency towards bouts of extreme instability.

Though Minsky developed what he described as his 'financial instability hypothesis' over many years, its essence is contained in a ten-page paper published in 1992 by the Jerome Levy Economics Institute of Bard College, New York. He saw banks and investment firms moving through three distinct phases. The first phase, so-called 'hedge' finance, is when they can meet all their obligations out of cash flow. They have not borrowed so much, in other words, that they cannot easily service their debt. In the second phase, 'speculative' finance, banks and investment firms are engaging in riskier behaviour. They can keep up the interest payments on their debt but they cannot begin to pay off their loans. Their response is thus typically to 'roll over' their debt. As long as lenders are happy with this, there should be no difficulty. Except that, typically, banks do not stop there. Their third and most dangerous phase Minsky called 'Ponzi' finance. This is not the kind of fraudulent behaviour that Bernie Madoff was found to have engaged in over the years or, in an earlier era, Ivar Kreuger, the so-called Match King. Rather, it describes the situation banks and investment firms get themselves into when their cash flow is insufficient either to keep up the interest payments or pay back their loans. They can cope only by borrowing more (using their borrowings to pay the interest) or by selling assets. The important thing about Minsky's hypothesis is that, while he is describing distinct types of behaviour, he is not describing distinct banks or investment firms. The key to the financial instability hypothesis is that the behaviour of banks changes, or progresses, through time. His economic units may start by engaging only in hedge finance but then migrate through to speculative and Ponzi behaviour. It is the fact that more and more firms do this that creates the inherent instability of capitalism that is central to his hypothesis.

How does it all end? Any value in Ponzi firms quickly evaporates when circumstances change even a little. They are forced to sell in order to try to meet their obligations. Asset values plunge. The sell-off process gathers pace, prompting financial collapses. This is the 'Minsky moment', which occurred in August 2007, the start of the crisis. The trouble is that few were ready for it.

A crisis for economics?
How much of a crisis for economics was the crisis in the global economy? Does it invalidate everything that went before? I think not. In the great debates the crisis produced between the different schools of economics, most agreed that the tools were there but people and policymakers did not necessarily know how and when to use them. When the eurozone succumbed to crisis in 2010, few economists were too surprised. They had long warned that it was a faulty construction. So economics may change rather less than

critics from outside the subject have suggested. Models that proved inadequate will be improved, re-estimated, or rebuilt from scratch. An industry will evolve around the proper modelling of money, banking and credit, which will become the discipline's new hot area. Behavioural economics, the crossover between psychology and economics, will become even more important. More attention will be paid to Keynes's 'animal spirits' – sentiment and mood – and to Keynes himself. Some of that, however, was happening anyway. The economics that will evolve from the Great Recession will be different from the economics that preceded it but probably not as much as some expect. The crisis did not throw up a new Keynes or, for that matter, any particularly new ways of thinking, though there was plenty of criticism of the old ways. Economists, like bankers, discovered that they were more fallible than they had previously thought – and for some that was a humbling experience. Only a few years ago, in 2005, American magazine *Newsweek* described economics as 'the sexiest trade alive'. It was good for economics to be brought down to earth.

It is worth remembering too that most economists do not engage in the kind of high-level macroeconomic modelling that helped leave policymakers under-prepared for the crisis. Most commercial economics is concerned with detail, with microeconomic questions that are useful and important to businesses and governments. Economists advise on competition, regulation, 'supply-side' policy design and company strategy. There are transport economists, health economists, education economists, labour market economists, and so on. They may all have had private views on the build-up to the crisis, and many did, but it was not their job to advise or warn. Similarly, most academic economists are not macroeconomists. Research tends to be concentrated on microeconomic questions. Tarring all economists with the same brush was never very sensible. The crisis exposed some of the subject's shortcomings but it remains very useful. But you would expect me to say that.

So there we are. It is unfortunate to end this *Free Lunch* with a nasty bout of indigestion. I hope, however, you remember the finer points of the meal rather than its after effects. I hope too that you persist with the interest in economics you have shown by reading this book.

Bite-size glossary

Aggregate demand: Total spending in the economy, or another way of describing gross domestic product. In a closed economy, aggregate demand would consist of spending by consumers and government and on investment (by business and government), as well as any change in stock levels. In an open economy aggregate demand also includes exports, but not imports.

Aggregate supply: The direct counterpart to aggregate demand, being the total of all goods and services produced in an economy over a given period.

Asymmetric information: The situation in which some people in the market have more information than others. In George Akerlof's classic article 'The Market for Lemons' sellers of second-hand cars will always know more about the quality of the vehicle than buyers.

Asymmetric shocks: Economic events that affect different countries, or different parts of countries, in distinct ways. It was long thought that Britain would be unable to participate in European economic and monetary union because of sterling's greater sensitivity to oil price changes as a result of North Sea production.

Automatic stabilisers: If governments allow public spending to rise and tax revenues to fall in a recession, without doing anything about it, they are allowing the economy's automatic stabilisers to operate. In a boom, tax revenues could be expected to be strong, public spending weaker.

Average cost: The cost to a firm of producing a product, measured simply by taking the number produced in a given period and dividing it by the total cost. It is distinct from the marginal cost – that of producing an extra unit of output – just as the average rate of income tax, which in Britain is likely to be around 30 per cent even for quite highly paid people, is distinct from the marginal rate of tax, which for top rate taxpayers is 45 per cent.

Balance of payments: The sum of all a country's transactions with the rest of the world. It builds up from trade in goods, exports and imports, and the trade gap beloved of headline writers, through to the current account. This measures trade in goods and services, as well as the so-called invisible items of trade, such as interest, profit and dividends paid to and received from abroad. The current account is the best overall measure of an economy's external position and whether it is 'paying its way' in the world. The capital account of the balance of payments is made up of long-term investment flows, such as the building of a factory by a foreign firm; portfolio flows, such as investment in stocks and shares in the country; and short-term speculative or 'hot' flows, perhaps attracted by the current interest rate. There are also official flows. A country that has a current account deficit and insufficient capital inflows to match it will probably suffer from a falling exchange rate, it may also have to borrow or run down its foreign exchange reserves. The balance of payments, as its name suggests, has to balance.

Base rate: The interest rate on which the banks base the rates they pay to depositors and charge borrowers. When the Bank of England changes interest rates it is common to refer to a base rate change, although the Bank alters a money-market rate, the Bank Rate at which it lends to financial institutions. The base rate is not to be confused with the basic rate, which is the standard rate of income tax.

Behavioural economics: A more sophisticated way of assessing and predicting economic decisions than merely assuming they are arrived at rationally. Behavioural economics uses social, cognitive and emotional factors to explain how individuals, businesses and other organisations reach decisions. It could be described as a psychological approach to economics.

Bretton Woods: The conference in 1944 that gave birth to the post-war international monetary system, including the International Monetary Fund, the World Bank and the 'gold exchange standard', a system of fixed-but-adjustable exchange rates that lasted until the early 1970s.

Bubble: From the time of the South Sea Bubble of 1720, bubble has been used as a term to describe an unsustainable rise in asset prices. Thus, the technology bubble burst in March 2000, while some commentators refer to a house price bubble. The Japanese economy of the late 1980s was subsequently known as the bubble economy. The global financial crisis of 2008–9 was described by some as the bursting of a worldwide debt bubble.

Budget: The main annual fiscal policy statement, which in Britain is held in March or April, and is mainly concerned with tax changes. An Autumn Statement may set out some of the measures beforehand, for consultation. Under current arrangements a Comprehensive Spending Review takes place every few years to agree public spending totals.

Budget deficit: What arises when the government's planned spending exceeds the amount it raises in taxation. A budget surplus occurs in the opposite situation, while a balanced budget matches government spending and tax revenues. Governments have adopted various rules over the years to limit their budget deficits. In Britain the Thatcher government ended up with the aim of balancing the budget over the economic cycle, while the Blair Labour government followed the 'golden rule' of borrowing only to fund public investment. The coalition government elected in May 2010 aimed to balance the 'current' budget (excluding capital/infrastructure spending by the government). Countries inside the euro were in theory required to meet the conditions of the Stability and Growth Pact, limiting their budget deficits to 3 per cent of gross domestic product and, in normal circumstances, aiming for a balanced budget or small surplus. There are many ways of measuring the budget deficit. For many years the 'public sector borrowing requirement' was the key measure in Britain. Now 'public sector net borrowing' is the accepted measure.

Business cycle: The tendency to show a regular pattern of faster and slower growth, usually over a four to five year period. The cycle has four phases – recovery, peak, slowdown and trough. When the recovery is particularly strong it becomes a boom, when the slowdown is sharp it may turn into a 'bust' or recession. Governments and central banks often try to dampen the effects of the cycle by using fiscal and monetary policy. Real business cycle theorists such as Robert Lucas advise against this. There are plenty of other types of business cycle. A Juglar cycle, after the French economist Clement Juglar, lasts nine to ten years. A Kondratiev cycle, after the Russian economist Nikolai Kondratiev, lasts around fifty years. There is considerable debate about the continued existence of all these cycles, though claims by Tony Blair and Gordon Brown that there would be no return to boom and bust while they were in charge eventually proved badly wrong.

Capital expenditure: Investment, by companies or governments, in plant, machinery, vehicles, buildings, or, in the case of governments, the infrastructure.

Central bank: The institution responsible for monetary policy and in most countries financial and banking regulation. The Bank of England, the European Central Bank, the Federal Reserve Board and the Bank of Japan are the world's major central banks, though in years to come we will hear far more about the People's Bank of China and the Reserve Bank of India.

Comparative advantage: The theory, developed by David Ricardo, in which countries can benefit from trade even if one has an absolute advantage in the production of all goods and services.

Competition policy: Measures taken by governments to break down monopolies or other dominant positions within markets by firms, thus encouraging competition. In Britain since 1997, the Office of Fair Trading has been given an enhanced role in investigating and recommending action against anti-competitive behaviour, while the Competition Commission, which polices monopolies, is effectively independent of government. It used to be thought that there were 'public interest' monopolies – companies that were dominant in the home market but could use this as a springboard in the world market. Such thinking, that a monopoly position for national champions should be permitted, is no longer fashionable.

Competitiveness: Essentially the ability of a country, or its exports, to compete internationally. Some economists argue that it is appropriate to measure competitiveness only among companies, not countries. Even so, a country that is uncompetitive will probably run a current account deficit, and may need a lower exchange rate, as well as more fundamental corrective measures.

Crowding out: The situation in which an increase in government activity results in a fall in private sector activity, either because the public sector lays claim on resources (particularly workers) that could have been used by private firms, or because increased government borrowing pushes up interest rates.

Current expenditure: Expenditure on non-capital items. Spending by governments on the wages and salaries of public sector workers, or on schoolbooks and medicines, all comes under the heading of current expenditure.

Deflation: A fall in the general price level, the opposite of inflation. The last persistent global deflationary episode was in the 1930s, although Japan has experienced deflation on and off since the early 1990s and global deflation was feared as a result of the crisis. Reference is sometimes made to deflationary policies. These are not aimed at bringing about deflation but, rather, slowing a strongly growing economy. A central bank raising interest rates or a government increasing taxes or cutting public spending could be said to be introducing deflationary policies.

Depreciation: Two distinct meanings, the first being the declining value of a capital asset due to wear and tear and obsolescence. The second is the right expression for a fall in the value of a currency during an era of floating rates. If the pound falls from $1.60 to $1.40 against the dollar, it has depreciated.

Depression: A prolonged economic downturn or period of stagnation, as distinct from a shorter recession. The last worldwide depression was in the 1930s. Some economists use depression for periods when economic activity is below normal.

Derivatives: Financial instruments or securities which are based on other instruments or assets. A currency future, an agreement to exchange, say, pounds for dollars at a specified rate in the future, is a derivative. So are much more complex financial instruments. Mortgage-backed securities, some of which caused huge problems in the global financial crisis, are a type of derivative.

Devaluation: The correct expression for a fall in the value of a currency during a fixed rate era, such as the Bretton Woods system that lasted from just after the Second World War until 1973. In November 1967 the pound was devalued from $2.80 to $2.40 against the dollar, remaining at the new lower level.

Diminishing returns: The situation in which a firm applies additional factors of production, for example extra workers, to increasing output but achieves a smaller increase in output for every additional worker employed. Diminishing marginal utility refers to the declining satisfaction each additional unit of consumption brings – one whisky might be enjoyable, the tenth much less so.

Direct taxation: Taxes on income, for example income tax or National Insurance contributions, or in the case of companies, corporation tax.

Disinflation: A reduction in the rate of inflation, not to be confused with deflation, a fall in prices.

Disposable income: Income after (direct) tax.

Econometrics: The application of mathematical and statistical techniques to economic theories and relationships. The equations that make up models of the economy are estimated using econometric techniques.

Economic growth: The rise in gross domestic product, or per capita GDP, from one year to the next. Growth is the ultimate aim of economic policy. The trend rate of economic growth in Britain, its average over time, is currently estimated by the Office for Budget Responsibility to be between 2.1 and 2.35 per cent.

Efficient market hypothesis: The theory that the level of the stock market, or any other financial market, reflects the efficient assessment and use by market participants of all the information available to them.

Elasticity of demand: The responsiveness of demand for a product to a change in its price, or to a change in the incomes of consumers.

Euroland: Popular name for the area covered by European economic and monetary union, the euro area. Euroland came into being on 1 January 1999 with eleven members (Austria, Belgium, Finland, France, Germany, Ireland, Italy, Luxembourg, the Netherlands, Portugal and Spain). Greece, Slovenia, Cyprus, Malta, Slovakia and Estonia joined later, with other countries also planning to join.

Exchange rate: The value of one currency, expressed in terms of another, for example the pound's exchange rate against the dollar is $1.50.

Externalities: Costs, or benefits, generated by firms or individuals but affecting others. Pollution is a common negative externality, which is why firms are subject to anti-pollution controls and penalties. An attractive garden might generate positive externalities – benefiting not only its owner but also passers-by.

Fiscal policy: Strictly speaking, matters pertaining to tax. The fiscal year is the tax year. In practice, fiscal policy refers to the tax and spending decisions by governments, usually taken annually in Budgets. The role of fiscal policy has changed over the years. In the 1950s and 1960s it was used for 'fine-tuning' purposes – managing demand in the economy. Now fiscal policy is usually framed in a medium-term context, with tax changes seen as impacting on economic performance and public spending also usually planned for some years in advance, though short-term fiscal 'stimulus' measures were adopted by many countries in 2008 and 2009. Fiscal drag is a technical term, describing the fact that in the absence of changes, the tax government takes from individuals will normally rise as a result of inflation as rising incomes move people into higher tax brackets. This is why income tax allowances, for example, are conventionally raised in line with inflation.

Floating currencies: The system that has existed since the early 1970s, in which currencies are not fixed in value against others. The dollar, the yen, the euro and the pound float freely. Not all currencies are floating. Some are tied to the dollar while European currencies were linked in the exchange rate mechanism of the European Monetary System prior to the adoption of the euro. One of the big international economic debates has been over China's tight control of her currency, the renminbi, which is not freely floating.

Full employment: In practice, an unemployment rate of 2 or 3 per cent – when everybody who could reasonably be in work is in employment. Why not zero? Because there will always be some people moving between jobs (frictional unemployment) and temporarily unemployed because of the weather or the state of the tourist trade (seasonal unemployment). Employment may still rise in a situation of full employment if more people can be lured into the workforce, for example married women or older people.

Game theory: The modelling of economic decision-making by means of games or strategies. Outcomes for firms and individuals depend not only on their decisions and strategies but also on what others do. The pioneers of game theory were John Von Neumann and Oskar Morgenstern, in their 1944 *Theory of Games and Economic Behaviour*. They gave us the idea of the 'zero sum game' in which one player's gain is another's loss. John Nash was responsible for demonstrating that the outcome of a game, in other words of any economic decision, could be a 'win–win' one.

Gini coefficient: The standard measure of inequality within or between countries. It varies between 0 and 1. A Gini coefficient of 0 would imply a perfectly equal distribution of income, with everybody getting the same; while a coefficient of 1 would mean that one person would receive everything.

Global financial crisis: The crisis that began in the summer of 2007 and, several years later, could not be said to be over. The crisis began with the freezing of funding markets and led to a fully-fledged banking crisis followed by a sovereign debt crisis, notably in the eurozone. Some said the crisis was the worst since the 1929 Crash, others that things had not been as bad since the outbreak of the First World War.

Gold standard: The international monetary system in which all currencies were fully backed by and convertible into gold.

Golden rule: A self-imposed fiscal rule that says the government should borrow only for investment, not current spending.

Government bonds: Interest-bearing bonds issued by the government to borrow from the financial markets or the public. Bonds are of short- (up to five years), medium-, or long-term duration – up to thirty years, sometimes longer. The yield, or interest, on government bonds is an important determinant of interest rates elsewhere in the economy. In Britain government bonds are called gilts (gilt-edged securities).

Great moderation: The period leading up to the global financial crisis, characterised by low inflation, low unemployment and steady growth. Policymakers appeared to have solved the macroeconomic problems of the past. The big build-up in public and private debt during the great moderation told a different story, however.

Great recession: The downturn that followed the great moderation and, since it was the worst for the global economy since the 1930s, economists called it the 'Great' recession. The Great Depression happened, of course, in the 1930s.

Gross domestic product: GDP, the most common measure of overall activity in the economy within a given period. GDP can be calculated three ways – it is the total of spending (GDP = C + I + G + X − M), the sum of production, and the total of all incomes received. All three should produce roughly the same answer. GDP at market prices includes taxation, while GDP adjusted for taxes and subsidies is GDP at factor cost. Gross national product is roughly similar to GDP, but also includes net property income from abroad. In some countries, such as Ireland, the GDP/GNP difference is quite significant, but not in the case of Britain.

Group of Seven: A grouping of the world's most powerful countries, the G7 started life as the Group of Five (America, Japan,

Britain, Germany and France) in the mid-1970s, with Canada and Italy added soon afterwards. The G7, which now includes Russia at some of its meetings, when it becomes the G8, holds annual summits and more frequent meetings between its finance ministers and central bankers. The G20, which includes China, India and several other 'emerging' economies, has gained greater prominence in recent years.

Human capital: Without a skilled and educated workforce, investment in the latest machinery will be futile. Investing in human capital, in education and training, can be as important as investing in equipment, although the returns may take longer to show through.

Hyperinflation: Runaway inflation, when the value of money falls at an alarming rate. Countries with inflation rates of 50 per cent or more *per month* are experiencing hyperinflation.

Indifference curve: A representation of a consumer's preferences between apples and pears, or income and leisure, or anything else. A consumer may be indifferent between five apples and five pears, or three apples and eight pears, and so on. Indifference curves can never cross.

Indirect taxation: Mainly taxes on spending, such as VAT and excise duties.

Inflation: A general increase in the price level, and one of the main targets for modern-day economic policy. The UK inflation target of 2 per cent sounds low but it means prices would double in thirty years. A 4 per cent target would mean a doubling of prices every fifteen years. Economists regard a small amount of inflation as desirable, not least to avoid the danger of deflation.

Strictly speaking, inflation should be used only to measure a general increase in prices but people often refer to house price inflation or wage inflation. The main measure of inflation now used in Britain is the consumer prices index, rather than the traditional retail prices index, although producer price inflation data (industry's input and output costs) are also published. The most comprehensive inflation measure is derived from GDP data, the GDP deflator.

Infrastructure: Roads, railways, telecommunications, hospitals, schools and other forms of public investment, these are usually but not necessarily built and maintained by government. An inadequate infrastructure has long been blamed for undermining Britain's economic performance.

Interest rate: The cost of borrowing, or the price of money. The amount that has to be paid to a lender for forgoing the use of money now. The rate of interest, more importantly, is the main weapon of monetary policy. Raising interest rates – increasing the cost of borrowing – tightens policy, and vice versa.

J-curve: A description of the likely balance of payments effects of currency devaluation. Initially the current account worsens because imports have become more expensive. Only later is there an improvement as exports benefit from the devaluation.

Keynesian policies: The use of a fiscal policy in an activist way, to manage demand in the economy. A recession would be tackled with higher public spending and tax cuts, and the opposite policies would be adopted in a boom. The heyday of Keynesian policies was in the 1950s and 1960s, though it made a comeback in the 2000s and, in particular, in 2008–9.

Laffer curve: A graphical demonstration of the fact that higher tax rates can result in lower tax revenues.

Liquidity trap: The situation, defined by Keynes, in which monetary policy becomes ineffective because interest rates cannot fall low enough to stimulate economic activity. When there is deflation or falling prices, there is also likely to be a liquidity trap.

Marginal rate of tax: The tax paid on an additional pound of income earned. From April 2013 a top rate taxpayer in Britain pays a marginal tax rate of 45 per cent on earnings above £150,000. Marginal cost, marginal revenue and marginal utility are all key concepts in economics. Firms produce to the point where marginal cost equals marginal revenue. In each case 'marginal' refers to an additional unit.

Monetarism: The belief that inflation is 'always and everywhere' a monetary phenomenon and that inflation results from increases in the money supply. While agreeing on this general position, monetarists argue among themselves about the choice of target measures for the money supply and about how best to control them. The modern heyday for monetarism was in the 1980s.

Monetary policy: Decisions that affect the cost and availability of money. Monetary policy, mainly exercised through interest rate changes, is regarded as the most effective tool for short-term economic management.

Monetary policy committee: A committee within the Bank of England of nine men and women that meets each month to agree the level of interest rates. The MPC, which is chaired by the Governor of the Bank, came into being in 1997 when the

Bank was given 'operational independence', control over interest rates. It is charged with achieving an inflation target set by the government, currently 2 per cent. Five members of the committee are Bank 'insiders', including the Governor and two deputies. Four are outside appointments, made by the Chancellor of the Exchequer.

Money supply: The stock of money is the amount of money in circulation; the money supply describes changes in that stock in a given period. Measures of the money stock (and money supply) range from the very narrow such as M0, mainly notes and coin, to the very broad, M4, which includes most forms of credit and deposits.

Monopoly: Strictly speaking a situation in which there is only one firm in an industry. A monopsony refers to a single buyer for an industry's products. In practice, monopoly situations develop when a firm establishes a dominant position within an industry. Oligopoly refers to dominance of an industry by a few large players, as is the case for Britain's supermarkets and banks.

Multiplier: Essential to Keynesian economics, the notion that an injection of spending has knock-on effects beyond the initial impact. An extra £5 billion of government spending will, in creating incomes for public sector workers and suppliers, create additional spending elsewhere in the economy. Keynesians have traditionally argued that these multiplier effects are large, while post-Keynesian economists say they will be neutralised by the fact that people will recognise that higher government spending will result, either in future tax rises, or inflation.

Natural rate of unemployment, Nairu: The level of

unemployment consistent with a stable rate of inflation. The Nairu, another way of describing the natural rate, is the non-accelerating inflation rate of unemployment. The idea, introduced by Milton Friedman, is that the natural rate is determined by supply-side factors, such as the skills of the workforce and how they are distributed around the country, together with factors such as the operation of the benefits system (over-generous benefits discourage the low-paid from taking jobs). Measures to expand the economy and reduce unemployment below the natural rate will result in inflation. Most economists accept the existence of a natural rate or Nairu, although they have found it difficult to estimate exactly where it is at any one time, making it an imprecise tool for policymakers.

Optimal currency area: An area or group of countries in which it is appropriate to have a single currency, this concept has been much used in the debate over the euro.

Output gap: A broad measure of spare capacity in the economy, the difference between actual GDP and its trend or long-run level. An economy which starts on trend, and has a trend rate of growth of 2.5 per cent, would have a positive output gap (i.e. spare capacity) after two years of 1 per cent growth, but a negative output gap – it would be operating above capacity – after two years of 4 per cent growth. Again, it would be a more useful tool for policymakers if economists were better at estimating it.

Perfect competition: The textbook model of a market, with many firms producing identical products and each having to accept the same market price for their product. Buyers have perfect information. For a time, some economists believed the Internet had characteristics of perfect competition.

Phillips curve: The relationship between unemployment and wage inflation developed by A.W. 'Bill' Phillips. The higher the level of unemployment, the lower the rate of wage inflation. In the late 1960s Milton Friedman introduced a new version of the Phillips curve, adjusted for expectations about inflation.

Productivity: An important determinant of prosperity. Labour productivity is output divided by the number of workers (or worker-hours) needed to produce it. The faster the rate of growth in productivity over time, the higher the trend rate of growth of GDP. Capital productivity is the same concept applied to investment. Total factor productivity is the combination of labour and capital productivity.

Quantitative easing: A policy, typically adopted when interest rates have reached very low levels, sometimes known as the 'zero bound', of injecting money directly into the economy. The Bank of England did this from 2009 by purchasing assets, mainly gilt-edged securities (UK government bonds) from the private sector. Other central banks have used variations on this method.

Quantity theory of money: The formal basis of monetarism, the link between the money supply and inflation. MV = PT (or PY), where M is the money stock, V its velocity of circulation, P the price level, T the number of transactions (Y is real GDP). Changes in M, money, will mostly be reflected in changes in P, prices.

Rational expectations: The important concept that says economic actors (people and businesses) learn from the past – they do not make the same mistake twice. Most associated with Robert Lucas, it demonstrated for example that governments would be unable to fool the public with an inflationary burst of extra state spending.

Real interest rate: The rate of interest adjusted for inflation. A depositor getting 5 per cent interest at a time of 2 per cent inflation is doing better than one earning 10 per cent interest when inflation is 8 per cent.

Real terms: Any economic variable adjusted for price changes, or inflation. Without such adjustments, comparisons would be meaningless. A 20 per cent rise in actual or 'nominal' GDP at a time of 20 per cent inflation represents zero real growth, while a 3 per cent rise at a time of 1 per cent inflation is equivalent to 2 per cent real growth.

Recession: Usually defined as two consecutive quarters of falling GDP, although it can apply to any pronounced slowdown. The National Bureau of Economic Research is the official recession arbiter in America. In 2009 the world economy experienced its worst recession in the post-war period, resulting in an actual fall in global GDP.

Saving ratio: The proportion of income saved during a given period. Traditionally, countries such as China have had a high saving ratio (as did Japan for a time), while Britain and America have had low saving ratios. In a closed economy, the amount of saving would determine the funds available for investment, although that is not the case where capital flows freely. Saving is usually divided into its discretionary components (deliberate decisions to save), and non-discretionary components (such as automatic pension contributions). Saving is also a net variable, so heavy borrowing by individuals will reduce the saving ratio.

Seasonal adjustment: Any economic variable adjusted for seasonal variations. Many indicators are adjusted in this way to allow meaningful comparisons between different times of year. Without such adjustment there would always be an apparent surge in consumer spending growth in November and December in anticipation of Christmas. Economists need to know how much of that surge is normal.

Structural deficit: That part of the budget deficit which does not reflect the impact of the economic cycle, in other words the underlying deficit. Governments accept that the budget deficit will increase during and after recessions. Setting their fiscal rules in terms of the structural deficit, as Britain's coalition government did in 2010, correctly targets the underlying deficit.

Supply-side economics: The branch of economics concerned with the factors that raise or lower the economy's long-run or trend growth rate. In the 1980s, the 'supply-siders', mainly free market economists in America, were concerned with matters such as tax cuts to restore incentives and deregulation to improve the workings of markets. Today, supply-side economics would be regarded as much wider than that, taking in the role of education and training, and 'active' labour market measures to encourage greater participation in the job market.

Symmetrical target: A target in which the penalties for undershooting are identical (symmetrical) to those for overshooting. The Bank of England's 2 per cent inflation target is symmetrical. If inflation falls below 1 per cent or rises above 3 per cent, the

Governor of the Bank of England has to write a letter of explanation to the Chancellor.

Tax credits: A form of payment by government to individuals or firms that normally reduces the amount of tax payable. Tax credits can also, in some circumstances, result in a net payment by the tax authorities to the non tax-paying recipient, effectively a welfare payment through the tax system.

Transfer payments: That part of government spending that consists of a transfer from taxpayers to benefit recipients, for example state pensioners or the unemployed.

Underlying inflation: A measure of inflation adjusted for special or temporary factors. The target measure of inflation used in Britain, the consumer prices index, is affected by temporary factors such as VAT changes or oil price hikes. 'Core' or underlying inflation measures strip out these temporary factors. A typical core measure would exclude food, energy and indirect taxes.

Unemployment rate: The percentage of eligible people who are not in work. Not as easy as it sounds. In Britain one measure of eligibility (the claimant count) is based on entitlement to benefit, the Jobseekers' Allowance; while another, the International Labour Office measure (The Labour Force Survey measure), counts all those who want to work, whether entitled to benefit or not.

Wealth: The stock of assets owned by, say, an individual, as distinct from income, which is the flow of money coming in each year. To the extent it is not spent, income adds to wealth.

Post-prandial reading

Economics, as I hope this book has demonstrated, is a living subject. There is a wealth of information, much of it good, in the newspapers, including of course the *Sunday Times*, www.thesundaytimes.co.uk, *The Times*, www.thetimes.co.uk, the *Financial Times*, www.ft.com, and the *Guardian*, www.guardian.co.uk, and in weekly magazines such as the *Economist*, www.economist.com. The Internet is also a wonderful source including, in Britain, the Bank of England, www.bankofengland.co.uk, the Treasury, www.hm-treasury.gov.uk, the Office for National Statistics, www.statistics.gov.uk, and organisations such as the Institute for Fiscal Studies, www.ifs.org.uk, the Royal Economic Society, www.res.org.uk, as well as my own site, www.economicsuk.com. Internationally, the Organisation for Economic Cooperation and Development, www.oecd.org, the International Monetary Fund, www.imf.org, the European Central Bank, www.ecb.int, and America's www.economy.com are all excellent resources.

There is a generous supply of books on economics, some of them very good, some quite hard work. Rather than litter this book with references, which serve only to clutter up the text, I decided to keep some recommendations until the end, which include those works I have referred to. Starting with the history of economic thought, readers have quite a choice, though some of these books will now be available only in libraries. William Barber's *A History of Economic Thought* (Penguin) is accessible, while Paul Strathern's *Dr Strangelove's Game: A Brief History of Economic Genius* (Hamish Hamilton) is quirky, informative and entertaining. *The Making of Modern Economics* by Mark Skousen (M. E. Sharpe) is full of anecdote, photographs of the great economists – and some of the not so great – and has a wonderfully light touch. More difficult, but useful for serious students, are Eric Roll's *A History of Economic Thought* (Faber & Faber) and Mark Blaug's *The History of Economic Thought* (Edward Elgar).

The lives of the great economists, as well as their original works, always repay reading. Various edited paperback versions of Adam Smith's *The Wealth of Nations* are in print, including one from Penguin. Ian Simpson Ross's *The Life of Adam Smith* (Clarendon Press) tells the life story. *The Condensed Wealth of Nations,* by Eamonn Butler, is published by the Adam Smith Institute. John Maynard Keynes merited a three-volume biography, by Robert Skidelsky. Volume One is *Hopes Betrayed, 1883–1920,* Volume Two is *The Economist as Saviour, 1920–37,* and the final volume is *Fighting for Britain, 1937–46.* All are published by Macmillan. Skidelsky's *The Return of the Master,* published by Penguin, came out after the global financial crisis hit. Keynes's *The General Theory of*

Employment, Interest and Money (Prometheus Books) is in print. Two other biographies are worth mentioning. Francis Wheen's *Karl Marx* (Fourth Estate) and, coming up to date, Sylvia Nasar's *A Beautiful Mind* (Faber & Faber), the story of the remarkable life of John Nash. Both are good reads.

The route to economic understanding is often through economic history. Eric Hobsbawm's *Industry and Empire* (Penguin), an economic history of Britain, has always been a favourite of mine. *Sterling, The Rise and Fall of a Currency* (Penguin) by Nicholas Mayhew, tells the pound's often-inglorious story. On a grander scale, *The Wealth and Poverty of Nations* by David Landes (Abacus) is excellent. As for modern UK economic history, Geoffrey Owen's *From Empire to Europe* (HarperCollins) tells the story of the post-war British economy from an industrial perspective. Two books of mine, *The Rise and Fall of Monetarism* and *From Boom to Bust*, both originally published by Penguin, do so from the perspective of economic policy. The policy perspective on economics has also been provided by some of those who have witnessed it at first hand. Nigel Lawson's *The View from No.11* (Corgi) is a great account of the Thatcher years and of how economic policy works in practice. The economic policies of the 1997–2010 Labour government are described in *Reforming Britain's Economic and Financial Policy* (Palgrave), written by the Treasury and edited by Ed Balls and Gus O'Donnell. A fun account of different Chancellors since 1945 is provided by Richard Holt in *Second Among Equals* (Profile Books). David Lipsey's *The Secret Treasury* (Viking) is also informative. Alistair Darling's *Back from the Brink: 1,000 Days at Number 11* (Atlantic Books) is an excellent first-hand account of the crisis. Other books on the crisis, apart from my own *The Age of Instability* (Profile), include *Too Big to Fail: Inside the Battle to Save Wall Street* (Penguin) by Andrew Ross Sorkin, and *The Big Short: Inside the Doomsday Machine* (Penguin) by Michael Lewis. *Fool's Gold: How Unrestrained Greed Corrupted a Dream, Shattered Global Markets and Unleashed a Catastrophe* (Abacus) by Gillian Tett, was one of the first of many books on the crisis. *This Time is Different: Eight Centuries of Financial Folly* (Princeton University Press), by Carmen Reinhart and Kenneth Rogoff, sets the crisis in context more than any other. The eurozone crisis will no doubt lead to many more books. In the meantime, my own *Will Europe Work?* (Profile) explains why the euro was doomed to difficulty from the start. *The Euro: The Battle for the New Global Currency* (Yale University Press), by David Marsh, tells the story of later developments for the single currency. Anybody who wants a perspective on a different part of the world and the shift in global economic activity might want to dip into my *The Dragon and the Elephant: China, India and the New World Order* (Profile).

There are plenty of excellent economics textbooks around. *Economics for Business* (McGraw Hill) by David Begg and Damian Ward; *Principles of Economics* (McGraw Hill), by Moore Mcdowell, Rodney Thom, Robert H. Frank and Ben Bernanke has at least one author most people will recognise; and *Economics* (Oxford University Press), by Richard Lipsey and Alec Chrystal, is the latest version of a book familiar to generations of students. Any list of economics texts would be incomplete without *Economics* (McGraw Hill) by Paul A. Samuelson and William D. Nordhaus. As a word of warning, these texts are generally to be read as part of formal courses of study.

Books that anybody can read and enjoy include *Economics: Making Sense of the Modern Economy* ed. Simon Cox (Economist Books); *The Undercover Economist* (Abacus) by Tim Harford; *The Armchair Economist: Economics and Everyday Life* (Pocket Books) by Steven E. Landsburg; *The Economic Naturalist: Why Economics Explains Almost Everything* (Virgin Books), by Robert H. Frank; and *The Soulful Science: What Economists Do and Why It Matters* (Princeton University Press) by Diane Coyle. *23 Things They Don't Tell You About Capitalism* (Penguin) by Ha-Joon Chang is fun, while *Nudge: Improving Decisions about Health, Wealth and Happiness* (Penguin) by Richard Thaler and Cass Sunstein is a good way into behavioural economics. *The Bottom Billion: Why the Poorest Countries are Failing and What Can Be Done About It* (Oxford University Press) by Paul Collier is good and thought-provoking. Also thought-provoking is E. F. Schumacher's classic *Small Is Beautiful: A Study of Economics as if People Mattered* (Vintage). There are very many more.

Index